The Thornton Romances.

THE

EARLY ENGLISH METRICAL ROMANCES

OF

PERCEVAL, ISUMBRAS, EGLAMOUR,

AND

DEGREVANT.

SELECTED FROM MANUSCRIPTS AT LINCOLN AND CAMBRIDGE.

EDITED BY

JAMES ORCHARD HALLIWELL-Phillips, ESQ. F.R.S.,

HON. M.R.I.A., HON. M.R.S.L., F.S.A., ETC.

CORRESPONDING MEMBER OF THE COMITE' DES ARTS ET MONUMENTS.

PRINTED FOR THE CAMDEN SOCIETY,

M.DCCC.XLIV.

Reprinted with the permission of the Royal Historical Society

AMS PRESS

NEW YORK • LONDON

First AMS EDITION published 1968
Manufactured in the United States of America

Series No. I, 30

DA
20
C17
no. 30
1968

AMS PRESS, INC.
NEW YORK, N.Y. 10003

COUNCIL

OF

THE CAMDEN SOCIETY,

FOR THE YEAR 1844.

President,
THE RIGHT HON. LORD BRAYBROOKE, F.S.A.

THOMAS AMYOT, ESQ. F.R.S., Treas. S.A. *Director.*
JOHN BRUCE, ESQ. F.S.A. *Treasurer.*
JOHN PAYNE COLLIER, ESQ. F.S.A.
THE LORD ALBERT CONYNGHAM, K.C.H., F.S.A.
C. PURTON COOPER, ESQ. Q.C., D.C.L., F.R.S., F.S.A.
T. CROFTON CROKER, ESQ. F.S.A., M.R.I.A.
SIR HENRY ELLIS, K.H., F.R.S., Sec. S.A.
HENRY HALLAM, ESQ. M.A., F.R.S., V.P.S.A.
THE REV. JOSEPH HUNTER, F.S.A.
SIR FREDERIC MADDEN, K.H., F.R.S., F.S.A.
THOMAS JOSEPH PETTIGREW, ESQ. F.R.S. F.S.A.
THOMAS STAPLETON, ESQ. F.S.A.
WILLIAM J. THOMS, ESQ. F.S.A., *Secretary.*
ALBERT WAY, ESQ. M.A., DIR. S.A.
THOMAS WRIGHT, ESQ. M.A., F.S.A.

The COUNCIL of the CAMDEN SOCIETY desire it to be understood that they are not answerable for any opinions or observations that may appear in the Society's publications; the Editors of the several Works being alone responsible for the same.

INTRODUCTION.

About the year 1440, or perhaps somewhat earlier, Robert Thornton, a native of Yorkshire, residing in the neighbourhood of Oswaldkirk, compiled a goodly volume of English treatises or translations, embracing the various subjects of history, romance, religion, and medicine. Nor must such a medley appear incongruous to the modern reader. At a time when the library of the University of Oxford is said to have contained no more than two or three hundred chained books, a folio volume which could afford amusement in hall, instruction at other times, religious information and perhaps consolation to the sick, and withall be produced as a medical authority for nearly every ill " that flesh is heir to," was not to be despised by a family resident in a remote part of the country, where, in all probability, literary luxuries were not readily accessible. It must not, however, be supposed that Robert Thornton was the *author* of this miscellany. Although in more than one instance the tracts are said to be " written " by him, we must be content, excepting perhaps a very few lines, with giving him the bare honour of a scribe; and if it be thought that by the title of this work we are conferring an unmerited posthumous reputation, it must be recollected that the real authors have not recorded their names, and thus, while no injustice is committed to any memory, we obtain the advantage of a short distinctive title, the value of which is known to every one in the habit of using works of reference.

As the reader will find a minute account of this venerable volume, which is now preserved in the library of Lincoln Cathedral, at the end of these observations, it will only be necessary to observe in this place that it contains copies of the four romances now printed. The texts of the two first, Sir Perceval and Sir Isumbras, are taken verbatim from Thornton's manuscript, but the other two are printed from MSS. at Cambridge, the copies made by Thornton unfortunately being imperfect. Collations with the latter are given in the notes; and it is believed that few variations of any importance afforded by the Lincoln manuscript have been omitted. A few remarks on these pieces will perhaps render their publication more acceptable.

The original of the English version of Perceval is an Anglo-Norman romance, containing about 20,178 lines,[*]

[*] Hist. Lib. de France, xv. 196. According to the Bibliothèque des Romans, 1734, p. 250, it contains 60,000 lines; but this difference is apparently owing to a mistake made by Borel, who took three romances for one. Tyrwhitt falls into the same error; Notes to Chaucer, p. 292.

written by Chrestien de Troyes at the end of the twelfth century, and continued by Gautier de Denet and Manessier, who published it between the years 1206 and 1212.* Chrestien de Troyes † appears to have derived some of the incidents in this romance from the prose Tristan. He dedicated his work to Philip ‡ Count of Flanders, at whose request it was written; but this nobleman having died before it was finished, his widow some time afterwards employed Manessier to complete it. The latter poet, speaking of a superb tomb raised to Perceval, says,—

" La sépulture puet véoir
Sor quatre pilers d'or séoir,
Si com Manesiers le tesmoigne
Que à fin traist ceste besoigne,
El non Jehane la contesse
Qui est de Flandres dame et maistresse.
Et por ce que tant ai apris
De ses bones mours à délivre,
Ai en son non finé mon livre.

* Roquefort, de l'état de la Poésie Françoise dans les xiie. et xiiie. siècles, 8vo. Paris, 1815, p. 194.

† Galland ascribes the romance to Raoul de Beauvais, an error which has been repeated more than once. See Warton's Hist. Engl. Poet., i. 137; Scott's Sir Tristrem, p. 42.

‡ See Fauchet, Recueil de l'origine de la langue et poesie Françoise, Paris, 1581, p. 103. Several writers have confused Manessier with Chrestien de Troyes. Among them is Bouhier, Notes sur Du Verdier, t. i. p. 315. Owing to the conflicting opinions of various writers, a curiously confused account of the authorship of the metrical Perceval is given in Dunlop's History of Fiction, ed. 1816, vol. i. pp. 201-2.

El non son aiol comencha,
Ne puis né fu dès lors en cha
Nus hom qui la main i mesist,
Ne de finer s'entremesist.
Dame, por vos s'en a peiné
Manesiers tant qu'il l'a finé
Selonc l'estoire proprement.
Et comencha al saldement
De l'espée sanz contredit ;
Tant en a et conté et dit
Si com en Salebiere trove,
Si com l'escris tesmoigne et prove
Que li rois Artus séoit là."

Hist. Lit. de France, xv. 252.

A person of the name of Gerbert also wrote a continuation of Perceval, beginning where Manessier did, as appears from the following extract :—

" Si con la matere descoevre
Gerbers qui a reprise l'oevre,
Quant chascuns trovere le laisse.
Mais or en a faite sa laisse,
Gerbers selonc le vraie estoire.
Diex l'en otroit force et victoire
De toute vilenie estaindre,
Et que il puist la fin ataindre
De Perceval que il emprent,
Si con li livres li aprent,
Où la matiere en est escripte,
Gerbers qui le nous traite et dite,
Puis en encha que Percevax
Qui tant ot paines et travax,

> La bone espée rasalsa,
> Et que du Graal demanda,
> Et de la lame qui saignoit
> Demanda que senefioit.
> Puis en encha le nous retrait
> Gerbers qui de son sens estrait
> La rime que je vois contant.
> Neis la luite de Tristant
> Amenda il tot à compas."
>
> *MS. Bib. de l'Arsenal*, 195, f. 171.

The Anglo-Norman romance has not been published, but several copies exist in MS.* Two of these have found their way into this country, one being at the College of Arms and another in the Advocates' Library at Edinburgh,† both unfortunately imperfect. The late Bishop Percy ‡ was possessed of another, which seems now to be missing. The commencement of the Arundel MS. is here given, in which it will be seen that Chrestien de Troyes compares his patron to Alexander the Great.

> " Qui petit seme, petit quielt;
> E qui aukes recoillir vielt,
> En tiel liu sa semence espande,
> Que fruit à cent doble li rende.

---

* Hist. Lit. de France, xv. 247.

† This is the MS. that was used by Galland. It contains 262 leaves, written on vellum, but imperfect at both ends. The Arundel MS. has only the first part.

‡ Reliques, ed. 1840, p. 189. See an early notice of another MS. in Devon's Issues of the Exchequer, 1837, p. 213, which may, however, be the St. Graal.

Car en terre que rien ne vaut
Bone semence seche e faut.
Cristiens seme e fait semence
D'un romanz qu'il comence,
E si le seme en si bon leu
Qu'il ne put estre sanz grant preu,
Qu'il est faitz pur le plus prodhome
Que seit en l'empire de Rome,
Ceo est li quens Phelipes de Flandres,
Qui vaut mielz ne fist Alixandres,
Cil que l'em dit que tant fu bons ;
Mais jeo proverai que li quiens
Vaut mielz que cil ne fist assez
Que cil ont en li amassez
Totes les vices e tuz les mals,
Dont li quiens est mondes e saufs.
Li quiens est tiels qu'il n'escoute
Vilain gab ne parole estoute ;
E s'il ot dire mal d'autri,
Qui qu'il soit, çeo peise li.
Li quiens aime dreite justise,
E lealté e seinte eglise,
E tote vilainie hiet,
Si est plus larges que hom ne siet.
Cil donc solom l'evaungile,
Sanz ypocrisie e sanz gile,
Que dit, ne sache ta senestre
Le bien quant le fera la destre ;
Cil le sache qui le receit,
Ceo est Deus qui tuz les secrez veit,
E siet totes les repostailles
Qui sont el queor et es entrailles.
La senestre, solom l'estoire,
Signifie la veine gloire,

> Que vient de fause ypocrisie ;
> E la destre que signifie
> Charité, qui de sa bone oevere
> Pas ne s'avante, eincois la covere,
> Si que nuls ne l' siet si cil non
> Qui Deus e charitez a non ;
> Deus est charitez e qui vit
> En charité, solom l'escrit.
> Seint Pol dit, jeo le vi e lui,
> Qui meint en Deu e Deu en lui.
> Donc sachez bien pur verité,
> Que li don sont de charité,
> Que li bons quiens Phélipes done,
> Que onques nuli n'en araisone,
> Fors son franc queor e debonaire,
> Que li loe le bien à faire ;
> Donc vaut mielz cil que ne valut
> Alixandres, qui ne chalut.
> De charité ne de nul bien
> S'il n'en ditez jà de rien,
> Donc avera bien sauvé sa paine
> Crestiens, qui entent e paine
> A rimoier le meillor conte,
> Par le comandement le conte,
> Que seit contez en court real,
> C'est li contes del Graal,
> Dont li quiens li bailla le livre ;
> Si orrez coment il s'en delivre."
> *MS. Arundel, Coll. Arm.* 14, f. 150.

The incidents in the Anglo-Norman romance follow in the same order, at the commencement, as in the abridged English version here printed. The death of the elder

Perceval, the retirement of the mother, taking the young hero with her to share her seclusion; his incitement to chivalry by accidentally meeting with some of Arthur's knights, his rude costume, and his victory over the knight who carried away the golden cup, are common to each. The English version, however, omits all mention of the Bleeding Lance and St. Graal, so conspicuous in the other; and Chrestien de Troyes relates a variety of adventures not there found. It is in fact an abridgment in the strictest sense of the term, the translator chiefly confining himself to the principal points of Perceval's career, with the exceptions above mentioned.

The metrical romance of Perceval was reduced into prose in the fifteenth century, and afterwards printed, 4to. Paris, 1530. It is a close copy of the original, and in many instances the same words are used. As the book is of great rarity, the prologue, which contains a brief history of the work, is here added.

Cy commence le Prologue de l'acteur.

Il est naturellement impossible à celuy qui en sa terre n'espand ou seme la semence à suffisance, qu'il y puisse recueillir le grain en habondance: parquoy est le proverbe veritable, disant, Qui petit seme petit recueille. Doncques celluy qui desire recepvoir d'aucune terre le grain à plenitude, regarde à mettre sa semence en terre utile et fertile, et si ainsi le faict, la terre luy rapportera à cent au double. Car en terre seiche, aride, et infertile, ne peult le grain profiter, mais y seicher et se deperdre. Pareillement la bonne parolle, dicte et alleguee devant ceulx qui ne la veullent retenir, ne humblement en leurs cueurs garder pour doctrine, ne peult aussi porter profit. Ce considerant, feu trehault et magnanime prince Philippes Conte de Flandres, fort charitable et convoiteux de veoir, lire, et ouyr les faictz et proesses des preux et hardis chevaliers, aymant leurs vertus et honorables enseignemens, ne voulut laisser perdre et perir la memoire de ceulx desquelz il avoit ouy ou entendu par escript l'honorable, vertueuse, et bien famée vie. Luy doncques, meu de telle affection, quelque jour se rememorant des merveilleuses entreprises et nobles faictz des chevalliers de la Table Ronde, print ung desir en son couraige de faire venir à lumiere la vie et faictz chevallereux du très preux, craint, et hardi chevallier Percevalle le Gallois. Car comme ayt dict, le dict Philippes Conte de Flandres estoit tant rempli de charité, que rien ne voioit où elle deust estre gardée, qu'il ne se meist en son debvoir de faire les choses à elle appartenantes, en suyvant la doctrine de Sainct Paul, qui dict, que Dieu est charité, et quiconques vit en charité, Dieu vit en luy. Car de toutes les vertus icelle est la principalle. Voyant doncques le dict Conte Philippes ceste vertu estre tant aggreable à Dieu, pour icelle ensuyvir, commanda à aucun docte orateur, de rediger et mettre par escript les faictz et vie du dict noble et preux chevallier Perceval le Gallois, suyvant la Chronique d'iceluy prince et traictie du Sainct Graal : mais parce que le Chroniqueur du dict Phelippes et luy trespasserent de ce siecle avant l'achevement et accomplissement du livre, et que leur intention vint à effect long temps après, passe que tres haulte et excellente princesse Madame Jehanne Contesse de Flandres eust veu le commencement de la chronique, sachant l'intencion du Conte Philippes son aieul, elle, meue de pareille charité, commanda à ung sien familier orateur nommé Menessier traduire et achever icelle chronique en la forme qu'elle estoit encommencée, ce que diligentement feist et acheva, suyvant le commandement et intention de sa dame et maitresse. Et parce que le langaige du dict Mennessier ne de son predecesseur n'est en usaige en nostre vulgaire Francoys, mais fort non acoustumé et estrange, je, pour satisfaire aux desirs, plaisirs, et voulontez des princes, seigneurs, et aultres, suyvans la maternelle langue de France, ay bien voulu m'employer à traduire et mettre de rithme en prose familiere les faictz et vie du dict vertueux chevallier Perceval, en ensuyvant au plus près selon ma possibilité et povoir le sens de mes predecesseurs translateurs, comme ay trouvé par leur escript, parquoy à tous auditeurs et lecteurs qui ce traictié liront et orront, de ce

que ay presumptueusement et tropt audacieusement mis, prie et requiers retenir et reserver le grain, et mettre au vent la paille.
Cy finist le prologue.

An analysis of this version, from a MS. of the fifteenth century, is given in the Bibliothèque des Romans, Novembre, 1775, pp. 37-83. Lady C. Guest has described the printed copy in her elegant edition of the Mabinogion, p. 395; and a more complete account of it is given in Dunlop's History, vol. i. pp. 223-233.

The tale of Perceval enjoyed great popularity, and was translated into most European languages. Perhaps the best known translation is that made by Wolfram von Eschenbach * into German at the commencement of the thirteenth century, consisting of 24,678 lines. It has been several times printed, but the best edition is that contained in Lachmann's collection of his works, 8vo. Berlin, 1833, pp. 13-388. The German version concludes as follows,—

> " Ob von Troys meister Cristjân
> Disem mære hât unreht getân,
> Daz mac wol zürnen Kyôt,
> Der uns diu rehten mære enbôt.
> Endehaft giht der Provenzâl,
> Wie Herzeloyden Kint den grâl
> Erwarp, als im daz gordent was,
> Dô in verworhte Anfortas.

* The late Mr. Bright possessed a fragment of an early MS. of this translation. See the sale catalogue of his Manuscripts, 8vo. 1844, art. 175.

> Von Provenz in tiuschiu lant
> Diu rehten mære uns sint gesant,
> Und dirre âventiur endes zil.
> Niht mêr dâ von nu sprechen wil
> Ich Wolfram von Eschenbach,
> Wan als dort der meister sprach.
> Sîniu kint, sîn hôch geslehte
> Hân ich iu benennet rehte,
> Parzivâls, den ich hân brâht
> Dâr sîn doch sælde het erdâht.
> Swes lebn sich sô verendet,
> Daz got niht wirt gepfendet
> Der sêle durch des lîbes schulde,
> Und der doch der werlde hulde
> Behalten kan mit werdekeit,
> Daz ist ein nütziu arbeit.
> Guotiu wîp, hânt die sin,
> Deste werder ich in bin,
> Op mir decheiniu guotes gan,
> Sît ich diz mær volsprochen hân.
> Ist daz durh ein wîp geschehn,
> Diu muoz mir süezer worte jehn."
> *Parzival, ed. Lachmann,* p. 388.

About the middle of the fourteenth century, a Flemish translation of the French Perceval was commenced by Penninc, and concluded by Peter Vostaert. It consists of 11,333 lines, and was completed in 1350, as appears from the following lines at the end :—

> " Dese boec was ghescreven int jaer,
> Dat segghic u wel vorwaer,
> Als men screef m.ccc. ende l. mede.
> God gheve ons sinen ewighen vrede."
> *Hoffmann's Horæ Belgicæ,* 8vo. 1830, p. 57.

Perceval was likewise translated into Icelandic. Two copies in this language are preserved in the Royal Library at Stockholm,* and another consisting of eighteen chapters, dated 1694, is in the British Museum, MS. Addit. 4859, ff. 46-60. In the same MS. ff. 61-65, is a short piece entitled, " Nu byriast Valvers [Valvens] þattur, sem var eirn af Artus Kauppum," which Sir F. Madden says " is evidently a short compilation from the Perceval."† This enumeration of the various translations may be concluded with the Welsh tale of Peredur ab Efrawc in the Mabinogion, in which some of the adventures of Perceval are taken from Chrestien de Troyes, and attributed to a chieftain who is said to have fallen in the battle of Cattraeth at the beginning of the sixth century.

The fame of our hero was by no means confined to foreigners. The allusion to him in Chaucer, hereafter quoted,‡ shows that his history was known in the land in which the incidents of the tale are laid; but that the title Perceval *le Galois* is a proof that the story came originally from Wales, seems too evident an absurdity to need refutation. Perceval is likewise mentioned, with other heroes of romance, in the following preface to an anonymous translation of Colonna, a MS. of the fifteenth century preserved in the Bodleian Library :—

* Described in the Mabinogion, p. 412.
† Introduction to Syr Gawayne, p. xliii.
‡ Notes, p. 257.

INTRODUCTION.

"Allemyghty God in Trinité,
Sothfaste God in persones thre,
Fadir, Sone, and Holi Gost,
In whom is witte and myghtes most,
Be at this tale begynny[n]g,
And also at the endyng.
So ende oure tale and so bygynne,
The joye of hevene al for to wynne,
After oure lyff at oure laste ende
To joye of hevene alle for to wende!
Many speken of men that romaunces rede,
That were sumtyme doughti in dede,
The while that God hem lyff lente,
That now ben dede, and hennes wente,
Off Bevis, Gy, and of Gauwayn,
Off Kyng Richard and of Owayn,
Off Tristam and of *Percyvale*,
Off Rouland Ris,* and Aglavale,
Off Archeroun and of Octovian,
Of Charles and of Cassibaldan,
Off Havelok, Horne, and of Wade,†
In romaunces that of hem ben made,
That gestoures often dos of hem gestes,
At mangerés and at grete festes.

---

* This hero is mentioned in Sir Tristrem, p. 141,—

"That on was Douk Morgan,
That other Rouland Rise."

† The loss of Wade's romantic history must ever be a source of regret. He is thus alluded to in the unpublished Morte Arthure,—

"Ware thow wyghttere thane *Wade*, or Wawayne owthire,
Thow wynnys no wyrchipe, I warne the before."
                                        MS. Lincoln A. i. 17, f. 63.

xviii   INTRODUCTION.

>Here dedis ben in remembraunce
>In many fair romaunce,
>But of the worthiest wyght in wede,
>That evere by-strod any stede,
>Spekes no man ne in romaunce redes,
>Off his batayle ne of his dedis;
>Off that batayle spekes no man,
>There alle prowes of knyghtes be-gan.
>   *MS. Laud.* 595, f. 1.

Sir Isumbras, our next romance, is likewise printed from the Lincoln MS. No French original of this or the two others has yet been discovered, but it is most probable that they are all derived from the Anglo-Norman. Sir Isumbras is somewhat similar to Robert of Sicily in its plot; both romances relating to the reclaiming of their heroes by divine interposition. The incident of the loss of the gold, and its recovery, will remind the reader of a well-known tale in the Arabian Nights' Entertainments. Isumbras seems to have been very popular in this country, if we may judge from the numerous copies still remaining, and the various allusions to it in early writers. It is thus mentioned in the prologue to the *Cursor Mundi*,* a metrical version of the Scriptures, several MSS. of which are preserved in our public libraries :—

>" *Here bigynneth the boke of storyes that men callen Cursor Mundi.*
>Men ȝernen jestes for to here,
>And romaunce rede in dyverse manere,

* See Notes, p. 259.

Of Alisaunder the conqueroure;
Of Julius Cesar the emperoure;
Of Greke and Troye the longe strif,
There mony mon lost his lif;
Of Bruyt, that baroun bolde of honde,
Furste conqueroure of Engelonde;
Of kyng Arthour that was so riche,
Was noon in his tyme him liche,
Of wondris that his knyʒtes felle,
And auntres duden men herde telle,
As Wawayn, Kay, and othere ful abul
For to kepe the rounde tabul;
How kyng Charles and Rouland fauʒt,
With Sarazenes nolde thei sauʒt;
Of Tristram and of Isoude the swete,
How thei with love firste gan mete;
Of kyng Jon, and of *Isombras*,
Of Idoyne, and of Amadas;
Storyes of dyverse thinges,
Of princes, prelatis, and of kynges,
Mony songes of dyverse ryme,
As Englisshe, Frensshe, and Latyne;
To rede and here mony are prest
Of thinges that hem liketh best."
MS. Coll. Trin. Cantab. R. iii. 8, f. 1.

There is another notice of Isumbras in the " Mirrour of Life," a metrical translation from a Latin work of John de Waldby.* The translator, at the commencement of his work, informs us,—

* MS. copies of this work are not uncommon. There is one in MS. Hatton 18, and, if I mistake not, part of another in MS. Sloane 1785, but I can scarcely judge from Ayscough's description, and have had no oppor-

> " I warne ȝow ferst ate benyngnyng,
> Y wyl make ȝow no veyn carpyng
> Of dethes of armes, ne of amours,
> As doth menstral' and jestoures,
> That maketh carpyng in many place
> Of Octovyane and *Ysambrace,*
> And of many other gestes,
> Namely when they cum to festes;
> Ne of the lyf of Bewys of Hamptone,
> That was a knyȝt of gret renone,
> Ne of syre Gy of Werewyke,
> Alle ȝif hit myȝte some men lyke."
>
> *MS. Bodl.* 48, f. 47.

The author of this translation was William of Nassington,* who flourished in the latter half of the fourteenth century. A copy of it in MS. Bodl. 446, contains the following curious colophon, which has escaped the notice of Warton and his editors:—

" Anno Domini Millesimo ccc^{mo} lxxxiiij°., compilatio ista hoc modo Cantabrigiæ erat examinata; dum a quodam sacerdote ad ligandum ibidem fuit posita a quibusdam scolaribus, diligenter erat intuita atque perlecta, et cancellario Universitatis ejusque concilio præsentata, propter defectus et hæreses examinanda, ne minus litterati populum per eam negligenter fallant, et in varios errores fallaciter inducant. Tunc jussu cancellarii, coram eo et

---

tunity of comparing it with MS. Bibl. Reg. 17 C. VIII., which contains another copy. There is also a copy among the Rawlinson MSS., the reference to which I am unable to add.

* See Sir F. Madden's note in the new edition of Warton, ii. 368. Can John de Wageby, in Walter's Account of the Clavis Scientiæ, 8vo. Lond. 1816, be an error for John de Waldeby? If so, it may be discovered that the Prick of Conscience is a translation from that author.

toto consilio universitatis, per quatuor dies, cum omni studio et diligentia fuit examinata, atque in omni collegio undique comprobata, die quinto, omnibus doctoribus utriusque juris et magistris theologiæ, cum cancellario, dicentibus et affirmantibus eam de sacris legibus et libris divinis bene ac subtiliter tractatam, et ex auctoritate omnium doctorum sacræ paginæ sapienter allegatam, id est affirmatam, necnon et fundatam. Ideo quicunque fueris, o lector, hanc noli contempnere, quia sine dubio si aliqui defectus in ea inventi fuissent, coram Universitate Cantabrigiæ combusta fuisset."

The romance of Isumbras was printed early in the sixteenth century,* and long sustained its popularity. It formed part of Captain Cox's celebrated library; and Drayton thus alludes to it in his poem called Dowsabell,—

"Farre in the countrey of Arden
There won'd a knight, hight Cassemen,
As bolde as Isenbras;
Fell was he and eger bent,
In batell and in tournament,
As was the good sir Thopas."

And in the "Cobler of Canterburie," 1608, mention is made of "the old wives that wedded themselves to the profound histories of Robin Hood, Clim of the Clough, *and worthie Sir Isembras.*"

Ellis† has analysed the romances of Isumbras and Eglamour in his usual entertaining manner. The latter is here printed from the Cambridge MS. Ff. ii. 38. Two

* Copland's edition, containing fifteen leaves, A to D iii, in fours, has been reprinted by Mr. Utterson. See Notes, p. 270. It was "Imprynted at London, by me Wyllyam Copland."
† Specimens of Early English Metrical Romances, vol. iii.

other MSS. of it are known to exist; one in MS. Cott. Calig. A. II., the other in the Percy MS. A single leaf of another early copy is preserved in a MS. belonging to Lord Francis Egerton.* It was printed at Edinburgh, in 1508, by Walter Chepman,† and subsequently at London by Copland and Walley. Shakespeare may possibly have had this hero in his mind when he calls one of his characters by his name in the Two Gentlemen of Verona, " What think'st thou of the fair Sir Eglamour ?" The name, however, appears to have passed into a kind of proverb. So, in Dekker's Satiromastix,—" Adieu, *Sir Eglamour*; adieu lute-string, curtain-rod, goosequill !"

The romance of Torrent of Portugal is partly founded upon the story related in Sir Eglamour. The names are changed, but the resemblance is too striking to have been the result of chance. The treachery of the sovereign, the prowess of the knight, the indiscretions and misfortunes of the lady, and the happy conclusion of her misfortunes, —these form the leading incidents of each romance. Torrent of Portugal‡ is preserved in an unique manuscript

* Todd's Illustrations of Gower and Chaucer, p. 167.

† Reprinted in 1827. Copland's edition is in the Bodleian, and Walley's in the British Museum. Copland is said to have printed two editions of Eglamour. Walley's edition contains twenty leaves, A to E iiij, in fours, " Imprynted at London in Foster Lane, at the sygne of the Harteshorne, by John Walley."

‡ Printed in 1842, 8vo. and published by Mr. J. Russell Smith of Old Compton Street.

of the fifteenth century, in the Chetham Library at Manchester,—

> " Here bygynneth a good tale
> Of Torrente of Portyngale."

And, although somewhat disfigured by the errors of the scribe, contains much that is curious and valuable. As this poetical tale has recently been published, there is no necessity for proving, in this place, a similarity that will be at once detected by the reader; but there is, perhaps, a secret history attached to the source of these romances that remains to be unravelled.

Sir Degrevant, the fourth and last romance in this collection, is printed from the Cambridge MS. Ff. i. 6, with collations from the Lincoln manuscript, and is, perhaps, more curious and valuable than the others. The descriptive notices of early costume and architecture, are of peculiar interest; and it would perhaps be difficult to select a romance of the kind of more merit. In the notes we have given some reasons for conjecturing that this romance relates to Agravain, if we can reconcile the supposition with the description given of his character in the *Roman de Lancelot*,[*] " Il fut sans pitié *et sans amour*, ne il n' eut oncques bonne grace fors que de chevalerie, et de beaulté, et la langue eut à delivre." An instance of his haughty behaviour is related in the prose Merlin,

[*] Notes to Syr Gawayne, p. 312.

a quality more apparent in the actions of the Earl than in those of Sir Degrevant; but still there scarcely seems to be sufficient dissimilarity to render our conjecture improbable, when we take into consideration how often the character of the same person is varied in different romances.

The contents of the present volume are entirely selected from the three manuscripts described in the following pages. Great pains have been taken in collating the texts, and every facility has been most liberally afforded me in the progress of my undertaking. To the Very Rev. the Dean of Lincoln, the Rev. G. D. Whitehead, the Rev. R. Pretyman, the Rev. J. J. Smith, Sir Charles Young, and David Laing, Esq., I beg to offer my best acknowledgments for the politeness with which they have aided my access to manuscripts in the libraries under their custody. In collecting materials for a lexicographical work, I have been deeply indebted to their liberality; and the treasures then placed at my disposal suggested the following publication, being unwilling to lose an opportunity that might not again present itself.

J. O. HALLIWELL.

Oxford, August 9th, 1844.

DESCRIPTION
OF THE
CAMBRIDGE AND LINCOLN MANUSCRIPTS.

I. MS. LINCOLN, A. i. 17.

THIS volume, generally known as the Thornton Manuscript, is written on 314 leaves of paper, in a somewhat small hand, in folio, measuring $11\frac{1}{2}$ inches by $8\frac{1}{4}$; but unfortunately imperfect both at the beginning and end, and also wanting leaves in a few other places. It was compiled by Robert Thornton, of East Newton, co. York, about the year 1440, and remained in the possession of the Thornton family till the close of the sixteenth century, as appears from several entries in different parts of the book. Thus in the sixteenth century, the name of Edward Thornton occurs three times, viz. at ff. 75, 137, 194; William Thornton twice, ff. 49, 144; and Ellenor Thornton once, f. 135. At the commencement of the seventeenth century, Dorothy Thornton inscribed her name on ff. 265, 266. On referring to the family pedigree, we find that Edward was the fifth son of William Thornton, great-grandson of our scribe, and that he lived to 1586; William was the father of this Edward; Eleanor was the daughter of Thomas Grimston, Esq. and married William Thornton, a grandson of the above-named William; and Dorothy was the daughter of Thomas Metham, and married Robert Thornton, son and heir of William, at the commencement of the seventeenth century. Dorothy died soon after the year 1616.* These entries, therefore, clearly connect the writer of the MS. with the Thorntons of East Newton; but, in addition to these evidences, we have the following important entry at f. 49, v°:—

"Isto die natus fuit, sancta Maria ante [Transfigurationem?] Domini nos-

---

* About this period, a person called Jhon Rokeby wrote the following proverb on f. 220, v°,—"Oft craving maikes sone forgittinge." At f. 29, r°, is the name of Robert Louson; and at f. 265, Roger Blande.

tri Jhesu Christi, Robertus Thornton *in Ridaylle*, anno Domini M.cccc.liij.' which relates to a grandson of the writer of the Lincoln MS., who married the daughter of William Layton of Sproxton. It may also be added that, in a collection of medical receipts at the end of the Lincoln MS., the rectors of Oswaldkirk and Appleton are referred to as authorities, both of which villages are in the neighbourhood of East Newton; and, about the period that MS. was written, the Thornton family were probably on intimate terms with Richard Pickering, the rector of Oswaldkirk. In 1444, Richard Thornton, Robert's third brother, had a legacy left him by that person; and in 1441, the same Pickering had granted *Roberto Thornetone de Newtone*, and others, certain lands in Oswaldkirk, *cum advocatione ecclesiæ Sancti Oswaldi ejusdem villæ, una cum terra mea arrabili vocata Milnehelme in territorio de Stanegrene, ac etiam omnia terras et tenementa mea, redditus et servitia, cum omnibus suis pertinentibus quæ habeo in villis et territoriis de Arnalle, Ristone, et Rowetone in Holderness, in comitatu Eboracensi.* See the Harleian Charters, 55 A. 43.

On the fly-leaves at the commencement of the MS. Sir F. Madden has drawn up an account of its contents, which has been printed with some additions in his Introduction to Syr Gawayne. This has been necessarily followed to some extent in the accompanying list, which is, however, rather more descriptive, and will be found to contain several additions and corrections.

1. Life of Alexander the Great, in prose. f. 1, r°. ακεφαλος.

Beg. .... downe into the dyke, and thare he felle, and was alle to-frusched; and thane Alexander said unto hym one this wyse.

Ad calcem. Explicit vita Alexandry magni conquestoris. Here endez the lyf of gret Alexander, conquerour of alle the worlde.

It commences imperfectly with the death of Nectanabus, or Anectanabus, as he is called in the MS., so that little can be wanting. It is imperfect between f. 18 and f. 19, and again between f. 19 and f. 20. Sir F. Madden says it is a literal translation of the Latin prose life, printed at Strasburgh in 1494. It agrees in substance with the alliterative Scotch romance in MS. Bodl. 264, and MS, Ashmole 44. There are some memoranda on f. 49, v°, which are quoted elsewhere.

2. Prognostications for each month of the year in which thunder falls. f. 50, r°.

This is written in a different and more recent hand, apparently temp. Hen. VIII. It occurs very frequently in MSS.

3. The lamentation of a sinner in Purgatory, entitled *Lamentacio Peccatoris.* f. 51, v°.

> *Beg.* Alle Crystyn men that wawkes me bye,
> Behold and see this dulfule seyght.

In twenty stanzas of four lines each, written in a later hand than Thornton's. Other copies of this poem are in MS. Lambeth 560; MS. Rawl. C. 258. On f. 52 are several very rude pen and ink drawings, part of which Sir F. Madden calls "a combat between a knight and a giant."

4. *Here begynnes Morte Arthure.* f. 53, r°.

> *Beg.* Now grett glorious Godd. thurgh grace of Hymselvene,
> And the precyous prayere. of hys prys modyr.

Ad calcem f. 53, r°.—Espoyez
Thornton, } ygl' En espyrance may.

At f. 93, v°, occurs the name of *Robart Thornton* in a scroll attached to an initial letter; and at f. 75, v°, is a small drawing of a combat. At the end of the poem is written, " Here endes Morte Arthure, writene by Robert of Thorntone." A later hand adds, " R. Thornton dictus, qui scripsit sit benedictus. Amen." A still more modern pen has written the well-known epitaph on King Arthur:—

" Hic jacet Arthurus, rex q[u]ondam rexque futurus."

Sir F. Madden considers this long alliterative romance to be the " Gret geste of Arthure," ascribed by Wyntown to Hucheon.

5. *Here bygynnes the romance off Octovyane.* f. 98, v°.

> *Beg.* Mekylle and littille, olde and ȝynge,
> Herkyns alle to my talkynge.

A leaf is wanting between f. 102 and f. 103; and f. 108 is much torn, leaving only part of col. 1 on the r°, and part of col. 2 on the v°. This version is different to that printed by Weber from the Cottonian MS., but agrees with that in MS. Cantab. Ff. ii. 38. See p. xlii.

6. *Here begynnes the romance off syr Ysambrace.* f. 109, r°.
Printed in this volume, pp. 88-120.

7. *Here bygynnes the romance off Dyoclicyane the emperour and the erle Berade of Tholous, and of the emprice Beaulilione.* f. 114, v°.

> *Beg.* Jhesu Criste, God and Lorde in Trynyté,
> Onely God and persones thre.

xix.

After the title is written, "Ky gray espoyere." This romance has been printed by Ritson from the Cambridge MS. See p. xli. The last leaf, f. 122, is destroyed, with the exception of a small fragment at the bottom, containing on the recto a few lines of the Erle of Tolous, corresponding to ll. 1119-1134 of Ritson's edition, and on the verso the commencement of the next article. By this accident, ll. 1094-1118 and ll. 1135 to the end are unfortunately wholly lost.

8. *Vita Sancti Christofori.* [*Her*]*e bygynnes the lyffe of the story of* [*s*]*aynte Christofre, to the heryng or the* [*se*]*yng of the whilke storye langes* [*gr*]*ete mede and it be done with devocione.* f. 122, v°.

> *Beg.* Lordynges, if it be ȝowre wille,
> And ȝe wille here and holde ȝow stille.

In couplets. It is imperfect between f. 122 and f. 123. The leaf marked f. 124 belongs to Sir Eglamour, and that which ought to be f. 124, belonging to this article, is marked f. 142. At the end is, "Explicit vita sancti Christofori. Thorntone." The last word is nearly obliterated.

9. *Syr Degrevante.* f. 130, r°.

> *Beg.* Jhesu, Lorde in Trynité,
> Graunte tham hevene for to see.

A leaf is wanting between f. 133 and f. 134. This romance is printed in the present volume from a MS. at Cambridge, but collations with this copy are given in the notes.

10. *Incipit syr Eglamour of Artasse.* f. 138, v°.

> *Beg.* Jhesu that es hevens kyng,
> Gyff us alle his blyssyng.

Printed in this volume from another MS. The leaf marked f. 142 belongs to Art. 8, but the right leaf is found at f. 124. This copy is slightly imperfect at the end, the lower corners of the leaves ff. 144, 145, 146, being torn off.

11. A tale of a wicked knight, who was converted by a friar, with the miraculous assistance of the Virgin Mary, entitled *De miraculo Beate Marie.* f. 147, r°.

> *Beg.* Jhesu Lorde in Trinyté,
> That was, and es, and aye schalle be.

In six-line stanzas. It is slightly imperfect, the lower corner of f. 147 having been torn away.

12. A tale called *Lyarde.* f. 148, r°.

Slightly imperfect, the lower corner of f. 148 having been torn off. This amusing but indelicate satire has been printed in the Reliq. Antiq. ii. 280-2.

13. *Tomas off Ersseldoune.* f. 149, v°.

> *Beg.* Lystyns, lordynges, bothe grete and smale,
> And takis gude tente what I wille saye.

In four-line stanzas. At the end is, " Explicit Thomas of Erseledownne." It is imperfect, the lower half of f. 152, and nearly the whole of f. 153, having been torn away. This copy has been printed by Mr. Laing in his " Early Popular Poetry of Scotland," 4to. 1822. There are four other MSS. of this ballad, MS. Cantab. Ff. v. 48, MS. Cott. Vitell. E. x., MS. Lansd. 762, and MS. Sloane 2578. The first of these has been printed by Jamieson and myself; and the commencement of the second by Sir W. Scott. The two others do not appear to have been hitherto noticed.

14. *Here bygynnes the Awnetyrs of Arthure at the Terne-Wathelyne.* f. 154, r°.

> *Beg.* In kyng Arthure tyme ane awntir by-tyde,
> By the Terne Wahethelyne, als the buke tellis.

Printed by Mr. Laing, and afterwards in Sir F. Madden's Syr Gawayne, pp. 95-128. There is another copy in MS. Douce 324, and a transcript made some time in the last century is at Middle Hill. Since the appearance of Syr Gawayne, another early MS. of this romance has been discovered, and printed for the Camden Society, under the care of Mr. Robson.

15. *Here bygynnes the Romance off Syr Perecyvelle of Gales.* f. 161, r°.

Printed in the present volume, pp. 1-87.

16. A charm for the tooth-ache, in verse. f. 176, r°.

Printed in the Reliq. Antiq. i. 126.

17. A similar charm. f. 176, r°.

Printed in the Reliq. Antiq. i. 126-7.

18. A charm for the tooth-ache, in Latin prose. f. 176, v°. Slightly imperfect.

19. *Epistola Sancti Salvatoris.* f. 176, v°.

Concerning this wonderful letter we are told: " Hec est epistola sancti Salvatoris, quam Leo papa transmisit Karolo regi, dicens quod quicunque eam secum portaverit, in die qua eam viderit vel legerit, ferro non occidetur, nec comburetur, nec aqua submergetur, nec malus homo, nec diabolus, nec aliqua alia creatura ei nocere poterit illo die."

20. A Latin orison, with a proeme in English. f. 176, v°.

Beg. He that devotely sayse this orysone dayly, salle hafe remyssyone of alle his synnys.

This proeme, which is much defaced, tells us that the Latin prayer was taught to St. Paul by the Holy Ghost, and that Pope Innocent granted three hundred days of pardon to whoever said it devoutly. It also enumerates a quantity of evils from which the orison was an efficient protection.

21. *A preyere off the ffyve joyes of owre Lady [in] Ynglys, and of the ffyve sorowes.* f. 177, v°.

22. *Psalmus, Voce mea ad Dominum clamavi.* f. 178, r°.

23. Five Latin prayers, *Here bygynnys fyve prayers to the wirchipe of the fyve wondys of oure Lorde Jhesu Cryste.* f. 178, r°.

24. A short prayer to our Saviour, entitled *Oracion in Ynglys.* f. 178, v°.

25. *A colett to owre lady Saynt Marye,* in Latin. f. 178, v°.

26. *Oracio in modo collecte, pro amico.* f. 178, v°.

27. *Antiphona sancti Leonardi cum collecta.* f. 178, v°.

28. *In nomine Patris, et Filii, et Speritus Sancti, Amen pro charite. Here begynnes the previté off the Passioune of owre Lorde Jhesu.* f. 179, r°.

Beg. Who so desyres to fynd comforthe and gostely gladnes in the Passione and in the Croysse of owre Lorde Jhesu.

Ad calcem. Explicit Bonaventure de misteriis Passionis Jhesu Christi.

29. Three lines. f. 189, r°.

> Of alle thynge it is the best,
> Jhesu in herte fast to fest,
> And lufe hym ower all thynge.

30. *Incipit tractatus Willelmi Nassyngtone, quondam advocati curiæ*

Eboraci, de Trinitate et Unitate, cum declaracione operum Dei, et de Passione Domini nostri Jhesu Christi, etc. f. 189, r°.

> *Beg.* A, Lord God of myghtes maste, Fadere and Sone and Haly Gaste!
> Fader, for thou ert Almyghtty, Sone, for thow ert alle wytty.

Warton has confused this poem, which has no merit, with Nassyngton's translation of Waldeby. See p. xx. The mistake was corrected by Sir F. Madden in Warton's Hist. ii. 368, where the commencing lines do not seem to be accurately given.

31. A prayer, in verse. f. 191, v°.

> *Beg.* Lorde Jhesu Cryste, Godd Almyghty,
> I thanke the with alle my herte hally.

32. Another prayer in verse, written as prose. f. 191, v°.

> *Beg.* Almyghty God in Trinité,
> Inwardly I thanke the.

33. Another poetical prayer. f. 191, v°.

> *Beg.* Jhesu that diede one the rude for the lufe of me.

This consists of twelve lines only, of which the first four, the 5th, 7th, 9th, and 11th rhyme, and the 6th, 8th, 10th, and 12th.

34. *Of the vertuz of the haly name of Jhesu. Ricardus Herimita super versiculo, Oleum effusum nomen tuum, in Cantic. etc.* f. 192, r°.

Beg. That es on Inglysce, Oyle owt-ʒettede es thi name.

Another copy is in MS. Harl. 1022, f. 62. The original Latin occurs in MS. Laud. 528.

35. *Narracio. A tale that Richerde Hermet [made].* f. 193, v°.

Beg. When I hade takene my syngulere purpos, and lefte the seculere habyte.

36. *A prayere that the same Richerd Hermet made, that es beried at Hampulle.* f. 193, v°.

A short Latin prayer.

37. *Ympnus quem composuit Sanctus Ambrosyus, et est valde bonus.* f. 193, v°.

38. Two tales from Hampole *de inperfecta contricione.* f. 194, r°.

Beg. Rycharde Hermyte reherces a dredfulle tale of unperfitte contrecyone.

Hampole appears to have taken these tales from Cæsarius.

39. *Moralia Richardi Heremite de natura apis; unde quasi apis argumentosa.* f. 194, r°.

Beg. The bee has thre kyndis. Ane es that scho es never ydille.

40. A tale from Hampole, *De vita cujusdam puelle incluse proptter amorem Christi.* f. 194, v°.

Beg. Alswa Heraclides the clerke telles, that a maydene forsuke hir ceté, and satte in a sepulcre.

41. Two short Latin extracts from *Richardus Herymyta.* f. 195, r°.

42. *A notabille tretys off the ten comandementys, drawene by Richerde the hermyte off Hampulle.* f. 195, v°.

Beg. The fyrste comandement es, Thy Lorde God thou salle loute.

43. *Item idem de septem donis Spiritus Sancti. Also of the gyftes of the Haly Gaste.* f. 196, r°.

Beg. The sevene gyftes of the Haly Gaste that ere gyfene to men and wymmene.

44. *Item idem de dilectacione in Deo. Also of the same delyte and ʒernyng of Gode.* f. 196, v°.

Beg. Gernyng and delite of Jhesu Criste, that has na-thyng of worldes thoghtes.

A short tract in prose, but at the end is written, *Explicit carmen. Qui scripsit sit benedictus! Amen.*

45. *Incipit Speculum Sancti Edmundi, Cantuar' Archi[e]piscopi, in Anglicis. Here begynnys the Myrrour of Seynt Edmonde the ersebechope of Canterberye.* f. 197, r°.

Beg. Videte vocacionem vestram. This wordes sayse saynte Paule in his pistylle.

The original Latin of this, by Edmund Rich, is printed in Biblioth. Patrum, Lugd. 1677, tom. xxv. p. 316.

46. A commentary on the Lord's prayer, called, *Tractatus de Dominica oracione secundum . . . . . . etc.* f. 209, v°.

Beg. Pater noster qui es in celis. In alle the wordes that er stabilled, and sett to say in erthe, than es the Pater Noster the beste.

47. A poetical address to Christ. f. 211, r°.

> *Beg.* Jhesu Criste, Saynte Marye sonne,
> Thurgh whayme this werlde was worthily wroghte.

In stanzas of four lines. At the end is, *Explicit tractatus. Explicit. Amen. Thorntone. Amen.*

48. Another metrical orison. f. 211, v°.

> Beg. Fadir, and Sone, and Haly Gaste,
> Lorde, to the I make my mone.

In stanzas of six lines, the alternate lines rhyming.

49. An orison to Christ. f. 212, r°.

Beg. Jhesu Criste, Goddes sune of hevene, Kyng of Kynges, and Lorde of Lordes.

This brief prayer seems to be partly in verse, and partly in prose.

50. *Incipit a meditacione of the fyve woundes of oure Lorde Jhesu Criste, with a prayere in the same, etc.* In Latin verse. f. 212, r°.

> Beg. Adoro te, piissime Jhesu, qui redimisti me!

51. *A medytacione of the Crosse of Criste, with a prayere.* In Latin verse. f. 212, v°.

Ad calcem. R. Thorntone dictus, qui scripsit sit benedictus. Amen.

52. A moral poem, in stanzas of four lines. f. 213, r°.

> Beg. When Adam dalfe and Eve spane, Go spire, if thou may spede.

53. Six lines of poetry. f. 213, v°.

> Beg. Jhesu Criste, have mercy one me,
> Als thou erte kynge of magesté.

54. *Here begynnes a sermone that dane Johan Gaytryge made, the whilke teches how scrifte es to be made and whareof, and in scrifte how many thyngez solde be consederide. Et est Petrus sentenciarum discrecione prima.* f. 213, v°.

Beg. Als a grete doctour schewes in his buke, of alle the creatours that Gode made in hevene and in erthe.

There is another copy in MS. Harl. 1022, a volume which seems to contain several pieces also found in this manuscript.

55. Hymn to Christ. f. 219, r°.

> Beg. Jhesu, thi swetnes wha moghte it se,
> And thareof hafe a clere knaweynge.

In eight-line stanzas. It was written, probably, by the author of Arts. 47, 48, and 49, none of which have much poetical merit.

56. A prose tract on the love of God. f. 219, v°.

Beg. Dere frende, wit thou wele that the ende and the soveraynté of perfeccione standes in a verray anehede of Godd.

57. A moral poem, ατελ. f. 222, r°.

> Beg. Thi joy be ilke a dele to serve thi Godd to paye,
> For alle this worldes wele, thou sese it wytes awaye.

Imperfect at the end, one leaf or more being wanting between f. 222 and f. 223, which renders the next article imperfect at the beginning.

58. A treatise on active and contemplative life, ακεφ. f. 223, r°.

Beg. . . . . . mene that ware in prelacye, and other also that ware haly temporalle mene.

59. A treatise on sin. f. 229, v°.

Beg. Wit thou wele, dere frende, that thof thou had never done syne with thi bodi.

60. *Of Sayne Johan the Evaungelist.* f. 231, r°.

> Beg. Of alle mankynde that He made, that maste es of myghte,
> And of the molde merkede and mesured that tyde.

An alliterative poem in 19 stanzas of 14 lines each, of which the first, third, fifth, and seventh rhyme, and the second, fourth, sixth, and eighth. At the close of each stanza are six shorter lines, of which the first, second, fourth and fifth rhyme, and the third and sixth.

61. A prose treatise on prayer. f. 233, v°.

Beg. Prayng es a gracyous gyfte of owre Lorde Godd tylle ylk mane.

One leaf or more is wanting between f. 236 and f. 237. The first letter is put S by mistake, but a P is written in the margin.

62. *De gracia Dei. Assit principio Sancta Maria meo.* f. 240, r°.

Beg. Off Goddis grace stirrand and helpand, and that na thyng may be done withowttene grace.

63. *Hic incipit quedam revelacio. A revelacyone schewed to ane holy womane now one late tyme.* f. 250, v°.

Beg. Alle manere of thyng that es bygune that may turne to the profyte of mannes saule.

A leaf is wanting between f. 253 and f. 254. This is a narrative by a woman of several visions of purgatory, revealed to her during sleep on the night of the Feast of St. Lawrence, 1422, and following evenings. She was visited by one Margaret, who was suffering pains in Purgatory, and who requested her to apply to the priests, Dane Perse Cowme, Sir Richerde Bowne, and Dane Johan Percy, f. 252, for assistance for her soul. The relator mentions two of her confessors at f. 253, viz. Mayster Foreste and Syr Johan Wynburne.

64, 65. Two Latin hymns. f. 258, r°.

66. *Here bygynnys Sayne Jerome Spaltyre*, in Latin. f. 258, v°.

67. *Religio Sancti Spiritus. Religio munda.* f. 271, r°.

Beg. Off the Abbaye of Saynte Spirite, that es in a place that es callede Conscyence.

A well-known allegorical treatise, common in manuscript, entitled, "The Abbaye of the Holy Goste." It is generally ascribed to Bishop Alcock, but Sir F. Madden clearly proves it to belong to an earlier period.

68. Part of a religious poem. f. 276, v°.

> *Beg.* The begynnyng es of thre,
> Fulle mekille therin men may see.

This is merely an extract from Hampole's Prick of Conscience. On f. 277 are two alphabets in different styles of writing.

69. *Ista oracio que sequitur est de vij. gaudia* Beate Marie Virginis per sanctum Thomam et martirem, Cantuariensem archiepiscopum, edita.* f. 277, v°.

This is the well-known hymn, commencing,—

> Gaude flore virginali,
> Honore quoque speciali.

70. *Another salutacioune tille oure lady of hir fyve joyes.* In Latin verse. f. 277, v°.

> *Beg.* Gaude, virgo, mater Christi,
> Que per aurem concepisti.

71. *Ane antyme to the Fadir of Hevene, with a colett*, in Latin. f. 278, r°.

72. *Another antyme of the Passyoune of Criste Jhesu,* in Latin. f. 278, r°.

73. *A colecte of grete pardone unto Crist Jhesu,* in Latin. f. 278, r°.

74. A hymn to our Saviour. f. 278, v°.

> *Beg.* Crucem coronam spiniam,
> Clavos diramque lanceam
> Devote veneremur.

---

* Sic in MS. pro *gaudiis*.

At the top of the page is written, " Thorntone. Misereatur mei Dei."

75. *A preyere to the wounde in Crystis syde*, in Latin. f. 278, v°.

76. *Memento, homo, quod sinis es, et in cenerem reverteris.* f. 279, r°.

> *Beg.* Erthe owte of erthe es wondirly wroghte,
> Erthe hase getyn one erthe a dignyté of noghte.

A poem in dialogue in four-line stanzas, each of which rhymes with the same syllable. Other copies, varying considerably from each other, are in MS. Porkington 10, art. 19; MS. Seld. supra 53; MS. Rawl. C. 307; MS. Rawl. Poet. 32: MS. Lambeth 853; MS. roll in the possession of Thomas Bateman, Esq. Jun., of Bakewell, Derbyshire.

77. *Hic incipit liber de diversis medicinis, et primo pro capite.* ατελ. f. 280, r°.

Beg. For werke and vanytee in the hede. Take vervayne, or vetoyne, or filles of wormod, and make lee therof, and wasche thi heved therwith thrys in a weke.

This is a very curious collection of medical receipts. The authority of the *Rector de Oswaldkirke* is frequently referred to, ff. 288, 291, &c. There is also a receipt at f. 299, *secundum Syr Apiltone;* and another at f. 282, v°, *secundum Magistrum Willelmum de Excestre*. The charms and many of the remedies are particularly curious. It is unfortunately imperfect, the MS. concluding abruptly with f. 314; but eight very small fragments of leaves belonging to the same treatise still remain after that folio. This may, however, have been originally, as now, the last piece in the volume; and, indeed, unless it were of unusual size, not much can be missing.

II. MS. CANTAB. Ff. ii. 38.

Formerly marked MS. More 690, under which reference it is mentioned by Percy, Ritson, Warton, and others. It is a folio volume on paper, containing 247 leaves, measuring $11\frac{3}{4}$ inches by $8\frac{1}{8}$, and written late in the reign of Henry VI.

1. A paraphrase on the seven penitential psalms, in verse. f. 1, r°.

Another copy is in MS. Sloane 1853, which was edited by Mr. W. H. Black for the Percy Society, June 1842. The commencement of this copy is wanting, the first line in the MS. being, " Ne cyrcumstaunce that long ther tylle," Mr. Black's ed. p. 22. This fragment agrees very closely with Mr. Black's edition; but the 88th, 90th, and 95th stanzas are much altered. Mr. Black mentions a fragment of another copy in MS. Harl. 1704. At the end is the following colophon:—" Here endyth the sevene salmes, and begynneth a Salutacion of oure Lady." The Latin sentences are entirely omitted in the present copy. A similar poem, in the same stanza, and with Latin sentences, is in MS. Digby 102.

2. A Salutation of Our Lady. f. 4, v°.

> *Beg.* Heyle, fairest that evyr God fonde!
> Heyle, modyr and mayden free!

Ad calcem. Here endyth the salutacion of oure lady, and begynneth the x. commaundementis of Almyȝty God.

Another copy in MS. Lambeth 853.

3. The Ten Commandments in verse. f. 5, r°.

> *Beg.* Thou schalt have oo God and no moo,
> And over alle thyng love hym also.

4. *Here suen the vij. werkis of merci bodili.* f. 5, r°.

> *Beg.* Seynt Poule the apostelle thus seyth he,
> Doyth alle youre werkys in charyté.

5. *Here suen the vij. werkis of merci gostli.* f. 5, v°.

> *Beg.* Teche eche man, with charyté,
> To kepe Goddes heestes, buxum to be.

6. *The v. bodyly wyttis.* f. 5, v°.

> *Beg.* Kepe thy syght fro vanyté,
> That thou noght coveyte that evelle may be.

7. *Here suen the v. goostly wyttys.* f. 5, v°.

> *Beg.* Have mynde on the blys that never schalle blyne,
> And on grete peyne that synners shalle wynne.

8. *Here suen the vij. deedly synnes.* f. 5, v°.

> *Beg.* Pryde ys hedd of alkyns synne,
> That makyth mannys soule fro God to twynne.

9. *The vij. vertues contrarie to the vij. dedli synnes.* f. 6, r°.

> *Beg.* Wyth scharpe thornes that weren fulle keene,
> Myn hedd was crowned, ȝe mone welle seene.

10. *Here suen the xij. Articulis of the Beleeve,* in prose. f. 6, r°.

Beg. The fyrste artycle of these twelve ys that God ys oon substaunce and thre persones in hymselfe.

11. *Here suen the vij. sacramentis schortly declarid of Seynt Edmonde of Pounteneye* [i. e. Edmund Rich], in prose. f. 6, v°.

Beg. Seynt Edmonde of Pountneye seythe that baptyme ys thee fyrste sacrament.

12. *Here bygynneth a tretice of thre arowis that schullen be schett on domesday aȝenste them that schullen be dampnedd,* in prose. f. 6, v°.

Beg. Who so wole have in mynde the dredefulle day of doome, so that hee may be movyd with drede.

Attributed in some MSS. to Wickliffe. Other copies in MS. Tanner 336, and MS. Bibl. Publ. Cantab. Ff. v. 45. It is common in MSS.

13. *Here suen the viij. tokenes of mekenes,* in prose. f. 8, r°.

Beg. The fyrste tokene ys, that a verry meke man or womman hath no dysdeyne, or ys evelle apayed.

14. *Here sueth the life of Marye Mawdelyn,* in prose. f. 8, v°.

Beg. This woman Mary Mawdelyn was the fyrste in the tyme of grace that dydd hur penaunce for hur synne.

15. *Here begynneth the lyfe of Seynte Margaret,* in prose. f. 10, r°.

Beg. This woman Seynte Margaret had a grete man to hur fadur, and was a paynym.

16. *Here foloweth the life of Seynt Thomas,* in prose. f. 11, r°.

Beg. Thys holi martyr Seynte Thomas, ye schalle knowe that he was borne in the cyté of London.

Like most copies of this, a pen has been drawn through it cross-ways. It contains nine columns, but the two last are found out of their place on the recto of fol. 32.

17. The *xij. profytes that men may gete in sufferyng of bodely anger.* f. 13, r°.

Beg. Almyghty God, that made alle thyng
Aftur hys own ordynaunce.

18. *The mirrour of vices and of vertues, which also ys clepid the sevene ages.* f. 14, v°.

Beg. How mankinde doith bigynne,
Ys wondre to dyscrye soo ;

> In game he ys begeten with synne.
> The chylde ys the modurs deedly foo
> Or they be fully partyd on twynne.

This ends imperfectly on the v° of fol. 15, and there appears to be some leaves wanting between f. 15 and f. 16, although the nearly obliterated signatures seem to follow consecutively. Another copy in MS. Lambeth 853.

19. *The compleynt of God.* f. 16, r°. ακεφ.

> *Beg.* And therfore, man, whyles thou may,
> Make amendys or that thou dye.

This poem is written in dialogue between our Saviour and a sinner, recounting the torments that Christ suffered for man's sake. Another copy is in MS. Lambeth 853.

20. *The ix. lessons of dyryge, whych ys clepyd Pety Joob.* f. 19, r°.

> *Beg.* Parce michy, Domine,
> Leef Lord, my sowle thou spare.

In stanzas of twelve lines, each ending with *Parce michy, Domine.* A copy is in MS. Harl. 1706, there ascribed to Hampole. See also MS. Douce 322. Another poem, with the same burden, generally follows this in most of the manuscripts.

21. *The proverbis of Salamon.* f. 23, r°.

> *Beg.* Wast bryngyth a kyngdome in nede,
> Nede makyth a man to travayle.

22. *The markys of medytacyouns.* f. 27, v°.

> *Beg.* Almyghty God in Trynyté,
> Fadur and Soone and Hooly Goost.

The two last columns of this are found out of their proper place on the recto of f. 13.

23. On the Assumption of the Virgin. f. 32, v°.

> *Beg.* A lovely tale y yow tell may,
> Of Seynt Mary that swete may ;
> The begynnyng of thys lesson
> Ys of hur Assumpcyon.

Other copies are in MS. Chetham 8009, f. 4; MS. Harl. 2382. See also Warton's Hist. Engl. Poet. ii. 276.

24. *Here foloweth the lyfe of Seynt Kateryn.* f. 37, r°.

> *Beg.* All tho that be crystenyd and dere,
> Lystenyth and ye may here

> The lyfe of a swete vyrgyne,
> Hur name ys clepydd Kateryn.

25. *Here foloweth the chartur of Criste.* f. 39, v°.

> *Beg.* Who so will over-rede this boke,
> And wyth hys goostly eye theron loke.

Other copies are in MS. Cott. Calig. A. II.; MS. Harl. 2382; MS. Bibl. Reg. 17 C. XVII.

26. *Here foloweth the xv. tokenys before the day of dome.* f. 42, v°.

> *Beg.* The grace of the Holy Goste,
> That ys ay stedfaste.

27. *Here foloweth How the goode man taght hys sone.* f. 45, r°.

> *Beg.* Lystenyth alle, and ye shall here
> How the godeman taght hys sone.

This is a better copy than that in MS. Harl. 5396 (misquoted by Ritson as 1596), printed in Ritson's "Pieces of Ancient Popular Poetry," 1791, pp. 83-91, and supplies several good corrections. It is singular that Ritson should have stated the Harl. MS. to be the only copy he had met with, as he prints in the same volume another piece from this very MS. See Art. 32. Perhaps, however, Ritson may have used Mr. Baynes' transcripts, without seeing the original. Other copies are in MS. Harl. 2399; MS. Lambeth 853; MS. Ashmole 61.

28. *Here foloweth a good ensaumple of a lady that was in dyspeyre.* f. 46, r°.

Printed from this MS. and collated with another copy in MS. Ff. v. 48, in Hartshorne's Ancient Metrical Tales, p. 134-144. "Wysdom," in l. 67, ought to be "mysdone," and l. 99 is, "And founde in a crysome oure Savyour swote." Several words also are omitted, but it would require too much space to give a corrected collation. Another copy is in MS. Harl. 3810.

29. The Lamentation of the Virgin. f. 47, r°.

> *Beg.* Lystenyth, lordynges, to my tale,
> And ye schalle here of oon story,
> Ys bettur then owthyr wyne or ale
> That ever was made in thys cuntré.

Other copies in MS. Ff. v. 48; MS. Harl. 5396.

30. Another poem on the same subject. f. 47, v°.

> *Beg.* Off alle wemen that ever were borne,
> That bere chylder, abyde and see.

Another copy is in MS. Ff. v. 48, and is printed from that MS. in the Reliq. Antiq. ii. 213-215. It is also found in MS. Chetham 8009, f. 119; MS. Ashmole 61, f. 106; MS. Rawl. C. 86.

31. A poem against adultery. f. 48, r°.

> *Beg.* Man for myschefe thou the amende,
> And to my talkyng thou take gode hede.

A curious tale of a visit to Purgatory. Two other copies are in the same library, Ee. iv. 35, and Ff. v. 48, from which Mr. Wright has made an interesting abstract in his "St. Patrick's Purgatory," pp. 85-87. The best copy is in MS. Ashmole 61, ff. 136-138, which has a long and curious preface, wanting, I believe, in all other copies, and where it is stated that it was the ghost of Sir William Basterfeld, that suffered for "spouse-breke." The copy in MS. Ff. v. 48, is printed in Hartshorne's Ancient Metrical Tales, pp. 169-178; and another copy is in MS. Harl. 5396.

32. *Here foloweth how a merchande dyd hys wyfe betray.* f. 49, v°.

Printed from this MS. in Ritson's "Pieces of Ancient Popular Poetry," 1791, pp. 69-79. At l. 44 *yn* ought to be *ynto*. Ritson mentions a fragment of another copy in MS. Harl. 5396, and another, apparently a different version, is in the Auchinleck MS. art. 28. An imperfect copy is in MS. Porkington 10, art. 54.

33. *Here foloweth a gode mater of the marchand and hys sone.* f. 51, r°.

> *Beg.* Lystenyth ye godely gentylmen and alle that ben here yn,
> Of a ryche franklyn of Ynglond a song y wylle begyn.

Another version of the same tale, the scene laid at Bristol, occurs in MS. Harl. 2382. The present copy has been printed by me in a Collection of Early English Poetry, 8vo. Lond. 1844.

34. *Here foloweth the Erle of Tolous.* f. 55, r°.

Printed from this MS. in Ritson's "Ancient Engleish Metrical Romanceës," vol. iii. pp. 93-144, with much correctness, but with inattention to the old contractions. Thus at l. 770, the common contraction w^t is interpreted in two different ways in the very same line. Among minor errors, *new* in l. 1021 should be *never*, and *Godd* in l. 1074 should be *Goddes*. *Gh* and *y* are substituted for the character ȝ. A copy of the time of Henry VIII. is in MS. Ashm. 45, ff. 3-31; and an earlier one in MS. Ashm. 61, ff. 27-38. See also p. xxvii.

35. *Syr Egyllamoure of Artas.* f. 63, r°.

Printed from this MS. in the present volume, pp. 121-176. A late MS. copy of this romance is contained in MS. Douce 261.

36. *Syr Tryamowre.* f. 71, v°.

> *Beg.* Heven blys that alle schalle wynne,
> Schylde us fro dedly synne.

Another copy in Bp. Percy's folio MS. It was twice printed by Copland; and has been published by Mr. Utterson from a printed copy in Garrick's Collection, in " Select Pieces of Early Popular Poetry," vol. i. pp. 5-72.

37. The tale of the Emperor Octavian. f. 82, r°.

Printed by me from this MS. for the Percy Society, Sept. 1844, with collations from the Lincoln MS. See p. xxvii.

38. Bevise of Hampton. f. 94, v°.

> *Beg.* Lordynges, lystenyth, grete and smale,
> Meryar then the nyghtyngale
> I wylle yow synge;
> Of a knyght y wylle yow rowne,
> That hyght Befyse of Hampton,
> Wythowt lesyng.

This romance is evidently alluded to in Sir Thopas. There are several other MSS. of it in our public libraries.

39. The Seven Sages. f. 126, r°.

> *Beg.* Some tyme ther was a nobleman,
> Whos name was clepyd Dyaclysyan.
> Of ryche Rome and that honour
> Lorde he was and emperour.
> An emperyce he had to wyfe,
> The fayrest that myght bere lyfe;
> A feyre lady and a gente,
> Hur name was clepyd Dame Ilacent.

Percy and others have placed this as an unique romance, under the title of " Dioclesian the Emperor." This is a different copy from that published by Weber, Met. Rom. vol. iii. pp. 3-153; but unfortunately two leaves are wanting, and one other has lost about half, being torn in the middle, and the lower part lost. The first deficiency occurs at fol. 127, the lower part of which leaf is wanting, whereby we lose part of the account of the wonderful proficiency the young prince made in science, and his discovery of the leaves which were placed under the corners of the bed. An entire leaf is wanting between f. 132 and f. 133, which contained the conclusion of the fourth tale and the commencement of the fifth. Another leaf is wanting between f. 134 and f. 135, which contained the conclusion of the seventh tale and nearly all the eighth. The conduct of the story is somewhat different from Weber's version. In the present copy, when the King goes " to hys towre" till his anger is somewhat abated, after he had heard of the supposed crime of his son, his steward comes and reminds him of his promise to grant him his first request, in consideration of certain favours performed in war. The steward then asked for the life of the prince for that day, a request which was immediately complied with. The tales are in the following order:—1. The pynote tree.—2. The Burgess of Rome.—3. The Boar and the herdsman.—4. The old wise man and his wife. The wife here kills her husband's favourite parrot as well as his hound. It is imperfect at the end.—5. The father murdered by his son. The beginning is wanting.—6. The widow who was comforted.—7. This tale does not appear to be in the copy printed by Weber. The greater part of it is wanting; but it commences with an account of a riotous son who kills his father in a wood, in order to inherit his estate.

> Hyt was a kny3t of thys contré,
> And a nobleman was he,
> And he had a sone feyre,
> A godely chylde, schulde be hys heyre :
> The chylde lovyd welle spendyng,
> And ryet yn alle thynge ;
> Taverns and dyces lovyd he,
> And horys lovyd he grete plenté !
> Thus he spendyd alle that he my3t wynne,
> Tylle that hys catelle waxe alle thynne.
> He hym bethoght yn alle wyse
> How he my3t hys fadur sle with some queyntyse.
> So hyt befelle upon a day,
> He feyned hym syke and yn hys bed he lay,

>And seyde ther was a boor yn that forest,
>That was a wondur vylous beest;
>" Fadur, but yf y have a brede of hym,
>I dye fro the and alle my kynne."
>The godemans hert was fulle sore,
>That hys sone shulde dye for the brede of a boor;
>He dyʒt hym on a gode palfray,
>And to the wode he went hys way.
>The chylde spekyth with felows xij.,
>And the xiij. was hymselfe,
>And mette hys fadur undur a tree,
>And assayle hym harde can he.
>He hewe hys fadur very smale,
>Alle yn pecys, as seyth thys tale,
>And home he went to bedd ageyn,
>And covyrd hym warme, hit ys not to layne.
>Tho tydynges come to that cyté,
>For hym was dele and grete pyté,
>For that noble knyght was sloon!

8. The concluding lines only of this tale remain, and are here given, as they may enable the reader to identify it.

>He set anon and solde hys londe,
>And gadurd hym sylvyr, y undurstonde,
>And sethen passyd he over the see,
>That never aftur they myʒt hym see.
>Thus schalle betyde of the, syr Emperour,
>And of thy wyfe so gret of honour;
>Yf thou do thy sone to dedd,
>Thorow councelle of thy wyvys redd,
>I beseche God that hyt betyde of the,
>As dud of the knyʒt of thys contré,
>That thus dud yn soche an entent,
>For sorowe yn pylgrymage he went.

9. The " squyer and hys borowe," the latter of whom betrayed him.—10. The magpie.—11. Herowdes and Merlin.—12. Hippocrates and his nephew.—14. The two dreams.—15. The three ravens.

40. The romance of Guy of Warwick. f. 147, r°.

>*Beg.* Sythen the tyme that God was borne,
>And Crystendome was set and sworne,

CAMBRIDGE MANUSCRIPTS. xlv

> Mané aventewres hathe be-falle,
> That ȝyt be not knowen alle.

This copy contains 12,156 lines, and is quite perfect. The conclusion, comprising the history of Heraud, commences on f. 217, v°, and has been erroneously described as a separate romance.

41. Le Bone Florence of Rome. f. 225, v°.

Printed from this MS. in Ritson's Met. Rom. vol. iii. pp. 1-92. Ritson's edition is generally very correct, but he has not used the character ȝ. Among the few errors of detail may be noticed l. 1108, which should be,— "Then Mylys made xij. armed knyȝtes."

42. The romance of Robert of Sicily. f. 240, r°.

Printed by me from this MS. in a Collection of Early Poetry, 8vo. 1844. Other copies are in MS. Harl. 525; MS. Harl. 1701; MS. Coll. Caii Cantab. D. 16; MS. Coll. Trin. Oxon. 57.

43. The romance of Sir Degaré. f. 243, v°.

> *Beg.* Lystenyth, lordynges, gente and fre,
> Y wylle yow telle of syr Degaré.

This copy ends imperfectly with p. 138 of Mr. Utterson's edition. Other copies are in MS. Auchinleck, Art. 18; MS. Douce 261; MS. Percy, p. 371.

In two places in this MS., some one has written a few lines from a curious song beginning, " Adewe, my prettye pussey." The entire song is preserved in Sheale's MS. in the Ashmolean Museum.

III. MS. CANTAB. Ff. i. 6.

An octavo volume, on paper, written in a very negligent hand, about the year 1450, containing 159 leaves, measuring $8\frac{1}{2}$ inches by $5\frac{3}{4}$. It was formerly marked MS. More 60, and is described in Bernard's Catalogue, p. 363, as, " Poema historicum lingua Anglica vetere, 8vo." In various parts of the book occur the names of Margery Hungelford, Anne Schyrley, Thomas Cotune, and W. Calverley. It is imperfect both at the beginning and end, and wants leaves in several places.

1. An extract from Gower. f. 1, r°. ακεφ.

 Beg. Thow hast thy tyrannye y-wroʒt;
    Lo, now yt ys sumdel y-boʒt!

2. A poem on pity. f. 9, r°.

 Beg. [P]itee that I have sogthe so yore ago,
    Wyth herte sore and fulle of bisy peyn.

Printed in Chaucer, ed. Urry, p. 421, under the title of, " How pyté is dede and buried in gentyle herte."

3. A lamentation of a lover. f. 11, r°.

 Beg. As ofte as syghes ben in herte trewe,
    And cristalle teres on dolefulle chekis trylle.

Thirteen stanzas of eight, with the burden, " So ofte and ofter I sygh for yowre sake." Another copy is in MS. Tanner 346.

4. A similar poem. f. 13, r°.

 Beg. For lac of sight grete cause I have to pleyne,
    Longe absense so sore me werreyth.

In eight-line stanzas, wanting a few lines at the end. Another copy is in MS. Tanner 346.

5. Another poem of the same nature. f. 14, r°.

 Beg. I may welle sygh, for grevous ys my payne,
    Now to deperte fram yow thys sodenly.

In 3 stanzas of 7, with the burden, " Alas for woo, depertynge hath me slayne."

6. A love song. ατελ. f. 14, v°.

 Beg. Where y have chosyne, stedefast wolle y be,
    Newyre to repente in wylle, thowth, ne dede.

7. The Cuckoo and the Nightingale. f. 15, r°.

Printed in Chaucer, ed. Urry, p. 543. This copy has several variations, and two additional stanzas.

8. Two stanzas, of seven lines each. f. 21, v°.

 Beg. As in yow resstyth my joy and comfort,
    Youre dissese ys my mortal payne.

9. The Parliament of Birds. f. 22, r°.

Printed in Chaucer, ed. Urry, p. 413. The last leaf is a little torn. At the end is written, "Explicit Parliamentum Avium quod W. Calverley." A good copy of this poem is in MS. Coll. S. Joh. Oxon. 57.

10. An extract from Gower. f. 36, r°.

> *Beg.* A king whylom was ȝonge and wys,
> The whyche sette of hijs wyt gret prys.

11. The Parliament of Love. f. 42, r°.

> *Beg.* What so evyr I syng or sey,
> My wylle is good too preyse here welle.

12. A roundel on fortune. f. 44, v°.

Printed in Ritson's Ancient Songs and Ballads, vol. i. p. 129.

13. Six lines, beginning, "Pees maketh plenté." f. 44, v°.

These lines are generally found at the end of Lydgate's Life of the Virgin Mary. They are printed in the Reliq. Antiq. vol. i. p. 315.

14. A ballad. f. 45, r°.

Printed in the Reliq. Antiq. vol. i. p. 23.

15. A poem, with the burden, *And gyf me lysens to lyve in ease.* f. 45, v°.

> *Beg.* As I walkyd apone a day,
> To take the eyre of fylde and floure.

Ad calcem. Explicit in veritate. Da michi quod merui. Quod Lewestone.

16. Chaucer's Complaint to his Purse. f. 48, r°.

Printed by Urry, p. 549. See also Wanley's note on MS. Harl. 2251, Art. 133.

17. Rough memoranda. f. 48, v°.

18. The Complaint of Annelida, f. 49, r°.

Printed by Urry, p. 432.

19. The Legende of Thisbe of Babylon, f. 52, r°.

Printed by Urry, p. 343. At the end is written, "Explicit Pyramus et Tesbe. Nomen scriptoris Nicholaus plenus amoris."

20. The Complaint of Venus. f. 56, r°.

Printed by Urry, p. 533. A copy of this in MS. Ashmole 59, is entitled, "A balade made by that worthy knight of Savoye in Frenshe, calde *ser Otes Graunsoun,* translated by Chauciers." There is another copy in MS. Fairfax 16.

21. A love song. f. 57, v°.
Printed in the Reliq. Antiq. vol. i. p. 169.
22. An inventory of goods at Fyndyrne. f. 58, r°.
23. *Incipit littera Cupidinis dei Amoris directa suis subditis amatoribus.* f. 59, r°.
Printed in Urry's Chaucer, p. 534. The present copy is differently arranged, and wants several stanzas. It is written in the following order, the lines referring to Urry's edition, — ll. 1 to 133, ll. 204 to 273, ll. 343 to 413, and ll. 134 to 196.
24. An extract from Gower. f. 65, r°.

> *Beg.* I rede that thou do right so.
> Ha, gude fadur, certus no.

25. *Sir Degrevvaunt and theynke and thanke.* f. 80, r°.
Printed in this volume, pp. 177-256.
26. *The cronekelys of seyntes and kynges of Yngelond.* f. 94, r°.
This is a brief chronological list from Brute to Henry VI.
27. An account of the arms borne by the sovereigns of Europe. f. 97, r°.
Beg. The emperour of Allmyene, he beryth goold ane egylle with ij. heedes.
28. La Belle Dame sans mercy. f. 98, r°.
Printed in Urry's Chaucer, p. 422.
29. A ballad of congratulation on the return of a lover. f. 116, r°.

> *Beg.* Welcome be ye, my sovereine,
> The cause of my joyfulle peine.

30. A song on an inconstant mistress. f. 117, v°.
Printed in Ritson's Ancient Songs and Ballads, vol. i. p. 129; and in the Reliq. Antiq. vol. i. p. 24.
31. Four lines of an old ballad. f. 118, r°.

> *Beg.* Sith fortune hath me set thus in this wyse.

32. A love song. f. 118, v°.
Printed in the Reliq. Antiq. vol. i. p. 25. At the end is written the name "A. Godwhen," in a scroll.
33. Another love song. f. 118, v°

> *Beg.* Alas, alas, and alas! why
> Hath fortune donne so crewely?

34. A ballad. f. 119, v°.

> Beg. Alas, what planet was y borne undir ?
> My hert ys set thus veray feythfully.

35. A love song. f. 119, v°.
Printed in the Reliq. Antiq. vol. i. p. 25. At the top of this song is written " Croca Dytyn."

36. A ballad. f. 120, r°.
Printed in the Reliq. Antiq. vol. i. p. 26. This also bears the name of " A. Godwhen."

37. Another ballad. f. 120, v°.
Printed in the Reliq. Antiq. vol. i. p. 202.

38. Musical notes. f. 120, v°, and f. 121, r°.

39. A ballad. f. 121, v°.

40. A moral poem. f. 122, v°.

> Beg. In fulle grett hevenesse myne hert ys pwyght,
> And sadely warpud mony a fowld.

41. A prayer to the Virgin. f. 124, r°.

> Beg. Most glorius quene reynyng yn hevene,
> Stere of the se, of alle this worldelle lady !

42. A ballad, with the burden, " A wikkyd tonge wole alwey deme amys." f. 125, r°.
Printed in Urry's Chaucer, p. 549.

43. Seven stanzas of seven lines each. f. 128, r°.

> Beg. Ther is no more dredfulle pestelens,
> Thane is tonge that can flatere and fage.

The fourth, fifth, and sixth stanzas, are taken from Troilus and Creseide, iii. 303—23, Urry's edition, p. 293.

44. Six lines from Lydgate. f. 129, r°.
Printed in Lydgate's Minor Poems, p. 74.

45. An allegorical poem. f. 129, r°.

> Beg. By sapience tempre thy courage,
> Of hasty ire daunte thy passions.

46. A short poem. f. 130, v°.

> Beg. Grettere mater of dol an hevynesse,
> Nor more cause haith no mane to complayne.

DESCRIPTION OF THE CAMBRIDGE MANUSCRIPTS.

47. A ballad. f. 132, r°.

> *Beg.* Veryly } I schalle nat fayne.
> And truly }

48. A poem against marriage. f. 133, r°.

> *Beg.* Take hede and lerne, lytulle chyld, and see
> That tyme passyd wulle not ayene retorne.

49. *How myschaunce regnyth in Ingeland.* f. 134, v°.

> *Beg.* Now God, that syttyst an hygh in trone,
> Help thy peple in here greet nede.

50. *A compleint onto dame Fortune.* f. 137, v°.

> *Beg.* O thou Fortune, why art thou so inconstaunt
> To make this land so to meeve.

51. Four stanzas, entitled, *Sanguinus, Colericus, Flemnaticus, Malencolicus.* f. 140, v°.

52. *A tretise for lavandres.* f. 141, r°.
Printed in the Reliq. Antiq. vol. i. p. 26.

53. A poem, imperfect at beginning. f. 142, r°.

> *Beg.* Cassamus roos aftre this talkynge,
> And took yn counsel Ydore and Betys.

54. A ballad. f. 154, r°.

> *Beg.* A ! mercy, Fortune, have pitee on me,
> And thynke that thou hast done gretely amysse.

55. A moral poem. f. 155, r°.

> *Beg.* Chaunge not thi freende that thou knowest of oolde,
> For eny newe in trust that thou shalt finde.

This is imperfect at the end, the last leaf being torn, and some leaves also are wanting.

ON THE TERMINAL CONTRACTIONS.

In the process of printing *in extenso* from early English manuscripts, it is obvious that no degree of care can exclude error, unless we are perfectly satisfied that our explanations of the various contractions which are almost invariably found in ancient documents are correct. This subject is one of great importance, and so few editors have paid any attention to it, that perhaps some observations on the plan pursued in the present work may not be unacceptable; more especially as considerable misapprehension seems to prevail respecting recent opinions on the terminal contractions, which, it must be admitted, have been somewhat dogmatically pronounced, and unaccompanied with explanations of the principles on which they have been established. It is, indeed, easier to affirm that Ritson, Weber, and others, have given us erroneous texts, than to offer intelligible reasons for differing from them to any great extent; and, although we now know that part of their system of reading is erroneous, we must look further into the grammatical construction of the Middle-English language than has yet been attempted, before we can decide positively on receiving all the innovations of this kind that have been proposed. Space will not permit us to enter at length into the latter question, but enough will be said to convince the reader of the caution that must be exercised before we can adopt a system that shall be permanent.

These remarks apply almost exclusively to a few of the terminal contractions in early English manuscripts. In Latin MSS. there are seldom any difficulties of precisely the same kind; and certain abbreviations are common to English and Latin MSS., the meanings of which have long been satisfactorily established and agreed upon by all writers on palæography. The following contractions are used in the MSS. employed for the present volume:—

ꝛ *er*, as þ̛, *ther*. toþ̛, *tother*. awñƀ, *awneter*.
þt *that*. þi *thei*. þs *this*. þu *thou*. þe *the*.

ON THE TERMINAL CONTRACTIONS.

wᵗ *with*, or *wyth*. In MS. More 690, f. 203, the same line is repeated, one copy of which has wᵗ, and the other *wyth*.

ꝑ *pre*, as ꝑued, *preved*. It is occasionally *per*, as ꝑsed, *persed*, though the same word must be read differently in Syr Gawayne, p. 32.

ꝫ *es*, as knyghtꝫ, *knyghtes*. In some MSS. it is exclusively used for the plural, not the genitive case.

hᵗ *hit*.

p *per*, as pcyuell, *Percyuelle*. It is occasionally *par*.

ſ *ser*, *sir*, *syr*. I have generally read *syr*, as more consonant with the usage of the Lincoln MS. Contractions for *words* represent those words in whatever way they may be spelt.

ꝑ *pro*, as ꝑmisede, *promisede*.

q qᵈ, *quod*, *quoth*.

ᵃ⁻ *ra*, as gᵘⁱꝥed, *graithed*.

ⁱ *ri*, as cⁱstmasse, *Cristmasse*.

ᵘ *ru*, as tᵘe, *true*.

spĩal, *special*.

᷊ *ur*, as goŭnoˆ, *governour*.

ʳ *ur*, as yoʳ, *your*.

ꝰ *us*, as ellꝰ, *ellus*.

⁊ *and*. In some manuscripts *ant*, but this of course depends on the practice of the MSS. themselves.

ā *am*, or *an*. A short stroke over a *vowel* generally denotes the absence of *m* or *n*. Sometimes in the Lincoln MS. this mark is erroneously placed, as in Sir Isumbras, 215, "thare þay sawe stŏrmes bloo," f. 110, vº, β. Compare also the following passage:—

> þe nõnnes of hȳ þay were full fayne,
> ffor þᵗ he hade þᵉ Saraȝenes slayne
> And þose haytheñ houndes;
> And of his pāynes sare guñ þam̄ rewe.
> *MS. Lincoln*, f. 112, vº, a.

Where the marks over the words *nonnes* and *paynes* must be superfluous.

m̃, ñ, sometimes *me*, *ne*. This prolongation of the last stroke is sometimes merely a flourish, but the final *e* is occasionally intended by it. In the Promptorium we have this prolongation with the other mark of contraction, m̃ or ñ. Compare the following lines :—

> Nay, sche seyde, sone myne,
> Ther ys neu͡ neyþyr of þem thyn͡.
> *MS. Cantab.* Ff. ii. 38, f. 83, r°, *a*.

But this mark is not so positive as the stroke over the letter, which latter can scarcely be considered a flourish. Sir F. Madden, however, in describing MS. Rawl. C. 86, which was written in 1508, reads " whan͡," at f. 106, *whanne*. See his Introd. to Syr Gawayne, p. lxvi.

łł, ł, lle, le. In later MSS. this contraction is even used with the final *e*. Concerning the explanation of this contraction there can be no reasonable doubt. The indications of the plural, or the infinitive, constantly depend upon it, and Mr. Wright is of opinion that before the fifteenth century, *ll* was never used at the end of a word without a final vowel, except by some very ignorant scribe. See his Anecdota Literaria, p. 26. In the MS. Ff. i. 6, little attention is paid to the final *e*, which will account for part of the grammatical errors to be found in our edition of Sir Degrevant; but some of our recent editors are scarcely more accurate than the scribes of the 15th century.

Joħn, *Johan*. We sometimes find the word written Joh{a}n. *Johan* is the proper form of the word, *John* being a more modern orthography. When a monosyllable is required, it is generally spelt *Jon*, or *Jhoñ*, *Jhone*, as in the Lincoln MS. f. 231, r°. See Wright's Anecdota Literaria, p. 27.

ñ, *ne*. Sometimes *nne*, as iñ, *inne*, A. S. innan, the adverbial form. So also in Sir Perceval, 260, " off Arthrus iñ," *inne*, A. S. inne: and in l. 264, kyñ, *kynne*, l. 268, skynñ, *skynne*, and l. 272, chynñ, *chynne*. In certain cases we may be guided in some measure by the practice of the scribes themselves. Later MSS. are very arbitrary in such matters. In the following passage, had we found the contracted forms syñ and atwyñ, we should hardly have hesitated at printing the duplication of the *n* in each instance :—

> So that deth fynde hym clene of *synne*,
> Whan the body and the soule schal *atwyne*.
> *MS. in Canterbury Cath. Library,* D. xiii.

In some cases we find the contraction ū for *un*, but this is not so usual in English MSS. An instance of it occurs in Sir Degrevant, l. 19, in the word knowũ, where *knowne* would not suit the construction of the verse; and our reading is confirmed by the other copy of the romance in the Lincoln MS.

m̃, *me*, as tham̃, *thame*.

d', sometimes *de*, as in verbs in the infinitive mood, but in the best MSS. we generally find the *e* written at length. The Cambridge MS. of Sir Degrevant is most uncertain in this respect; as in the following passage:—

>Now to fforest he ffounde
>Both wyt horne ⁊ w^t hound,
>To breyng þe deere to þe grond
>Was hys most glew.

Where *hound* and *grond* should both strictly have the final *e*, or the contractive mark above given. Again:—

>fforþy they name hē þ^t stounde
>A knyght of tabuℏ round,
>As maked is in þe mappe moũd.

And, in the following instance, each final word should properly have an *e*:—

>ffor he was in þ^e holy lond,
>Dede of armes for to ffond,
>The heþ^{e}nemen⁹ w^t hys hond.

r⁹ *re*, as þer⁹, *there*.

According to Sir F. Madden, the stroke through the top of the *h*, ħ, indicates the final *e;* but, as far as the Thornton MS. can be considered a fair guide, neither that mark, nor a similar one in words ending with *ght*, seem necessarily to imply an additional letter. On the contrary, I have observed words unnecessarily written with this mark, and adverbs with the *e* at length; and this is the only instance in which I differ wholly from the conclusions to which Sir F. Madden has arrived in his list of marks of abbreviations prefixed to Syr Gawayne. Here, again, it may happen that other MSS. vary; and, indeed, we constantly find MSS. of the fifteenth century most irregularly written, bidding defiance to the criteria of any grammatical system. In such cases, unless we attempt a bold and extensive system of conjectural correction, our only plan is to be guided by the best explanations of the terminal contractions as they are used in more correct MSS. Our copy of Sir Degrevant, as has been already noticed, is often grammatically incorrect, and shows that, after the middle of the fifteenth century, the scribes gradually lost sight of the real use and importance of the terminal contractions. We have a curious instance of this at f. 81, r°, a.:—

> And also sede for sowe,
> Wyght horse for to *drow*,
> And thought werke be lawe,
> And wyth non͡ oþ' schore.

Where the grammatical construction of course requires *drowe*. In the same manner, at f. 80, v,° β, the word *about* should be *aboute*, the adverb, not the preposition:—

> He was sterne and stoute,
> And rode in a gay route,
> And brak hys parkę *about*,
> The best that he hade.

Various other instances of similar negligence might be quoted, but what is here before us is sufficient for our present purpose. The MSS. themselves, especially those of a later date, are not, therefore, to be always implicitly trusted; and we see how dangerous a plan it is to mix the texts of different manuscripts, the forms of the words and sometimes the construction of the sentences being so much at the mercy of the scribes. Thus, the text of the copy of Sir Degrevant in the Lincoln MS. is preferable to the one we have selected, but then we should have been reduced to the necessity of supplying the *lacuna* from an inferior MS., and thus have made up a text in two different styles of our language. In editing such pieces, we must remember that we are not dealing with a classical author, the scribes of whose works dealt with a language they were not accustomed to alter; but in early English manuscripts, whether taken from recitation or transcribed from others, the copyists do not appear to have proceeded on any regular system. This is particularly the case with our ancient popular literature; and even in the MSS. of so standard a work as the Canterbury Tales, Mr. Wright has satisfactorily proved how fatal an error was Tyrwhitt's plan of selecting readings from a number of copies, without a proper regard to grammatical construction.

The Cambridge MS. of Sir Degrevant is written in two different hands of nearly the same period. In the first part, the terminal contractions are generally exhibited, especially the *tt*; but, in the remaining portion, they are with few exceptions altogether omitted, and the *ll* has neither the contraction nor the final *e*. The pieces from Chaucer in the same MS. seem to be more carefully transcribed in this respect.

P. xxv. l. 26. *Sancta Maria.*—I have proposed *ante Transfigurationem* to fill the evident *lacuna*, because *sancta Maria* would hardly refer to the Blessed Virgin, but more probably to St. Mary ad Nives, whose day is August 5th, the day before the Transfiguration. Mr. J. G. Nichols suggests to me that *sancta Maria* may be an error for *septimana*, a very plausible conjecture, and, to judge from the careless way the memorandum is written, not unlikely to be correct.

P. xxxii. l. 4. *Proptter.*—The Latin is given exactly as it is found in the MSS. themselves. In like manner, we have *inperfecta* for *imperfecta*, *spiniam* for *spineam*, *sinis* for *cinis*, and various other erroneous forms of a like kind.

THE ROMANCE

OF

SIR PERCEVAL OF GALLES.

[f. 161.] *Here bygynnes the Romance off Syr Perecyvelle of Gales.*

I.

Lef, lythes to me
Two wordes or thre
Off one that was faire and fre,
  And felle in his fighte;
His righte name was Percyvelle,   5
He was fosterde in the felle,
He dranke water of the welle,
  And ȝitt was he wyghte!
His fadir was a noble-mane,
Fro the tyme that he begane,   10
Miche wirchippe he wane,
  Whenne he was made knyghte;
In kyng Arthures haulle
Beste by-luffede of alle,

Percyvelle thay gane hym calle,   15
    Who so redis ryghte.

II.

Who that righte cane rede,
He was doughty of dede,
A styffe body one a stede
    Wapynes to welde;   20
Thare-fore kyng Arthoure
Dide hym mekille honoure,
He gaffe hym his syster Acheflour,
    To have and to holde;
Fro thethyne tille his lyves ende,   25
With brode londes to spende,
For he the knyght wele kende,
    He bytaughte hir to welde;
With grete gyftes to fulfille,
He gaffe his sister hym tille,   30
To the knyght at ther bothers wille,
    With robes in folde.

III.

He gaffe hym robes in folde,
Brode londes in wolde,
Mony mobles untolde,   35
    His syster to take;
To the kirke the knyghte ȝode
For to wedde that frely fode,
For the gyftes that ware gude,
    And for hir ownne sake;   40

Sythene, withowttene any bade,
A grete brydale thay made,
For hir sake that hym hade
    Chosene to hir make;
And after, withowttene any lett,   45
A grete justyng ther was sett,
Off alle the kempes that he mett
    Wolde he none forsake.

IV.

Wolde he none forsake,
The rede knyghte ne the blake,   50
Ne none that wolde to hym take
    With schafte ne with schelde;
He dose als a noble knyghte,
Wele haldes that he highte,
Faste preves he his myghte,   55
    Deres hym none elde.
Sexty schaftes I say
Syr Percyvelle brake that ilke day,
And ever that riche lady lay
    One walle and byhelde;   60
Thofe the rede knyghte hade sworne,
Oute of his sadille is he borne,
And almoste his lyfe forlorne,
    And lygges in the felde.

V.

There he lygges in the felde,   65
Many mene one hym byhelde,

Thurgh his armour and his schelde
  Stoneyde that tyde.
That arghede alle that ther ware,
Bothe the lesse and the mare,   70
That noble Percyvelle so wele dare
  Syche dynttys habyde;
Was ther nowthir more ne lasse
Off alle those that ther was,
That durste mete hym one the grasse,   75
  Agaynes hyme to ryde;
Thay gaffe syr Percyvelle the gree,
Beste worthy was he,
And hamewardez thanne rode he,
  And blythe was his bryde.   80

VI.

And thofe the bryde blythe be
That Percyvelle hase wone the gree,
ȝete the rede knyghte es he
  Hurte of his honde;
And therfore gyffes he a gyfte,   85
That if he ever covere myghte,
Owthir by day or by nyghte,
  Inne felde for to stonde,
That he scholde qwyte hym that dynt,
That he of his handes hynte;   90
Salle never this travelle be tynt,
  Ne tolde in the londe,
f. 162] That Percyvelle in the felde
  Schulde hym schende thus undire schelde,

Bot it scholde agayne be ȝolden,   95
    If that he were leveande!

VII.

Now than are thay leveande bathe,
Was noȝte the rede knyghte so rathe
For to wayte hym with skathe,
    Er ther the harmes felle;   100
Ne befelle ther no stryffe,
Tille Percyvelle had in his lyffe
A sone by his ȝonge wyffe,
    Aftir hym to duelle.
Whenne the childe was borne,   105
He made calle it one the morne,
Als his fadir highte byforne,
    ȝonge Percyvelle:
The knyghte was fayne, a feste made
For a knave childe that he hade,   110
And sythene, withowttene any bade,
    Offe justyngez thay telle!

VIII.

Now of justyngez thay telle;
Thay sayne that syr Percyvelle,
That he wille in the felde duelle,   115
    Als he hase are done.
A grete justynge was ther sett
Of alle the kempes that ther mett,
For he wolde his sone were gette
    In the same wonne;   120

Theroff the rede knyghte was blythe,
Whenne he herde of that justynge kythe,
And graythed hym armours ful swythe,
  And rode thedir riȝte sone:
Agayne Percyvelle he rade   125
With schafte and with schelde brade,
To holde his heste that he made
  Of maistres to mone.

IX.

Now of maistres to mone,
Percyvelle hase wele done   130
For the love of his ȝonge sone,
  One the firste day.
Ere the rede knyghte was bownne,
Percyvelle hase borne downne
Knyght, duke, erle, and baroune,   135
  And vencusede the play!
Right als he hade done this honour,
So come the rede knyghte to the stowre,
Bot "wo worthe wykkyde armour!"
  Percyvelle may say;   140
For ther was syr Percyvelle slayne,
And the rede knyghte fayne,
In herte is noȝte for to layne,
  Whenne he went one his way!

X.

Whenne he went one his way,   145
Durste ther no mane to hym say,

Nowther in erneste ne in play,
  To byd hym habyde;
For he had slayne riȝte thare
The beste body at thare ware, 150
Syr Percyvelle with woundez sare,
  And stonayed that tyde.
And thanne thay couthe no better rede,
Bot put hym in a prevee stede,
Als that mene dose with the dede, 155
  In erthe for to hyde.
Scho that was his lady
Mighte be fulle sary,
That lorne hade siche a body,
  Hir aylede no pryde! 160

XI.

And now is Percyvelle the wighte
Slayne in batelle and in fyghte;
And the lady hase gyffene a gyfte,
  Holde if scho may,
That scho schalle nevermare wonne 165
In stede with hir ȝonge sonne,
Ther dedez of armez schalle be donne,
  By nyghte ne be daye;
Bot in the wodde schalle he be,
Salle he nothyng see 170
Bot the leves of the tree,
  And the greves graye:
Schalle he nowther take tent
To justez ne to tournament,

Bot in the wilde wodde went 175
  With bestez to playe.

XII.

With wilde bestez for to playe,
Scho tuke hir leve and went hir waye,
Bothe at barone and at raye,
  And went to the wodde. 180
Byhynde scho leved boure and haulle;
A maydene scho tuke hir withalle,
That scho myȝte appone calle,
  Whenne that hir nede stode:
Other gudez wolde scho nonne nayte; 185
Bot with hir tuke a tryppe of gayte,
With mylke of thame for to bayte
  To hir lyves fode;
Off alle hir lordes faire gere
Wolde scho noȝte with hir bere, 190
Bot a lyttille Scottes spere,
  Agayne hir sone ȝode.

XIII.

And whenne hir ȝong sone ȝode,
Scho bade hym walke in the wodde,
Tuke hym the Scottes spere gude 195
  And gaffe hym in hande;
"Swete modir," sayde he,
"What manere of thyng may this bee,
That ȝe nowe hafe takene mee?
  What calle ȝee this wande?" 200

Thanne byspakke the lady,
" Sone," scho sayde, " sekerly
It es a dart doghty;
  In the wodde I it fande."
The childe es payed of his parte,   205
His modir hase gyffene hym that darte,
Therwith made he many marte
  In that wodde lande.

XIV.

Thus he welke in the lande
With hys darte in his hande;   210
Under the wilde wodde wande
  He wexe and wele thrafe:
He wolde schote with his spere
Bestes and other gere,
As many als he myghte bere;   215
  He was a gude knave!
Smalle birdes wolde he slo,
Hertys, hyndez also;
Broghte his moder of thoo,
  Thurte hir none crave;   220
So wele he lernede hym to schote,
Ther was no beste that welke one fote,
To fle fro hym was it no bote,
  Whenne that he wolde hym have.

XV.

Evene whenne he wolde hym have;   225
 Thus he wexe and wele thrave,

And was reghte a gude knave
        With-in a fewe ȝere;
Fyftene wynter and mare
He duellede in those holtes hare,   230
Nowther nurture ne lare
        Scho wolde hym none lere:
Tille it byfelle on a day,
The lady tille hir sone ganne say,
"Swete childe, I rede thou praye   235
        To Goddez sone dere,
That he wolde helpe the,
Lorde, for his poustee,
A gude mane for to bee,
        And longe to duelle here!"   240

XVI.

"Swete moder," sayde he,
"Whatkyns a Godd may that be,
That ȝe nowe bydd mee
        That I schalle to pray?"
Thenne byspakke the lady evene,   245
"It es the grete Godd of hevene,
[f. 163] This worlde made he with-in sevene
        Appone the sexte d[a]y."
"By grete Godd," sayde he thanne,
"And I may mete with that manne,   250
With alle the crafte that I kanne
        Reghte so schalle I pray!"
There he levede in a tayte
Bothe his modir and his gayte,

The grete Godd for to layte, 255
    Fynde hyme whenne he may.

XVII.

And as he welke in holtes hare,
He sawe a gate as it ware,
With thre knyghtis mett he thare
    Off Arthrus inne; 260
One was Ewayne fytz Asoure,
Another was Gawayne with honour,
And Kay the bolde baratour,
    And alle were of his kynne.
In riche robes thay ryde; 265
The chylde hadd nothyng that tyde,
That he myȝte inne his bones hyde,
    Bot a gaytes skynne;
He was burely of body and therto riȝt brade,
One ayther halfe a skynne he hade, 270
The hode was of the same made
    Juste to the chynne.

XVIII.

His hode was juste to his chynne,
The flesche halfe tourned with-inne,
The childes witt was fulle thynne 275
    Whenne he scholde say oughte;
Thay were clothede alle in grene,
Siche hade he never sene,
Wele he wened that thay had bene
    The Godd that he soghte! 280

He said, " Wilke of ȝow alle three
May the grete Godd bee,
That my moder tolde mee
  That alle this werlde wroghte ?"
Bot thanne ansuerde syr Gawayne, 285
Faire and curtaisely agayne,
" Sone, so Criste mote me sayne,
  For swilke are we noghte !"

XIX.

Thanne saide the fole one the filde,
Was comene oute of the woddez wilde, 290
To Gawayne that was meke and mylde
  And softe of ansuare,
" I salle sla ȝow alle three,
Bot ȝe smertly now telle mee
Whatkyns thyngez that ȝe bee, 295
  Sene ȝe no Goddes are !"
Thenne ansuerde syr Kay,
" Who solde we thanne say
That hade slayne us to day
  In this holtis hare ?" 300
At Kayes wordes wexe he tene,
Bot he a grete bukke had bene,
Ne hadd he stonde thame bytwene,
  He hade hym slayne thare !

XX.

Bot thanne said Gawayne to Kay, 305
" Thi prowde wordes pares ay,

I scholde wynne this childe with play,
   And thou wolde holde the stille."
" Swete sone," thanne said he,
" We are knyghtis alle thre,   310
With kyng Arthoure duelle wee
   That hovyne es on hylle."
Thenne said Percyvelle the lyghte,
In gayte skynnes that was dyghte,
" Wille kyng Arthoure make me knyghte, 315
   And I come hym tille ?"
Thanne saide syr Gawayne riȝte thare,
" I kane gyffe the nane ansuare,
Bot to the kynge I rede thou fare
   To wete his awenne [wille]." 320

XXI.

To wete thus the kynges wille,
Thare thay hovene ȝitt stille,
The childe hase takene hym tille
   For to wende hame.
And als he welke in the wodde,   325
He sawe a fulle faire stode
Offe coltes and of meres gude,
   Bot never one was tame;
And sone said he, " Bi seyne John,
Swilke thynges as are ȝone   330
Rade the knyghtes apone,
   Knewe I thaire name;
Als ever mote I thryffe or thee,
The moste of ȝone that I see

Smertly schalle bere mee 335
    Tille I come to my dame!"

XXII.

He saide, "Whenne I come to my dame,
And I fynde hir at hame,
Scho wille telle the name
    Off this ilke thynge." 340
The moste mere he thare see
Smertly over-rynnes he,
And saide, "Thou salle bere me
    To morne to the kynge."
Kepes he no sadille gere, 345
Bot stert up one the mere;
Hamewarde scho gunne him bere
    Withowttene faylynge:
The lady was never more sore bygone,
Scho wiste never whare to wonne, 350
Whenne scho wiste hir ȝonge sonne
    Horse hame brynge!"

XXIII.

Scho saw hym horse hame brynge,
Scho wiste wele by that thynge
That the kynde wolde oute-sprynge, 355
    For thynge that be moughte.
Thanne als sone saide the lady,
"That ever solde I sorowe dry
For love of thi body,
    That I hafe dere boghte!" 360

"Dere sone," saide scho [hym to],
"Thou wirkeste th[ise]lfe mekille unroo,
What wille thou with this mere do,
  That thou hase hame broghte?"
Bot the boye was never so blythe,   365
Als whenne he herde the name kythe
Of the stode-mere stythe,
  Of na thyng thanne he roghte!

XXIV.

Now he calles hir a mere,
Als his moder dide ere;   370
He wened alle other horsez were,
  And hade bene callede soo.
"Moder, at ȝonder hille hafe I bene,
Thare hafe I thre knyghtes sene,
And I hafe spokene with thame, I wene,   375
  Wordes in throo;
I have highte thame alle thre
Before thaire kyng for to be,
Siche one schalle he make me
  As is one of tho!"   380
He sware by grete Goddez myȝte,
"I schalle holde that I hafe highte,
Bot if the kyng make me knighte
  To morne I salle hym sloo!"

XXV.

Bot thanne by-spakke the lady,   385
That for hir sone was sary,

Hir thoghte wele that scho myȝt dy,
  And knelyde one hir kne;
"Sone, thou has takyne thi rede
To do thiselfe to the dede,   390
In everilke a strange stede
  Doo als I bydde the!
To morne es forthirmaste ȝole day,
And thou says thou wille away
To make the knyghte if thou may,   395
  Als thou tolde mee;
Lyttille thou cane of nurtoure,
f. 164] Luke thou be of mesure
Bothe in haulle and in boure,
  And fonde to be fre!"   400

XXVI.

Than saide the lady so brighte,
"There thou meteste with a knyghte,
Do thi hode off, I highte,
  And haylse hym in hy!"
"Swete moder," sayd he thenne,   405
"I saw never ȝit no menne;
If I solde a knyghte kenne
  Telles me wharby."
Scho schewede hym the menevaire,
Scho had robes in payre,   410
"Sone, ther thou sees this fare
  In thaire hodes lye."
"Bi grete God," sayd he,
"Where that I a knyghte see,

Moder, as ȝe bidd me 415
    Righte so schalle I !"

XXVII.

Alle that nyȝte tille it was day
The childe by the modir lay,
Tille on the morne he wolde away,
    For thyng that myȝte betyde. 420
Brydille hase he righte nane;
Seese he no better wane,
Bot a wythe hase he tane,
    And kenylles his stede.
His moder gaffe hym a ryng, 425
And bad he solde agayne it bryng,
" Sonne, this salle be oure takynnyng,
    For here I salle the byde."
He tase the rynge and the spere,
Stirttes up appone the mere, 430
Fro the moder that hym bere
    Forthe ganne he ryde!

Here is a Fytt of Percyvelle of Galles.

XXVIII.

One his way, as he ganne ryde,
He fande an haulle ther besyde,
He saide, " For oghte that may betyde, 435
    Thedir inne wille I."

He went inne withowttene lett,
He fande a brade borde sett,
A bryghte fire wele bett
  Brynnande therby;   440
A mawnger ther he fande,
Corne therin lyggande,
Therto his mere he bande
  With the withy.
He saide, " My modir bad me   445
That I solde of mesure bee,
Halfe that I here see
  Stylle salle it ly."

XXIX.

The corne he pertis in two,
Gaffe his mere the tone of thoo,   450
And to the borde ganne he goo
  Certayne that tyde.
He fande a lofe of brede fyne,
And a pychere with wyne,
A mese of the kechyne,   455
  A knyfe ther besyde;
The mete ther that he fande
He dalte it evene with his hande,
Lefte the halfe lyggande
  A felawe to byde!   460
The tother halfe ete he;
How myȝte he more of mesure be?
Faste he fonded to be free,
  Thofe he were of no pryde.

XXX.

Thofe he were of no pryde, 465
Forthirmore ganne he glyde
Tille a chambir ther besyde,
  Moo sellys to see;
Riche clothes fande he sprede,
A lady slepande on a bedde, 470
He said, "Forsothe, a tokyne to wedde
  Salle thou lefe with mee."
Ther he kyste that swete thynge,
Of hir fynger he tuke a rynge,
His awenne modir takynnynge 475
  He lefte with that fre.
He went forthe to his mere,
Tuke with hym his schorte spere,
Lepe one lofte as he was ere,
  His way rydes he. 480

XXXI.

Now on his way rydes he,
Moo selles to see;
A knyghte wolde he nedis bee
  Withowttene any bade.
He come ther the kyng was 485
Servede of the firste mese,
To hym was the maste has
  That the childe hade;
And thare made he no lett
At ȝate, dore ne wykett, 490

Bot in graythely he gett,
    Syche maistres he made!
At his first in comynge,
His mere withowttene faylynge
Kyste the forhevede of the kynge,   495
    So nerehande he rade!

XXXII.

The kyng had ferly thaa,
And up his hande ganne he taa,
And putt it forthir hym fraa
    The mouthe of the mere.   500
He saide, " Faire childe and free,
Stonde stille besyde mee,
And telle me wythene that thou bee,
    And what thou wille here."
Thanne saide the fole of the filde,   505
" I ame myne awnne modirs childe
Comene fro the woddez wylde
    Tille Arthure the dere;
ȝisterday saw I knyghtis three,
Siche one salle thou make mee   510
On this mere by-for the,
    Thi mete or thou schere!"

XXXIII.

Bot thanne spak syr Gawayne,
Was the kynges trenchepayne,
Said, " Forsothe, is noȝte to layne,   515
    I ame one of thaa;

Childe, hafe thou my blyssyng
For thi feres folowynge,
Here hase thou fondene the kynge,
   That kane the knyghte maa!"   520
Thanne sayde Perċyvelle the free,
"And this Arthure the kyng bee,
Luke he a knyghte make mee,
   I rede at it be swaa!"
Thofe he unborely were dyghte,   525
He sware by mekille Goddes myȝte,
"Bot if the kyng make me knyghte,
   I salle hym here slaa!"

XXXIV.

Alle that ther werene, olde and ȝynge,
Haddene ferly of the kyng,   530
That he wolde suffre siche a thyng
   Of that foulle wyghte.
On horse hovande hym by,
The kyng byholdez hym one hy;
Thanne wexe he sone sory,   535
   Whenne he sawe that syghte!
The teres oute of his eghne glade,
Never one another habade,
"Allas!" he sayde, "that I was made
   Be day or by nyghte!   540
f. 165] One lyve I scholde after hym bee,
That methynke lyke the,
Thou arte so semely to see,
   And thou were wele dighte!"

XXXV.

He saide, " and thou were wele dighte, 545
Thou were lyke to a knyghte
That I lovede with alle my myghte,
  Whilles he was one lyve;
So wele wroghte he my wille
In alle manere of skille, 550
I gaffe my syster hym tille
  For to be his wyfe;
He es moste in my mane,
Fiftene ȝere es it gane
Sene a theffe hade hym slane 555
  Abowte a littille stryffe!
Sythene hafe I ever bene his fo,
For to wayte hym with wo,
Bot I myȝte hym never slo,
  His craftes are so ryfe!" 560

XXXVI.

He sayse, " his craftes are so ryfe,
Ther is no mane apone lyfe,
With swerde, spere, ne with knyfe,
  May stroye hym allane,
But if it were syr Percyvelle sone; 565
Who so wiste where he ware done,
The bokes says that he mone
  Venge his fader bane."
The childe thoghte he longe bade
That he ne ware a knyghte made, 570

For he wiste never that he hade
    A fader to be slayne;
The lesse was his menynge,
He saide sone to the kynge,
"Syr, late be thi jangleynge,   575
    Of this kepe I nane!"

XXXVII.

He sais, "I kepe not to stande
With thi jangleyns to lange,
Make me knyghte with thi hande,
    If it salle be donne!"   580
Thanne the kyng hym hendly highte
That he schold dub hym to knyghte,
With thi that he wolde doune lyghte
    And ete with hym at none.
The kyng biholdez the vesage free,   585
And evermore trowed hee
That the childe scholde bee
    Syr Percyvelle sonne:
It ranne in the kynges mode,
His syster Acheflour the gude,   590
How scho went in to the wodde
    With hym for to wonne.

XXXVIII.

The childe hadde wonnede in the wodde,
He knewe nother evylle ne gude,
The kynge hym-selfe understode   595
    He was a wilde manne;

So faire he spakke hym withalle,
He lyghtes doune in the haulle,
Bonde his mere amonge thame alle,
  And to the borde wanne! 600
Bot are he myghte bygynne
To the mete for to wynne,
So commes the rede knyghte inne
  Emangez thame righte thanne,
Prekande one a rede stede, 605
Blode rede was his wede,
He made thame gammene fulle gnede,
  With craftez that he canne.

XXXIX.

With his craftez ganne he calle,
And callede thame recrayhandes alle, 610
Kynge, knyghtes in-with walle,
  At the bordes ther thay bade;
Fulle felly the coupe he fett
Before the kynge that was sett,
Ther was no mane that durste hym lett, 615
  Thofe that he ware fadde.
The couppe was filled fulle of wyne,
He dranke of that that was ther-inne:
Alle of rede golde fyne
  Was the couppe made; 620
He tuke it up in his hande
The coupe that he there fande,
And lefte thame alle sittande,
  And fro thame he rade!

XL.

Now fro thame he rade, 625
Als he says that this made;
The sorowe that the kynge hade
    Mighte no tonge telle.
"A! dere God," said the kyng thanne,
"That alle this wyde werlde wanne, 630
Whethir I salle ever hafe that manne
    May make ȝone fende duelle;
Fyve ȝeres hase he thus gane,
And my coupes fro me tane,
And my gude knyghte slayne, 635
    Mene calde syr Percyvelle;
Sythene takene hase he three,
And ay awaye wille he bee,
Or I may harnayse me
    In felde hym to felle!" 640

XLI.

"Petir!" quod Percyvelle the ȝynge,
"Hym thanne wille [I] downe dynge,
And the coupe agayne brynge,
    And thou wille make me knyghte."
"Als I am trewe kyng," said he, 645
"A knyghte salle I make the,
For-thi thou wille brynge mee
    The coupe of golde bryghte!"
Up ryses syr Arthoure,

Went to a chamboure 650
To feche doune armoure
  The childe in to dyghte;
Bot are it was doune caste,
Ere was Percyvelle paste,
And on his way folowed faste 655
  That he solde with fyghte.

XLII.

With his foo for to fighte;
None other gates was he dighte
Bot in thre gayt skynnes, righte
  A fole als he ware; 660
He cryed, "How, mane, on thi mere,
Bryng agayne the kynges gere,
Or with my dart I salle the fere,
  And make the unfere!"
And after the rede knyghte he rade 665
Baldely, withowttene bade,
Sayd, "A knyght I salle be made
  For some of thi gere!"
He sware by mekille Goddez payne,
"Bot if thou brynge the coupe agayne, 670
With my dart thou salle be slayne,
  And slongene of thi mere."
The knyghte byhaldez hym in throo,
Calde hym fole that was hys foo,
For he named hyme soo 675
  The stede that hym bere;

XLIII.

And for to see hyme with syghte,
He putt his umbrere on highte,
To byhalde how he was dyghte
   That so tille hym spake; 680
He sayde, " Come I to the, appert fole,
I salle caste the in the pole,
For alle the heghe days of ȝole,
   Als ane olde sakke !"
Thanne sayd Percyvelle the free, 685
" Be I fole or whatte I bee,
Now sone of that salle wee see
   Whose browes schalle blakke !"
Of schottyng was the childe slee,
At the knyghte lete he flee, 690
Smote hym in at the eghe
   And oute at the nakke.

XLIV.

For the dynt that he tuke,
Oute of sadille he schoke,
Who so the sothe wille luke, 695
   And ther was he slayne.
f. 166] He falles downe one the hille,
His stede rynnes whare he wille :
Thanne saide Percyvelle hyme tille,
   " Thou art a lethir swayne !" 700
Then saide the childe in that tyde,
" And thou woldeste me here byde,

After thi mere scholde I ryde,
And brynge hir agayne.
Thenne myȝte we bothe with myȝte 705
Menskfully togedir fyghte,
Ayther of us as he were a knyghte,
Tille tyme the tone ware slayne."

XLV.

Now es the rede knyghte slayne,
Lefte dede in the playne, 710
The childe gone his mere mayne
After the stede;
The stede was swifter than the mere,
For he hade no-thynge to bere
But his sadille and his gere, 715
Fro hym thofe he ȝede.
The mere was bagged with fole,
And hir-selfe a grete bole,
For to rynne scho myȝte not thole
Ne folowe hym no spede; 720
The childe saw that it was soo,
And tille his fete he ganne hym too,
The gates that he scholde goo
Made he fulle gnede.

XLVI.

The gates made he fulle gnede, 725
In the waye ther he ȝede,
With strenght tuke he the stede
And broghte to the knyghte;

" Methynke," he sayde, " thou art fele,
That thou ne wille away stele,   730
Now I houppe that thou wille dele
    Strokes appone hyghte !
I hafe broghte to the thi mere,
And mekille of thyne other gere,
Lepe on hir as thou was ere,   735
    And thou wille more fighte !"
The knyghte lay stille in the stede,
What sulde he say whenne he was dede ?
The childe couthe no better rede,
    But downe gunne he lyghte.   740

XLVII.

Now es Percyvelle lyghte
To unspoyle the rede knyghte,
Bot he ne couthe never fynd righte
    The lacynge of his wede ;
He was armede so wele   745
In gude iryne and in stele,
He couthe not gett of a dele
    For nonkyns nede.
He sayd, " My moder bad me,
Whenne my dart solde brokene be,   750
Owte of the irene brenne the tree,
    Now es me fyre gnede !"
Now he getis hym flynt,
His fyre-irene he hent,
And thenne withowttene any stynt   755
    He kyndilt a glede.

XLVIII.

Now he kyndils a glede,
Amonge the buskes he ȝede,
And gedirs fulle gude spede
  Wodde a fyre to make;   760
A grete fyre made he thanne,
The rede knyghte in to brenne,
For he ne couthe nott kenne
  His gere off to take.
Be thanne was syr Gawayne dyght,   765
Folowede after the fyghte
Betwene hym and the rede knyghte,
  For the childes sake.
He fande the rede knyght lyggand,
Slayne of Percyvelle hande,   770
Besyde a fyre brynnande
  Off byrke and of akke.

XLIX.

Ther brent of birke and of ake
Gret brandes and blake,—
"What wylt thou with this fyre make?"   775
  Sayd Gawayne hym tille;
"Peter!" quod Percyvelle thenne,
"And I myghte hym thus kenne,
Out of his irene I wolde hym brenne
  Righte here on this hille."   780

Bot thenne sayd syr Gawayne,
" The rede knyghte for thou has slayne,
I salle unarme hym agayne,
  And thou wille holde the stille!"
Thanne syr Gawayne doun lyghte,   785
Unlacede the rede knyghte,
The childe in his armour dight
  At his awnne wille!

L.

Whenne he was dighte in his atire,
He tase the knyghte bi the swire,   790
Keste hym reghte in the fyre
  The brandes to balde:
Bot thenne said Percyvelle one bost,
" Ly stille therin now and roste,
I kepe nothynge of thi coste   795
  Ne noghte of thi spalde."
The knyghte lygges ther on brede,
The childe es dighte in his wede,
And lepe up apone his stede,
  Als hym-selfe wolde.   800
He luked doune to his fete,
Saw his gere faire and mete,
" For a knyghte I may be lete,
  And myghte be calde."

LI.

Thenne sayd syr Gawayne hym tille,   805
" Goo we faste fro this hille,

Thou hase done what thou wille,
   It neghes nere nyghte!"
"What! trowes thou," quod Percyvelle the ȝynge,
"That I wille agayne brynge 810
Untille Arthoure the kynge
   The golde that es bryghte?
Nay, so mote I thryfe or thee,
I ame als grete a lorde als he,
To day ne schalle he make me 815
   None other gates knyghte!
Take the coupe in thy hande,
And mak thiselfe the presande,
For I wille forthire in-to the lande
   Are I doune lyghte!" 820

LII.

Nowther wolde he doune lyghte,
Ne he wolde wende with the knyght,
Bot rydes forthe alle the nyghte,
   So prowde was he thanne!
Tille one the morne at forthe dayes, 825
He mett a wyche, as mene says;
His horse and his harnays
   Couthe scho wele kenne.
Scho wende that it hade bene
The rede knyghte that scho hade sene, 830
Was wount in those armes to bene
   To gerre the stede rynne.

In haste scho come hym agayne,
Sayde, " It is not to layne,
Mene tolde me that thou was slayne   835
  With Arthours mene !

LIII.

" Ther come one of my mene,
Tille ȝonder hille he gane me kenne,
There thou sees the fyre brene,
  And sayde that thou was thare."   840
Ever satt Percyvelle stone stille,
And spakke nothynge hir tille,
Tille scho hade sayde alle hir wille,
  And spakke lesse ne mare.
" At ȝondere hille hafe I bene,   845
f. 167] Nothynge hafe I there sene
Bot gayte skynnes I wene,
  Siche ille farande fare."
" Mi sone, and thou ware thare slayne,
And thyne armes of drawene,   850
I couthe hele the agayne
  Als wele als thou was are !"

LIV.

Than wist Percyvelle by thatt,
It servede hym of somwhatt
The wylde fyre that he gatt,   855
  Whenne the knyghte was slayne ;

And righte so wolde he thare
That the olde wiche ware,
Oppone his spere he hir bare
  To the fyre agayne;   860
In ille wrethe and in grete
He keste the wiche in the hete,
He sayde, " Ly stille and swete
  Bi thi sone, that lyther swayne !"
Thus he leves thayme twoo,   865
And one his gates gane he goo;
Siche dedis to do moo
  Was the childe fayne.

LV.

Als he come by a wodd syde,
He sawe tene mene ryde,   870
He said, " For oughte that may betyde,
  To thame wille I me."
Whenne those tene saw hym thare,
Thay wende the rede knyghte it ware,
That wolde thame alle for-fare,   875
  And faste gane thay flee;
For he was so gates cledde,
Alle belyffe fro hym thay fledde,
And ever the faster that thay spedde
  The swiftlyere sewed hee,   880
Tille he was warre of a knyghte,
And of the menevaire he had syght,
He put up his umbrere one hight,
  And said, " Syr, God luke thee !"

LVI.

The childe sayde, " God luke the !" 885
The knyght said, " Now wele the be !
A ! lorde Godd, now wele is mee,
  That ever was I made !"
For by the vesage hym thoghte
The rede kny3te was it no3te, 890
That hade theme alle by-soughte,
  And baldely he bade ;
It semede wele bi the syghte
That he had slayne the rede kny3t,
In his armes was he dighte 895
  And one his stede rade.
Sone sayde the knyghte tho,
And thankede the childe fulle thro,
" Thou hase slayne the moste foo
  That ever 3itt I hade !" 900

LVII.

Thenne sayde Percyvelle the free,
" Wherefore fledde 3ee
Lange are, whenne 3e sawe mee
  Come rydande 3ow by ?"
Bot thanne spake the olde knyghte, 905
That was paste out of myghte
With any mane for to fyghte,
  He ansuerde in hy ;
He sayde, " Theis childrene nyne,
Alle are thay sonnes myne, 910

For ferde or I solde thame tyne,
    Therfore fledd I.
We wende wele that it had bene
The rede kny3te that we hade sene;
He walde hafe slayne us by-dene   915
    With-owttene mercy.

LVIII.

" Withowttene any mercy
He wolde hafe slayne us in hy;
To my sonnes he hade envy
    Moste of any menne.   920
Fiftene 3eres es it gane
Syne he my brodire hade slane,
Now hadde the theefe undirtane
    To sla us alle thenne;
He was ferde lesse my sonnes sold hym slo,   925
Whenne thay ware eldare and moo,
And that thay solde take hym for thaire foo,
    Where thay my3te hym kenne;
Hade I bene in the stede
Ther he was done to the dede,   930
I solde never hafe etyne brede
    Are I hade sene hym brenne!"

LIX.

" Petir!" quod Percyvelle, " he es brende,
I haffe spedde better thanne I wend."
Ever at the laste ende   935
    The blythere wexe the knyghte!

By his haulle thaire gates felle,
And ȝerne he prayed Percyvelle
That he solde ther with hym duelle,
  And be ther alle that nyghte.   940
Fulle wele he couthe a geste calle,
He broghte the childe in-to the haulle,
So faire he spake hym with-alle
  That he es doune lyghte;
His stede es in stable sett,   945
And hymselfe to the haulle fett,
And thanne, withowttene any lett,
  To the mette thay thame dighte.

LX.

Mete and drynke was ther dighte,
And mene to serve thame fulle ryghte,   950
The childe that come with the knyghte
  Enoghe ther he fande;
At the mete as thay beste satte,
Come the portere fro the ȝate,
Saide a mane was theratte   955
  Of the Maydene-lande;
Saide, " Syr, he prayes the
Off mete and drynke for charyté,
For a messagere es he,
  And may nott lange stande."   960
The knyght badde late hym inne,
For he sayde, " It es no synne,
The mane that may the mete wynne
  To gyffe the travellande."

LXI.

Now the travellande mane 965
The portere lete in thane,
He haylsede the knyghte as he cane,
  Als he satt on dese;
The knyghte askede hym thare,
Whase mane that he ware, 970
And how ferre that he walde so fare,
  Withowttene any lese.
He saide, "I come fro the lady Lufamour,
That sendes me to kyng Arthoure,
And prayes hym, for his honoure, 975
  Hir sorowes for to sesse;
Up-resyne es a sowdane,
Alle hir landes hase he tane,
So by-seges he that womane
  That scho may hafe no pese." 980

LXII.

He sayse that scho may have no pese,
"The lady, for hir fayrenes,
And for hir mekille reches,
  He wirkes hir fulle woo;
He dose hir sorow alle hir sythe, 985
And alle he slaes doune rythe;
He wolde have hir to wyfe,
  And scho wille noȝte soo.
Now hase that ilke sowdane
Hir fadir and hir eme slane, 990

f. 168] And hir brethir ilkane,
  And is hir moste foo;
So nere he hase hir now soughte,
That tille a castelle es scho broghte,
And fro the walles wille he noghte   995
  Ere that he may hir too.

LXIII.

" The sowdane sayse he wille her ta;
The lady wille hir-selfe sla,
Are he that es hir maste fa
  Solde wedde hir to wyfe!   1000
Now es the sowdane so wyghte,
Alle he slaes doune ryghte,
Ther may no mane with hym fyghte,
  Bot he were kempe ryfe."
Thane sayde Percyvelle, " I the praye   1005
That thou wolde teche me the waye
Thedir als the gates laye,
  Withowttene any stryfe;
Mighte I mete with that sowdane,
That so dose to that womane,   1010
Al-sone he solde be slane,
  And I myȝte hafe the lyfe!"

LXIV.

The messangere prayed hym mare
That he wolde duelle stille thare,
" For I wille to the kynge fare   1015
  Myne erandez for to say."

" For thenne mekille sorowe me betyde,
And I lenger here habyde,
Bot ryghte now wille I ryde
  Als so faste als I may !"   1020
[T]he knyghte herde hym say so,
ȝerne he prayes hyme to-too
His nyne sonnes with hym to goo;
  He nykkes hyme with nay.
Bot so faire spekes he,   1025
That he takes of thame three
In his felawchipe to be,
  The blythere were thay !

LXV.

Thay ware blythe of ther bade,
Busked thame and forthe rade,   1030
Mekille myrthes thay made,
  Bot lyttille it amende ;
He was paste bot a while
The montenance of a myle,
He was by-thoghte of a gyle,   1035
  Wele werse thane thay wende.
Thofe thay ware of thaire fare fayne,
Forthwarde was thaire cheftayne ;
Ever he sende one agayne
  At ilke a myle ende,   1040
Untille thay ware alle gane ;
Thane he rydes hym allane,
Als he ware sprongene of a stane,
  Thare na mane hym kende.

LXVI.

For he walde none sold hym kene, 1045
Forthe rydez he thenne,
Amangez uncouthe mene
    His maystrés to make.
Now hase Percyvelle in throo
Spokene with his emes twoo, 1050
Bot never one of thoo
    Took his knawlage:
Now in his way es he sett,
That may hym lede, withowttene lett,
Thare he and the sowdane salle mete, 1055
    His browes to blake.
Late we Percyvelle the ȝynge
Fare in Goddes blessynge,
And untille Arthoure the kynge
    Wille we agayne take. 1060

LXVII.

The gates agayne we wille tane,
The kyng to Carebedd es gane,
For mournynge es his maste mane,
    He syghes fulle sore.
His wo es wansome to wreke, 1065
His hert es bownne for to breke,
For he wend never to speke
    With Percyvelle no more.
Als he was layde for to ly,
Come the messangere on hy 1070

With lettres fro the lady,
   And schewes thame righte thare.
A fote my3te the kyng no3t stande,
Bot rede thame thare lyggande,
And sayde, "Of thyne erande   1075
   Thou hase thyne answare."

LXVIII.

He sayde, "thou wote thyne ansuare,
The mane that es seke and sare,
He may fulle ille ferre fare
   In felde for to fyghte."   1080
The messangere made his mone,
Saide, "Wo worthe wikkede wone!
Why ne hade I tournede and gone
   Agayne with the knyghte?"
"What knyghte es that," said the kyng, 1085
"That thou mase of thy menynge?
In my londe wot I no lordyng
   Es worthy to be a knyghte."
The messangere ansuerd agayne,
"Wete 3e his name es for to layne, 1090
The whethir I wolde hafe wetene fayne
   What the childe highte.

LXIX.

"Thus mekille gatt I of that knyght,
His dame sonne he said he hight;
One what maner that he was dight 1095
   Now I salle 3ow telle:

He was wighte and worthly,
His body bolde and borely,
His armour bryghte and blody,
      Hade bene late in batelle: 1100
Blode rede was his stede,
His aktone and his other wede,
His cote of the same hede,
      That tille a knyghte felle."
Thane comanded the kyng   1105
Horse and armes for to brynge,—
"If I kane trow thi talkynge,
      That ilke was Percyvelle!"

LXX.

For the luffe of Percyvelle
To horse and armes thay felle,   1110
Thay wolde no lengare ther duelle,
      To fare ware they fayne;
Faste forthe gane thay fare,
Thay were aferde fulle sare,
Ere thay come whare he ware   1115
      The childe wolde be slayne.
The kyng tase with hym knyghtis thre,
The ferthe wolde hym-selfe be;
Now so faste rydes hee,
      May folowe hym no swayne.   1120
The kyng es now in his waye,
Lete hym come whenne he maye,
And I wille forthir in my playe
      To Percyvelle agayne.

LXXI.

Go we to Percyvelle agayne, 1125
The childe paste oute on the playne,
Over more and mountayne,
    To the Maydene-lande;
Tille agayne the evene tyde,
Bolde bodys sawe he byde, 1130
Pavelouns mekille and unryde
    Aboute a cyté stonde;
On-huntyng was the sowdane,
He lefte mene many ane,
Twenty score that wele kane, 1135
    Be the ȝates ȝemande;
And ellevene score one the nyghte,
And tene one the daye lighte,
Wele armyde at alle righte,
    With wapyns in hande. 1140

LXXII.

With thaire wapyns in thaire hande,
There wille thay fight ther thay stande,
Sittande and lyggande
    Ellevene score of mene.
In he rydes one a rase, 1145
Or that he wiste where he was,
In-to the thikkeste of the prese
    Amanges thame thanne;
And up stirt one that was bolde,
By-gane his brydille to holde, 1150

And askede whedire that he wolde
    Make his horse to rynne.
He said, "I ame hedir come
For to see a sowdane;
In faythe righte sone he salle be slane,   1155
    And I myghte hym kene!

LXXIII.

"If I hym oghte kene may,
To morne, whenne it es lighte daye,
Then salle we togedir playe
    With wapyns unryde."   1160
They herde that he had undirtane
For to sle thaire sowdane;
Thay felle aboute hym everilkane
    To make that bolde habyde.
The childe sawe that he was fade,   1165
The body that his bridille hade,
Evene over hym he rade
    In gate there bisyde:
He stayred about hym with his spere,
Many thurgh gane he bere;   1170
Ther was none that myȝt hym dere
    Percevelle that tyde.

LXXIV.

Tide in townne who wille telle,
Folkes undir his fete felle,
The bolde body Percevelle   1175
    He sped thame to spille;

Hym thoghte no spede at his spere,
Many thurgh gane he bere,
Fonde folke in the here
  Feghtyng to fille;   1180
Fro that it was mydnyghte
Tille it was evene at daye lighte,
Were thay never so wilde ne wighte,
  He wroghte at his wille.
Thus he dalt with his brande, 1185
There was none that myght hym stande
Halfe a dynt of his hande,
  That he stroke tille!

LXXV.

Now he strykes for the nonys,
Made the Sarazenes hede bones 1190
Hoppe, als dose hayle stones,
  Abowtte one the gres;
Thus he dalt thame on rawe
Tille the daye gunne dawe,
He layd thaire lyves fulle law, 1195
  Als many als there was.
Whenne he hade slayne so many mene,
He was so wery by thenne,
I telle ȝow for certene
  He roghte wele the lesse 1200
Awther of lyfe or of dede,
To-medis that he were in a stede,
Thar he myghte riste hym in thede
  A stownde in sekirnes!

LXXVI.

Now fonde he no sekirnes, 1205
Bot under the walle ther he was
A faire place he hym chese,
  And downe there he lighte.
He laide hym doune in that tyde,
His stede stode hym besyde, 1210
The fole was fayne for to byde,
  Was wery for the fyght.
Tille one the morne that it was day,
The wayte appone the walle lay,
He sawe an uggly play 1215
  In the place dighte:
ȝitt was ther more ferly,
Ther was no qwyk manne left therby;
Thay called up the lady
  For to see that sighte. 1220

LXXVII.

Now commes the lady to that sight,
The lady Lufamour the brighte,
Scho clambe up to the walle one hight
  Fulle faste to beholde;
Hedes and helmys ther was, 1225
I telle ȝow withowttene lese,
Many layde one the gresse,
  And many schelde brode;
Grete ferly thaym thoghte
Who that wondir had wroghte, 1230

That had thame to dede broghte,
    That folke in the felde :
And wold come none innermare,
For to kythe what he ware,
And wist the lady was thare   1235
    Thaire warysonne to ȝelde.

LXXVIII.

Scho wold thaire warysone ȝelde ;
Fulle faste forthe thay bihelde,
If thay myghte fynde in the felde
    Who hade done that dede :   1240
Thay luked undir thair hande,
Sawe a mekille horse stande,
A blody knyghte liggande
    By a rede stede.
Then said the lady so brighte,   1245
" ȝondir ligges a knyghte
That hase bene in the fighte,
    If I kane righte rede ;
Owthir es ȝone mane slane,
Or he slepis hym allane,   1250
Or he in batelle es tane,
    For blody are his wede !"

LXXIX.

Scho says, " Blody are his wede,
And so es his riche stede,
Siche a knyght in this thede   1255
    Saw I never nane ;

What so he es and he maye ryse,
He es large there he lyse,
And wele made in alle wyse,
   Ther als mane salle be tane."   1260
Scho calde appone hir chaymbirlayne,
Was called hende Hatlayne,
The curtasye of Wawayne
   He weldis in wane;
Scho badd hym wende and see,   1265
" ȝif yone mane one lyfe be,
Bid hym com and speke with me,
   And pray hym als thou kane."

LXXX.

Now to pray hym als he kane
Undir the wallis he wane,   1270
Warly wakend he that mane,
   The horse stode stille;
Als it was tolde un-to me,
He knelid downe one his kne,
Hendely hailsed he that fre,   1275
   And sone said hym tille,—
" My lady, lele Lufamour,
Habyddis the in hir chambour,
Prayes the for thyne honour
   To come, ȝyf ȝe wille."   1280
So kyndly takes he that kyth,
That up he rose and went hym wyth,
The mane that was of myche pyth,
   Hir prayer to fulfille.

LXXXI.

Now hir prayer to fulfille 1285
He folowed the gentilmans wille,
And so he went hir untille,
  Forthe to that lady.
Fulle blythe was that birde brighte,
Whenne scho sawe hym with syghte, 1290
For scho trowed that he was wighte,
  And askede hym in hy;
f. 170] At that fre gan scho frayne,
Thoghe he were lefe for to layne,
If he wiste who had thame slayne 1295
  Thase folkes of envy.
He sayd, " I soghte none of tho,
I come the sowdane to slo,
And thay ne wolde noghte late me go;
  Thaire lyfes there refte I !" 1300

LXXXII.

He sayd, " Belyfe thay solde aby !"
And Lufamour, that lele lady,
Wist fulle wele ther-by
  The childe was fulle wighte.
The birde was blythe of that bade, 1305
That scho siche an helpe hade,
Agayne the sowdane was fade
  With alle for to fighte.
Faste the lady hym byhelde,
Scho thoght hym worthi to welde, 1310

And he myghte wyne hir in felde
    With maystry and myghte.
His stede thay in stabille set,
And hymselfe to haulle was fet,
And than, with-owttene any let,   1315
    To dyne gunne thay dighte.

LXXXIII.

The childe was sett one the dese,
And served with reches,
I telle ȝow with-owttene lese,
    That gaynely was get;   1320
In a chayere of golde,
Bi-fore the fayrest to byholde,
The myldeste maydene one molde,
    At mete als scho satt;
Scho made hym semblande so gude,   1325
Als thay felle to thaire fude,
The maydene mengede his mode
    With myrthes at the mete:
That for hir sake righte tha,
Sone he gane undir-ta   1330
The sory sowdane to sla,
    Withowttene any lett.

LXXXIV.

He sayd, "Withowttene any lett,
When the sowdane and I bene mett,
A sadde stroke I salle one hym sett   1335
    His pride for to spylle!"

Then said the lady so free,
"Who that may his bon be,
Salle hafe this kyngdome and me,
   To welde at his wille!"   1340
He ne hade dyned bot smalle,
Whenne worde come in-to the haulle,
That many mene with-alle
   Were hernyste one the hille;
For tene thaire felawes were slayne,   1345
The cité hafe thay nere tane;
The mene that were with-in the wane,
   The comone belle gunne knylle.

LXXXV.

Now knyllyne thay the comone belle.
Worde come to Percevelle,   1350
And he wold there no lengere duelle,
   Bot lepe fro the dese;
Siche wilde gerys hade he mo,
Sayd, " Kinsmene, now I go,
For alle ȝone salle I slo   1355
   Longe are I sese!"
Scho kiste hym withowttene lett,
The helme one his hede scho sett;
To the stabille fulle sone he gett,
   There his stede was.   1360
There were none with hym to fare;
For no mane thenne wolde he spare,
Rydis furthe withowttene mare
   Tille he come to the prese.

LXXXVI.

Whenne he come to the prese, 1365
He rydes inne one a rese,
The folkes that by-fore hym was
  Thaire strenght hade thay tone:
To kepe hym thane were thay ware,
Thaire dynttis deris hym no mare, 1370
Thenne who so hade strekyne sare
  One a harde stone:
Were thay wighte, were thay woke,
Alle that he tille stroke,
He made thaire bodies to roke, 1375
  Was ther no better wone.
I wote he sped hym so sone,
That day by heghe none
With alle that folke hade he done,
  One lefe lefte noghte one! 1380

LXXXVII.

Whenne he had slayne alle tho,
He loked forthir hyme fro,
If he myghte fynde any mo
  With hym for to fyghte:
And als that hardy bihelde, 1385
He sese ferre in the felde
Fowre knyghtis undir schelde
  Come rydand fulle righte.
One was kyng Arthour,
Anothir Ewayne the floure, 1390

The thirde Wawayne with honoure,
  And Kay the kene knyghte.
Percevelle saide withowttene mare,
" To ȝondir foure wille I fare,
And if the sowdane be thare,   1395
  I salle holde that I highte!"

LXXXVIII.

Now to holde that he hase highte,
Agaynes thayme he rydis righte,
And ay lay the lady brighte
  One the walle, and byhelde   1400
How many mene that he had slane,
And sythene gane his stede mayne
Foure kempys agayne,
  Forthir in the felde.
Then was the lady fulle wo,   1405
Whenne scho sawe hym go
Agaynes foure knyghtys tho,
  With schafte and with schelde.
They were so mekyl and unryde,
That wele wende scho that tyde,   1410
With bale thay solde gare hym byde,
  That was hir beste belde.

LXXXIX.

Thofe he were beste of hir belde,
As that lady byhelde,
He rydes forthe in the felde   1415
  Evene thame agayne.

Then sayd Arthoure the kyng,
" I se a bolde knyghte owt spryng,
For to seke feghtyng
    Forthe wille he frayne;   1420
If he fare forthe to fighte,
And we foure kempys agayne one knyght,
Littille menske wold to us lighte,
    If he were sone slayne."
They fore forthward right faste,   1425
And sone kevelles did thay caste,
And evyr felle it to frayste
    Untille syr Wawayne.

XC.

Whenne it felle to syr Wawayne
To ryde Percevelle agayne,   1430
Of that fare was he fayne,
    And fro thame he rade;
Ever the nerre hym he drewe,
Wele the better he hym knewe
Horse and hernays of hewe,   1435
    That the childe hade.
"A! dere God," said Wawayne the fre,
" How gates may this be,
If I sle hym, or he me,
    That never ȝit was fade?   1440
And we are sister sones two,
And aythir of us othir slo,
He that lifes wille be fulle wo
    That ever was he made!"

XCI.

Now no maistrys he made,   1445
Syr Wawayne there als he rade,
Bot hovyde stylle and habade,
    His concelle to ta.
" Ane unwyse mane," he sayd, " am I,
That puttis myselfe to siche a foly,   1450
Es there no mane so hardy
    That ne anothir es alswa?
Thogfe Percevelle hase slayne the rede knyght,
ȝitt may another be als wyghte,
And in that gere be dyghte,   1455
    And takene alle hym fra!
If I suffire my sister sone,
And anothir in his gere be done,
And gete the maystry me appone,
    That wolde do me wa!   1460

XCII.

f. 171] " It wolde wirke me fulle wa,
So mote I one erthe ga,
It ne salle noghte be-tyde me swa,
    If I may righte rede;
A schafte salle I one hym sett,   1465
And I salle fonde firste to hitt;
Thenne salle I kene be my witt
    Who weldys that wede."
No more carpys he that tyde,
Bot sone to-gedyr gone thay ryde,   1470

Mene that bolde were to byde,
    And styff appone stede;
Thaire horse were stallworthe and strange,
Thair scheldis were un-failande,
Thaire speris brake to thaire hande,   1475
    Als thame byhoved nede.

XCIII.

Now es brokene that are were hale,
And thane by-gane Percevale
For to telle one a tale,
    That one his tonge laye.   1480
He sayde, " Wyde whare hafe I gane,
Siche anothir sowdane
In faythe sawe I never nane,
    By nyghte ne by daye!
I hafe slayne, and I the kene,   1485
Twenty score of thi mene,
And of alle that I slewe thenne,
    Me-thoghte it bot a playe;
Agayne that dynt that I hafe tane,
For siche one aughte I never nane,   1490
Bot I qwyte two for ane,
    Forsothe and I maye!"

XCIV.

Then spake syr Wawayne,
Certanely is noghte to layne,
Of that fare was he fayne,   1495
    In felde there thay fighte;

By the wordis so wylde
At the fole one the felde,
He wiste wele it was the childe,
  Percevelle the wighte!   1500
He sayse, " I ame no sowdane,
Bot I am that ilke mane,
That thi body bygane
  In armours to dighte;
I giffe the prise to thi pyth,   1505
Unkyndely talked thou me with,
My name es Wawayne in kythe,
  Who so redys righte."

XCV.

He sayse, "Who that wille rede the aryghte,
My name es Wawayne the knyghte."   1510
And than thay sessene of thaire fighte,
  Als gude frendes scholde.
He sayse, "Thynkes thou noghte whenne
That thou woldes the knyghte brene,
For thou ne couthe noghte kene   1515
  To spoyle hym alle colde."
Bot thenne was Percevelle the free
Als blythe als he myghte be,
For thenne wiste he wele that it was he,
  By takens that he tolde.   1520
He dide thenne, als he gane hym lere,
Putt up hys umbrere,
And kyste togedir with gud chere
  Those beryns so bolde.

XCVI.

Now kissede the beryns so bolde, 1525
Sythene talkede what thay wolde;
Be thenne come Arthour the bolde,
  That there was knyghte and kyng,
Als his cosyns hadd donne,
Thankede God also sone, 1530
Off mekille myrthis thay mone
  At thaire metyng.
Sythene, withowttene any bade,
To the castelle thay rade
With the childe that thay hade, 1535
  Percevelle the ȝynge.
The portere was redy thare,
Lete the knyghtis in fare,
A blythere lady thane
  1540

XCVII.

" Mi grete socour at thou here sende,
Off my castelle me to diffende,
Agayne the sowdane to wende,
  That es my moste foo."
Theire stedis thay sett in the stalle; 1545
The kyng wendis to haulle,
His knyghtis ȝode hym with-alle,
  Als kynde was to go:
Thaire metis was redy,
And ther-to went thay in hy, 1550

> The kyng and the lady,
>> And knyghtis also.

XCVIII.

> Wele welcomed scho the geste
> With riche metis of the beste,
> Drynkes of the derreste   1555
>> Dightede by-dene.
> Thay ete and dranke what thay wolde;
> Sythene talked and tolde
> Off othir estres fulle olde,
>> The kyng and the qwene.   1560
> At the firste by-gynnyng,
> Scho frayned Arthour the kyng
> Of childe Percevelle the ȝyng,
>> What life he had in bene?
> Grete wondir had Lufamour   1565
> He was so styffe in stour,
> And couthe so littille of nurtour,
>> Als scho had there sene.

XCIX.

> Scho had sene with the childe
> Nothyng bot werkes wylde,   1570
> Thoghte grete ferly one filde
>> Of that foly fare.
> Then said Arthour the kyng
> Of bold Percevelle techyng,
> Fro the firste bygynnyng,   1575
>> [Ti]lle that he come thare.

[Whenne that] his fadir was slayne,
[Thenne his modi]r to the wode gane,
. . . . . here hir allane,
       [In the holtis hare]   1580
Fully feftene ȝere
To play hym with the wilde dere,
Littille wonder it were
       Wilde if he ware!"

C.

When he had tolde this tale   1585
To that semely in sale,
He hade wordis at wale
       To thame ilkane.
The[n] said Percevelle the wighte,
"ȝif I be noghte ȝitt knyghte,   1590
Thou salle halde that thou highte
       For to make me ane."
Than saide the kyng fulle sone,
"Ther salle other dedis be done,
And thou salle wynne thi schone   1595
       Appone the sowdane."
Then said Percevelle the fre,
"Als sone als I the sowdane see,
Righte so salle it sone be,
       Als I hafe undirtane."   1600

CI.

He says, "Als I hafe undirtane
For to sla the sowdane,

THE ROMANCE OF

So salle I wirke als I kanne
  That dede to bygynne."
That day was ther no more dede   1605
With those worthily in wede,
Bot buskede thame and to bedde ȝede,
  The more and the mynne;
Tille one the morne erely
Comes the sowdane with a cry,   1610
Fonde alle his folkes hym by
  Putt unto pyne!
Sone asked he wha
That so durste his mene sla,
And wete hym one lyfe gaa,   1615
  The maystry to wynne?

CII.

Now to wynne the maystry;
To the castelle gane he cry
If any were so hardy
  The maistry to wynne,   1620
f. 172] "A man for ane,
Thoghe he hadd alle his folke slane,
Here salle he fynde Golrotherame
  To mete hym fulle ryghte;
Appone siche a covenande,   1625
That ȝe hefe up ȝour hande,
Who that may the better stande
  And more es of myghte,
To bryng that other to the dede,
Browke wele the londe on brede,   1630

And hir that is so faire and rede,
　　Lufamour the brighte!"

CIII.

Thenne the kyng Arthour,
And the lady Lufamour,
And alle that were in the towre,　　1635
　　Graunted ther-with.
Thay called Percevelle the wight,
The kyng doubbed hym to knyghte;
Thofe he couthe littille in sighte,
　　The childe was of pith:　　1640
He bad he solde be to prayse,
Therto hende and curtayse,
Syr Percevelle the Galayse
　　Thay called hym in kythe!
Kyng Arthour in Maydene-lande　　1645
Dubbid hym knyghte with his hande,
Bad hym ther he his fo fande,
　　To gyff hym no grythe!

CIV.

Grith takes he nane;
He rydes agayne the sowdane　　1650
That highte Gollerotherame,
　　That felle was in fighte.
In the felde so brade
No more carpynge thay made,
Bot sone togedir thay rade　　1655
　　Theire schaftes to righte!

Gollerotheram, thofe he welde wede,
Percevelle bere hym fro his stede
Two londis one brede,
    With maystry and myghte!   1660
At the erthe the sowdane lay,
His stede gunne rynne away,
Thane said Percevelle one play,
    "Thou haste that I the highte!"

CV.

He sayd, "I highte the a dynt,   1665
And now methynke thou hase it hynt,
And I may als I hafe mynt,
    Thou schalt it never mende!"
Appone the sowdane he duelled
To the grownde ther he was felled,   1670
And to the erthe he hym helde
    With his speres ende:
Fayne wolde he hafe hym slayne
This uncely sowdane,
Bot gate couthe he get nane,   1675
    So ille was he kende!
Thane thynkes the childe
Of olde werkes fulle wylde,
"Hade I a fire now in this filde,
    Righte here he solde be brende!" 1680

CVI.

He said, "Righte here I solde the brene,
And thou ne solde never more thenne

Fighte for no wymmane,
  So I solde the fere!"
Thenne said Wawayne the knyghte,   1685
"Thou myghte and thou knewe righte,
And thou woldes of thi stede lighte,
  Wynne hym one were."
The childe was of gamene gnede,
Now he thynkes one thede,   1690
"Lorde! whethir this be a stede,
  I wende had bene a mere!"
In stede righte there he in stode,
He ne wiste nother of evylle ne gude,
Bot then chaunged his mode,   1695
  And slaked his spere.

CVII.

Whenne his spere was up tane,
Then gane this Gollerothiram,
This ilke uncely sowdane,
  One his fete to gete.   1700
Than his swerde drawes he,
Strykes at Percevelle the fre,
The childe hadd no powsté
  His laykes to lett:
The stede was his awnne wille,   1705
Saw the swerde come hym tille,
Leppe up over an hille
  Fyve stryde mett:
Als he sprent forby,
The sowdane keste up a cry,   1710

The childe wanne owt of study,
    That he was inne sett.

CVIII.

Now ther he was in sett;
Owt of study he gett,
And lightis downne withowttene lett, 1715
    Agaynes hym to goo.
He says, " Now hase thou taughte me
How that I salle wirke with the."
Than his swerde drawes he,
    And strake to hym thro: 1720
He hitt hym evene one the nekk-bane,
Thurgh ventale and pesane,
The hede of the sowdane
    He strykes the body fra!
Then fulle wightly he ȝode 1725
To his stede there he stode;
The milde maydene in mode
    Mirthe may scho ma!

CIX.

Many mirthes then he made,
In-to the castelle he rade, 1730
And boldly he there habade
    With that maydene brighte;
Fayne were thay ilkane
That he had slane the sowdane,
And wele wonne that wymmane 1735
    With maystry and myghte!

Thay said Percevelle the ȝyng
Was beste worthy to be kyng,
For wele, withowttene lesyng,
  He helde that he highte.   1740
Ther was no more for to say,
Bot sythene appone that other day,
He weddys Lufamour the may,
  This Percevelle the wighte!

CX.

Now hase Percevelle the wight   1745
Wedded Lufamour the bright,
And is a kyng fulle righte
  Of alle that lande brade.
Thane kyng Arthour in hy
Wolde no lengare ther ly,   1750
Toke lefe at the lady,—
  Fro thame than he rade;
Left Percevelle the ȝyng
Off alle that lande to be kyng,
For he had with a ryng   1755
  The maydene that it hade.
Sythen, appone the tother day
The kyng went on his way,
The certane sothe als I say,
  Withowttene any bade.   1760

CXI.

Now thane ȝong Percevelle habade
In those borowes so brade,

For hir sake that he hade
    Wedd with a ryng.
Wele weldede he that lande,   1765
Alle bewes to his honde,
The folke that he byfore fonde
    Knewe hym for kyng.
Thus he wonnes in that wone
Tille that the twelmonthe was gone,   1770
With Lufamour his lemmane,
    He thoghte on no thyng:
Now on his moder that was,
How scho levyde with the gres,
With moste drynke and lesse,   1775
    In welles there thay spryng.

CXII.

f. 173] Drynkes of welles ther thay spryng,
And gresse etys withowt lesyng,
Scho liffede with none othir thyng
    In the holtes hare.   1780
Tille it byfelle appone a day,
Als he in his bedd lay,
Tille hymselfe gunne he say,
    Syghande fulle sare,
"The laste ȝole day that was,   1785
Wilde wayes I chese,
My modir alle manles
    Leved I thare!"
Thane righte sone saide he,
"Blythe salle I never be,   1790

Or I may my modir see,
  And wete how scho fare."

CXIII.

Now to wete how scho fare,
The knyght busked hym ȝare,
He wolde no lengare duelle thare   1795
  For noghte that myghte bee;
Up he rose in that haulle,
Tuke his lefe at tham alle,
Bot at grete and at smalle,
  Fro thaym wendis he.   1800
Faire scho prayed hym evene thane,
Lufamour his lemmane,
Tille the heghe dayes of ȝole were gane
  With hir for to bee.
Bot it served hir of nothyng: 1805
A preste he made forthe bryng
Hym a messe for to syng,
  And aftir rode he.

CXIV.

Now fro thame gunne he ryde:
Ther wiste no mane that tyde   1810
Whedirwarde he wolde ryde,
  His sorowes to amende;
Forthe he rydes allone,
Fro tham he wolde everichone,
Mighte no mane with hym gone,   1815
  Ne whedir he wolde lende.

Bot forthe thus rydes he ay,
The certene sothe als I 30w say,
Tille he come at a way
    By a wode ende;   1820
Then herde he faste hym by,
Als it were a womane cry,
Scho prayed to mylde Mary
    Som socoure hir to sende.

CXV.

Scho sende hir socour fulle gude,   1825
Mary that es mylde of mode!
As he come thurgh the wode
    A ferly he fande;
A birde brighteste of ble
Stode faste bondene tille a tre,   1830
I say it 30w certanly,
    Bothe fote and hande.
Sone askede he who,
Whenne he sawe hir tho,
That had served hir so,   1835
    That lady in lande.
Scho said, " Syr, the blake knyghte,
Solde be my lorde with righte,
He hase me thus gates dighte
    Here for to stande!"   1840

CXVI.

Scho says, " Here mone I stande,
For a faute that he fande,

That salle I warande
    Is my moste mone!
Now to the I salle say, 1845
Appone my bedd I lay
Appone the laste ȝole day,
    Twelve monethes es gone:
Were he knyghte, were he kyng,
He come one his playnge, 1850
With me he chaungede a ryng,
    The richeste of one!
The body myght I noghte see,
That made that chaungyng with me,
Bot what that ever he be, 1855
    The better hase he tone!"

CXVII.

Scho says, "The better hase he tane,
Siche a vertue es in the stane,
In alle this werlde wote I nane
    Siche stone in a rynge; 1860
A mane that had it in were,
One his body for to bere,
There scholde no dyntys hym dere,
    Ne to the dethe brynge."
And then wiste syr Percevale 1865
Fulle wele by the ladys tale,
That he had broghte hir in bale
    Thurgh his chaungyng.
Thane also sone sayd he
To that lady so fre, 1870

"I salle the louse fro the tre,
  Als I ame trewe kyng!"

CXVIII.

He was bothe kyng and knyght;
Wele he helde that he highte,
He loused the lady so brighte,   1875
  Stod bowne to the tre.
Downe satt the lady,
And ʒong Percevalle hir by,
For-waked was he wery,
  Rist hym wolde he: 1880
He wende wele for to ryst,
Bot it wolde nothyng laste;
Als he lay althir-best
  His hede one hir kne,
Scho putt on Percevelle wighte,   1885
Bad hym fle with alle his myghte,
"For ʒonder comes the blake knyghte,
  Dede mone ʒe be!"

CXIX.

Scho sayd, "Dede mone ʒe be,
I say ʒow, syr, certanly,   1890
ʒonder out comes he
  That wille us bothe sle!"
The knyghte gane hir answere,
"Tolde ʒe me noghte lang ere,
Ther solde no dynttis me dere,   1895
  Ne wirke me no woo?"

The helme on his hede he sett,
Bot or he myght to his stede get,
The blak knyght with hym mett
    His maistrys to mo.   1900
He sayd, " How ! hase thou here
Fondene now thi playfere ?
ȝe schalle haby it fulle dere
    Er that I hethene go !"

CXX.

He said, " Or I hethyn go   1905
I salle sle ȝow bothe two,
And alle siche othir mo,
    Thaire warysone to ȝelde."
Than sayd Percevelle the fre,
" Now sone thane salle we see,   1910
Who that es worthy to bee
    Slayne in the felde !"
No more speke thay that tyde,
Bot sone togedir gane thay ryde,
Als mene that wolde were habyde,   1915
    With schafte and with schelde.
Thane syr Percevelle the wight
Bare downe the blake knyght;
Thane was the lady so bright
    His best socour in telde.   1920

CXXI.

Scho was the beste of his belde;
Bot scho had there bene his schelde,

He had bene slayne in the felde
Right certeyne in hy;
Ever als Percevelle the kene 1925
Sold the knyghtis bane hafe bene,
Ay went the lady by-twene,
And cryed, "Mercy!"
Than the lady he forbere,
And made the blak knyghte to swere 1930
Of alle evylles that there were
Forgiffe the lady:
And Percevelle made the same othe,
That he come never undir clothe
To do that lady no lothe, 1935
That pendid to velany.

CXXII.

f. 174] "I did hir never no velany;
Bot slepande I saw hir ly,
Than kist I that lady,
I wille it never layne; 1940
I tok a ryng that I fande,
I left hir, I undirstande,
That salle I wele warande,
Anothir ther agayne."
Thofe it were for none other thyng, 1945
He swere by Jhesu hevene kyng,
To wete withowttene lesyng,
And here to be slayne!
"And alle redy is the ryng,
And thou wille myne agayne bryng, 1950

SIR PERCEVAL OF GALLES.

Here wille I make the chaungyng,
  And of myne awnne be fayne!"

CXXIII.

He saise, " Of myne I wille be fayne."
The blak knyghte ansuers agayne,
Sayd, " For sothe it is noghte to layne,   1955
  Thou come over late;
Als sone als I the ryng fande,
I toke it sone off hir hande,
To the lorde of this lande
  I bare it one a gate;   1960
That gate with grefe hafe I gone,
I bare it to a gude mone,
The stalwortheste geant of one
  That any mane wate:
Es it nowther knyghte ne kyng,   1965
That dorste aske hym that ryng,
That he ne wolde hym downe dyng
  With harmes fulle hate!"

CXXIV.

" Be thay hate, be thay colde,"
Thane said Percevelle the bolde;   1970
For the tale that he tolde
  He wex alle tene!
He said, " Heghe one galous mote he hyng,
That to the here giffes any ryng,
Bot thou myne agayne brynge,   1975
  Thou haste awaye gevene;

76 THE ROMANCE OF

And ȝif it may no nother be,
Righte sone thane telle thou me
The sothe whilke that es he,
   Thou knawes that es so kene! 1980
There es no more for to say,
Bot late me wynne it, ȝif I may,
For thou hase giffene thi part of bothe away,
   Thof thay had better bene."

CXXV.

He says, "Thofe thay had better bene." 1985
The knyghte ansuerde in tene,
"Thou salle wele wete withowttene wene,
   Wiche that es he:
If thou dare do als thou says,
Sir Percevelle de Galays, 1990
In ȝone heghe palays
  Therinne solde he be!
The riche ryng with that grym,
The stone es bright and nothyng dym,
For sothe ther salle thou fynd hym, 1995
   I toke it fro me;
Owthir with-in or with-owt,
Or one his play ther abowte,
Of the he giffes littille dowte,
   And that salle thou see!" 2000

CXXVI.

He says, "That salle thou see,
I say the fulle sekirly."

And than forthe rydis he
    Wondirly swythe.
The geant stode in his holde,   2005
That had those londis in wolde,
Saw Percevelle that was bolde,
    One his lande dryfe.
He calde one his portere,
" How gate may this fare?   2010
I se a bolde mane ȝare
    One my lande ryfe!
Go reche me my playlome,
And I salle go to hym sone;
Hym were better hafe bene at Rome,   2015
    So ever mote I thryfe!"

CXXVII.

Whethir he thryfe or he the,
Ane iryne clobe takes he;
Agayne Percevelle the fre
    He went than fulle right.   2020
The clobe wheyhed reghte wele,
That a freke myght it fele,
The hede was of harde stele,
    Twelve stone weghte!
There was iryne in the wande,   2025
Ten stone of the lande,
And one was by-hynde his hande,
    For holdyng was dight.
Ther was thre and twenty in hale,
Fulle evylle myght any mene smale,   2030

That mene telles nowe in tale,
With siche a lome fighte.

CXXVIII.

Now are thay bothe bowne,
Mett one a more browne,
A mile withowt any towne, 2035
Boldly with schelde.
Thane saide the geant so wight,
Als sone als he sawe the knyght,
" Mahowne, loved be thi myght !"
And Percevelle byhelde. 2040
" Art thou hym that," saide he thane,
" That slew Gollerothirame ?
I had no brothir bot hym ane,
Whenne he was of elde."
Than said Percevelle the fre, 2045
" Thurgh grace of God so salle I the,
And siche geantez as ȝe,
Sle thaym in the felde !"

CXXIX.

Siche metyng was seldom sene,
The dales dynned thaym by-twene, 2050
For dynttis that thay gaffe by-dene,
Whenne thay so mett :
The gyant with his clobe-lome
Wolde hafe strekyne Percevelle sone,
Bot he ther-under wightely come 2055
A stroke hym to sett.

The geant missede of his dynt,
The clobe was harde as the flynt;
Or he myght his staffe stynt,
  Or his strengh lett,   2060
The clobe in the erthe stode,
To the midschafte it wode;
Then Percevelle the gode,
  Hys swerde owt he get.

CXXX.

By then hys swerde owt he get,   2065
Strykes the geant withowttene lett,
Merkes evene to his nekk,
  Reght evene there he stode;
His honde he strykes hym fro,
His lefte fote also,   2070
With siche dyntis as tho
  Nerre hym he ȝode.
Then sayd Percevelle, " I undirstande
Thou myghte with a lesse wande
Hafe weledid better thi hande,   2075
  And hafe done the some gode;
Now bese it never for ane
The clobe of the erthe tane,
I telle thi gatis alle gane,
  Bi the gude rode!"   2080

CXXXI.

He says, " By the gud rode!
As evylle als thou ever ȝode,

Of thi fote thou getis no gode,
    Bot lepe if thou may!"
The geant gan the clobe lefe,   2085
And to Percevelle a dynt he ȝefe
In the nekk with his nefe,
    Sone neghede thay.
At that dynt was he tene,
He strikes off the hande als clene   2090
As ther hadde never none bene,
    That other was alwaye:
Sythen his hede gane he off hafe;
He was ane unhende knave
A geant berde so to schafe,   2095
    For sothe als I say!

CXXXII.

f. 175] Now, for sothe als I say,
He lete hym ly there he lay,
And rydis forthe one his way
    To the heghe holde.   2100
The portare saw his lorde slayne,
The kayes durste he noght layne,
He come Percevelle agayne,
    The ȝatis he hym ȝolde.
At the firste bygynnyng,   2105
He askede the portere of the ryng,
If he wiste of it anythyng;
    And he hym than tolde.
He taughte hym sone to the kiste,
Ther he alle the golde wiste,   2110

Bade hym take what hym liste
    Of that he hafe wolde.

CXXXIII.

Percevelle sayde hafe it he wolde,
And schott owtt alle the golde;
Righte there appone the faire molde   2115
    The ryng owte glade.
The portare stode besyde,
Sawe the ryng owt glyde,
Sayde ofte, "Wo worthe the tyde
    That ever was it made!"   2120
Percevelle answerde in hy,
And asked where-fore and why
He banned it so brothely,
    Bot if he cause hade?
Thenne alsone said he,   2125
And sware by his lewté,
"The cause salle I telle the,
    Withowttene any bade!"

CXXXIV.

He says, "Withowtten any bade,
The knyghte that it here hade,   2130
Theroff a presande he made,
    And hedir he it broghte;
Mi mayster tuke it in his hande,
Ressayved faire that presande;

He was chefe lorde of this lande, 2135
  Als man that mekille moghte!
That tyme was here fast by
Wonnede a lady,
And hir wele and lely
  He luffede, als me thoghte; 2140
So it byfelle appone a day,
Now the sothe als I salle say,
Mi lorde went hym to play,
  And the lady bysoghte.

CXXXV.

" Now the lady byseches he 2145
That scho wolde his lemane be,
Fast he frayned that free
  For any kyns aughte.
At the firste bygynnyng,
He wolde hafe gyffene hir the ryng, 2150
And whenne scho sawe the tokynyng,
  Thenne was scho unsaughte.
Scho gret and cried in hir mone,
Sayd, " Thefe, hase thou my sone slone,
And the ryng fro hym tone 2155
  That I hym bitaughte?"
Hir clothes ther scho rafe hir fro,
And to the wodd gane scho go;
Thus es the lady so wo,
  And this is the draghte! 2160

CXXXVI.

" For siche draghtis als this,
Now es the lady wode i-wys,
And wilde in the wodde scho es
   Ay sythene that ilke tyde:
Fayne wolde I take that free, 2165
Bot alsone als scho sees me,
Faste away dose scho flee,
   Wille scho noghte abyde!"
Then sayde syr Percevelle,
" I wille assaye fulle snelle 2170
To make that lady to duelle,
   Bot I wille noghte ryde:
One my fote wille I ga
That faire lady to ta;
Me aughte to bryng hir of wa, 2175
   I laye in hir syde!"

CXXXVII.

He sayse, " I laye in hir syde;
I salle never one horse ryde
Tille I hafe sene hir in tyde,
   Spede if I may! 2180
Ne none armoure that may be
Salle come appone me,
Tille I my modir may see
   Be nyghte or by day!
Bot reghte in the same wode 2185
That I firste fro hir ȝode,

That salle be in my mode,
   Aftir myne other play;
Ne I ne salle I never mare
Come owt of ȝone holtis hare,   2190
Tille I wete how scho fare,
   For sothe als I saye.

CXXXVIII.

"Now for sothe als I say!"
With that he helde one his way,
And one the morne, whenne it was day, 2195
   Forthe gonne he fare.
His armour he leved therin,
Toke one hym a gayt skynne,
And to the wodde gane he wyne
   Among the holtis hare.   2200
A sevenyght long hase he soghte,
His modir ne fyndis he noghte,
Of mete ne drynke he ne roghte,
   So fulle he was of care!
Tille the nynte day byfelle,   2205
That he come to a welle
Ther he was wonte for to duelle,
   And drynk take hym thare.

CXXXIX.

When he had dronkene that tyde,
Forthirmare gane he glyde,   2210

Than was he warre hym besyde
    Of the lady so fre:
Bot whenne scho sawe hym thare,
Scho byganne for to dare,
And sone gaffe hym answare,   2215
    That brighte was of ble.
Scho bigan to calle and cry,
Sayd, "Siche a sone hade I!"
His hert lightened in hy
    Blythe for to bee.   2220
Be that he come hir nere,
That scho myght hym here,
He said, "My modir fulle dere,
    Wele byde ȝe me!"

CXL.

Be that so nere getis he,   2225
That scho myghte nangatis fle,
I say ȝow fulle certeynly
    Hir byhoved ther to byde;
Scho stertis appone hym in tene,
Wote ȝe wele withowttene wene,   2230
Had hir myghte so mekille bene,
    Scho had hym slayne that tyde:
Bot his myghte was the mare,
And up he toke his modir thare,
One his bake he hir bare,   2235
    Pure was his pryde.
To the castelle, withowttene mare,
The righte way gone he fare,

86   THE ROMANCE OF

The portare was redy ȝare,
  And lete hym inne glyde. 2240

CXLI.

In with his modir he glade,
Als he sayse that it made;
With siche clothes als thay hade,
  Thay happed hir forthy.
The geant had a drynk wroghte, 2245
The portere sone it forthe broghte,
For no mane was his thoghte,
  Bot for that lady;
Thay wolde not lett long thone,
Bot lavede in hir with a spone, 2250
Then scho one slepe felle also sone,
  Reght certeyne in hy.
Thus the lady there lyes
Thre nyghttis and thre dayes,
And the portere alwayes 2255
  Lay wakande hir by.

CXLII.

f. 176] Thus the portare woke [by],
Ther whills hir luffed s[icurly],
Tille at the laste the lady
  Wakede, als I wene. 2260
Thenne scho was in hir awenne [wate],
And als wele in hir gate,
Als scho hadde nowthir arely ne late
  Never ther owte bene.

Thay sett thame downe one thaire kne, 2265
Thanked Godde alle three,
That he wolde so appone thame see,
  As it was there sene.
Sythene aftir gane thay ta
A riche bathe for to ma, 2270
And made the lady in to ga,
  In graye and in grene.

CXLIII.

Thane syr Percevelle in hy
Toke his modir hym by,
I say ȝow than certenly, 2275
  And home went hee;
Grete lordes and the qwene
Welcomed hym al-bydene,
Whenne thay hym one lyfe sene,
  Than blythe myghte thay bee! 2280
Sythen he went into the Holy Londe,
Wanne many cités fulle stronge,
And there was he slayne, I undirstonde,
  Thus gatis endis hee.
Now Jhesu Criste, hevens kyng, 2285
Als he es Lorde of alle thyng,
Grante us alle his blyssyng!
  Amene for charyté!

Quod Robert Thorntone.

Explicit Syr Percevelle de Gales. Here endys the Romance of Syr Percevelle of Gales, cosyne to Kyng Arthoure.

THE ROMANCE

OF

SIR ISUMBRAS.

f. 109] *Here begynnes the Romance off Syr Ysambrace.*

I.

Jhesu Crist, Lorde of hevene kynge,
Graunte us alle his dere blyssynge,
  And hevene unto oure mede!
Now, hende in haule, and ȝe wolde here
Of eldirs that by-fore us were,   5
  That lyffede in arethede,
I wille ȝow telle of a knyghte,
That bothe was stalworthe and wyghte,
  [And worth]ily undir wede:
His name was hattene syr Ysambrace, 10
Swilke a knyghte als he was
  Now lyffes nowrewhare in lede.

II.

He was mekille mane and lange,
With schuldirs brode and armes strange,
  That semly were to see;   15
So was he bothe faire and heghe,
Alle hym loffede that hym seghe,
  Se hende a mane was hee!
He luffede glewmene wele in haulle,
He gafe thame robis riche of palle,   20
  Bothe golde and also fee;
Of curtasye was he kynge,
Of mete and drynke no nythynge,
  One lyfe was none so fre.

III.

Als fayre a lady to wyefe had he   25
Als any erthly mane thurte see,
  With tunge als I ʒow nevene;
Knave childire had thay thre,
Thay were the faireste that myghte be
  Undir the kynge of hevene!   30
Bot in his hert a pride was broghte,
Of Goddis werkes gafe he noghte,
  His mercys for to nevene;
So longe he reyngned in his pride,
That God wolde no lenger habyde,   35
  To hym he sent a stevene.

IV.

It felle so appone a daye,
The knyghte went to the wode hym to playe,
  His foreste for to see;
And als he come by a derne sty,   40
A fowle herde he synge one hy
  Fulle heghe upone a tree,
And said, " Welcome, syr Ysambrace,
Thou hafes forgetyne whate thou was,
  For pride of golde and fee!   45
The kyng of hevene gretis the soo,
Werldes wele the bus for-goo,
In elde or ȝouthe thou salle dry woo,
  Chese whethir es lever to thee!"

V.

With carefulle herte and sygheyngez sare,   50
The knyghte felle on his knes al bare,
  And bothe his handis uphelde:—
" Werldes wele I wille for-sake,
And to Goddes mercy I me bytake,
  To hym my saule I ȝelde!   55
In ȝouthe I maye bothe ryde and goo,
When I ame alde I may nott so,
  My lymmes wille waxe unwelde;
Now, Lorde, ȝif it thi wille bee,
In ȝowthede penance send thou mee,   60
  And welthe appone myne elde!"

VI.

The foule thane toke ane heghe flyghte,
Alle-one he leved that drery knyghte,
   And sone he went awaye;
And whenne he of the fowle had no syghte, 65
His stede, that was bothe stronge and wyghte,
   Sone dede downe undir hym laye.
His hawkes and his howndis bothe,
Wente to the wode, als thay were wrothe,
   Ilkone a dyverse waye.   70
Whate wondir was thofe hym ware wo,
One fote now moste hym nedis goo,
   To pyne turnes alle his playe!

VII.

And als he wente by a wod schawe,
Thare mett he with a lyttille knave 75
   Come rynnande hym agayne;
And wele wers tythynges he hym tolde,
Brynned were alle his byggynges bolde,
   His bestes werene alle slayne!
"A! Lorde, ther es no thyng lefte one lyfe 80
Bot thi thre childir and thi wyfe,
[f. 110]   The sothe es noghte to layne!"
The knyghte thane ansuerde with herte so vey,
"With thi that I may one hir see,
My wyfe and my childire thre,   85
   ȝitt was never mane so fayne."

VIII.

Bot als he wente by hym allone,
His hirde-mene mett he everylkone,
  With a fulle drery swoghe,
And saide thaire fee was fro thame revede, 90
" Certis, syr, us es noghte levyde
  A stotte unto ȝoure plowghe !"
Thay wepede sare and gaffe thame ille ;
The knyghte bad thay solde be stylle,
  " I wytte ȝow noghte this woghe ; 95
God that sent me alle this woo,
Wele hase he sent me also,
  And ȝitt may send y-noghe !"

IX.

A dolefulle syghte the knyghte gane see
Of his wyfe and his childir three, 100
  That fro the fyre were flede ;
Alle als nakede als thay were borne
Stode togedir undir a thorne,
  Braydede owte of thaire bedd.
Bot changede never the knyghttes blee, 105
To he sawe thame so nakede bee
  He levyde so comly clede.
The lavedy bade hir childir be blythe,
" I see ȝoure fadir ȝondir one lyve,
  For nothynge that ȝe drede !" 110

X.

They wepede alle and gafe thame ille,
The knyghte bad thay solde be stylle,
      "And wepe ȝe noghte so sore;
For alle the sorowe that we aryne inne,
It es ilke dele for oure syne,   115
      We ware worthi wele more!
Bot we kane nonekyns werkes wyrke,
Owre frendis of us wille sone be irke,
      Of lande I rede we fare;
Of my-selvene hafe I no thoghte,   120
Bot I may helpe my childir noghte,
      For thame es alle my kare!"

XI.

The knyghte offe his mantille of palle,
And over his weyfe he lete it falle
      With a fulle drery mode;   125
His riche surcote i-wysse schare he,
And gafe his pore childir thre,
      That nakede byfore hym stode.
"Now salle ȝe alle," he said, "do my rede,
To seke thare God was qwike and dede,   130
      That done was one the rode;
For Jesus Criste so hende es he,
That who so sekes hym with herte fre,
      He sendis thame lyves fode."

XII.

And with a knyfe son gerte he schare   135
A crose appone his schuldir bare,
      In storye als I ȝowe saye;
Alle those that there his frendis ware,
They wepid alle and syghede sare,
      Thayre sange was waylawaye!   140
The knyghte and his lady hende
Toke lefe at thaire dere frendes,
      And made thaire fondynge daye;
For thame weped bothe olde and ȝynge,
Thare was a carefulle departynge,   145
      And sythene thay went thaire waye.

XIII.

With thame tuke thay fulle littille gude
That myghte helpe tham to thaire lyves fode,
      Nowther golde ne fee;
Bot in the lande to begge thaire mete,   150
Were so that thay myghte any gete
      For saynte charité.
Fyve wokes thus them gunne thay over-passe,
Als it Jhesu Cristes wille was,
      With thaire childir three;   155
Tho that are was wonte to wele and wyne,
The myschevous poverte that thay were inne
      Grete dole it was to see!

XIV.

ȝitt in a wode thay were gone wylle,
Towne ne myghte thay none wyne tille,   160
      Als wery als thay were;
Bot whenne thre dayes tille ende was gane,
Mete ne drynke ne hade thay nane,
      Thay weped for hungre sore!
Nothynge sawe thay that come of corne,   165
Bot the floures of the thorne,
      Up-one those holtes hore;
Thay entirde thane to a water kene,
The bankes were fulle ferre bytwene,
      And watirs breme als bare.   170

XV.

The knyghte his eldeste sone tase there,
And over the water he hym bare,
      And sett hym one the bryme;
And sayde, "Luke, my sone, that thou be stylle,
To whils I feche thi brother the tille,   175
      And playe the with the blome."
The knyghte that was bothe hend and gude,
Agayne swythe over the water he wode,
      His medille sone over to brynge;
So come a lyonne with latys un-mylde,   180
And in hir pawes scho hent the childe,
      And to the wode faste gane rynne.

XVI.

Thane with carefulle herte and syghynge sare,
His medilmaste sone ȝit lefte he thare,
    [And went wepynge aweye.]   185
Thus with sorowfulle chere and drery mode,
Agayne over the water he wode,
    To pyne tornes alle his playe!
A labarde ther come and tuk that othir,
To the wode he bare hym to his brother,   190
    Wyghtly he wente awaye!
The lady grette and gafe hir ille,
Nere scho wolde hir-selvene spille
    One lande righte whare scho laye.

XVII.

The knyghte mase dole and sorowe y-noghe,   195
Nerehand he hym-selvene sloghe
    Are he come to the banke;
And the lady grett and gafe hir ille,
Nowther of tham myghte other stille,
    Thaire sorowe it was fulle ranke!   200
Thay sayd, allas that thay were borne,
"Felle werdes es layde us by-forne,
    That are were wele and wanke!"
The knyghte bad scho sulde be stille,
And gladly suffir Goddes wille,   205
    "Us awe hym alle to thanke!"

XVIII.

Littille wondir thofe thame wo were,
For bothe thaire childir leve thay there,
    [Hys lovely sonnes two.
Hys wyfe thane toke he there,]   210
And over the water he thane bare
    His ʒongeste sone also.
And thurgh a foreste ʒode thay three,
And entred in towardeʒ the Greckes see,
    Thare thay sawe stormes bloo: 215
And appone the lond thus als thay stude,
Thay sawe come saylande over the flode
    A thowsand schippes and moo.

XIX.

And als thay stode so appone the lande,
And lokede in-to the see strande,   220
    Those schippes sawe thay ryde
With toppe-castelles sett one lofte,
Of riche golde thame semed wroghte,
    Stremours fro thame ferre gane glyde.
The sowdanne hym-selfe was therinne,   225
That Cristendome was commene to wynne,
    Thare wakkyns woo fulle wyde!
The knyghte thoghte that he wolde wende
In-to that havene at ferrere ende,
    A littille ther bysyde.   230

XX.

Those schippes landed by that land syde,
The folke come up with mekille pryde,
  ȝaa moo thene I kane nevene;
The knyghte thane karpede to the lady free,
"What maye thiese ferly folkkes bee?" 235
  He spake with lowde stevene:
f. 111.] "In this foreste lange hafe we gane,
Mete ne drynke myghte we gete nane
  More thane thiese dayes sevene;
Aske we thiese folkes of thaire mete, 240
And luke ȝife we maye any gete
  For Goddis lufe of hevene!"

XXI.

Untille a galaye thus gane thay wynne,
There the sowdane of those Sarazenes was inne,
  That fulle richely was wroghte; 245
Thay askede hym some lyves fode
For His lufe that dyede on the rode,
  And made this worlde of noghte!
The Sarazens said he was a spye,
Whenne that thay herde hym swa gates crye, 250
  That thaire schippes had soghte;
The sowdane bade do hym awaye,
"For thay lefe nott on owre laye,
  Loke that ȝe gyffe hym noghte!"

XXII.

A knyghte saide to the sowdane kynge, 255
" Now certis, syr, it es a wondir thynge
    ʒone pore mane for to see;
For he es bothe lange and heghe,
The faireste mane that ever I seghe,
    A knyghte hym semes to bee. 260
His wyfe es whitte as walles bone,
Hir lyre es als the see fome,
    And bryghte als any blee."
The sowdane than gret rewthe thoghte,
And command that thay solde be broghte, 265
    He wolde hymselfe thame see.

XXIII.

Whenne he hir sawe, hym rewed sare,
So semly als thay bothe ware,
    If thay were robed riche.
The sowdane byddes hym gold and fee, 270
" If thou wille duelle and be with me,
    And helpe me to my fyghte;
If thou be doghty mane of dede,
Thou salle be horssede on a stede,
    My-selfe salle dube the knyghte!" 275

XXIV.

Fulle stille thane stode syr Ysambrace,
A Sarazene he sawe wele that he was,
    And sone he sayde hym naye:

"Certis, that salle I never mare
Agayne Crystyndomme fyghte no fare,   280
  And lefe appone thi laye.
Now in this foreste hafe we gane,
Mete ne drynke we myghte gete nane,
  This es the sevent daye;
I aske ȝow some lyves fode   285
For His lufe that dyed on rode,
  And late us wende oure waye."

XXV.

The sowdane sawe that lady thare,
Hym thoghte als scho an angelle ware,
  That ware commene owte of hevene. 290
He saide, "Wille thou selle thi wyffe to me?
And I wille gyff the golde and fee,
  ȝaa more than thou kane nevene:
I salle the gyffe tene thowsand pownde
Of florence that bene rede and rownde,   295
  And gud robes sevene;
And scho salle be lady of alle my lande,
And alle salle bowe hir to fote and hande,
  And noghte withstande hir stevene."

XXVI.

Sir Ysambrace sayd thane schortly, "Naye, 300
My wyfe wille I nott selle awaye,
  Bot mene me for hir slaa;

I wedded hir in Goddes laye,
To halde hir to myne endyng daye,
  ȝaa bothe in wele and waa."   305
The gold thane on his mantille thay talde,
And tille hyme-selfene thay gane it falde,
  His wyefe thay tuke hym fraa;
And appone the lande thay hym kaste,
And bett hym tille his rybbis braste,   310
  And made his flesche fulle blaa!

XXVII.

The littille childe one lande was sett,
And sawe how mene his fadir bett,
  He wepid and was fulle waa.
The lady grete and gafe hir ille,   315
Unnethes thay myght halde hir stille,
  That ne scho hir-selve walde slaa.
Hir armes scho sprede and lowde gane crye,
And ofte scho cryed one oure lady,
  " Salle we departe in two?   320
Allas! for salle I never blythe be,
My weddede lorde salle I never see,
  Now wakyns alle my woo!"

XXVIII.

Whenne the wounded knyght myght up-stande,
He tok his childe by the hande,   325
  Wepande awaye went hee.

A riche schippe was dighte righte ȝare,
The sowdane bad that lordes solde fare
  With that lady so free;
The sowdane with his ownne honde   330
Crownned hir qwene of alle his londe,
  And sent hir to his conntré:
A chartir was mad fulle wele farande,
The sowdane selide it with his hande,
That thofe he never come in his lande,   335
  That scho solde qwene bee.

XXIX.

When the lady in schippe was ȝare,
Ever scho weped fulle selly sare,
  And knelis byfore the kynge.
"Sir kynge," scho sayde, "I pray the   340
A bowne that thou wille graunt to me,
  Now at oure parttynge;
Mete and drynke thou gare tham gyfe,
A sevenyghte that thay myght with lyfe,
  That littille childe and he."   345
The sowdane grauntes, scho was fulle fayne;
[Scho callyd hir lorde to hir agayne,]
  A rynge was thaire takynnyng.

XXX.

The lady was curtayse and mylde,
Scho blyssede hir lorde and hir childe,   350
  And felle downe one hir knee.

Thay drewe up sayle of ryche hewe,
The wynde thame sonne owte of havene blewe
  With that lady so free.
The wonded knyghte hym downe sett,   355
And for his wyfe fulle sare he grett,
  Whils he thaire schipe myghte see.
And whenne the knyght myghte upstande,
He toke his childe by the hande,
  And awaye thane faste went hee.   360

XXXI.

Sythene sett he hym downe undir a tree,
Unnethes myghte he with ehgne see,
  So had he wepede sare!
Mete and drynke forthe he droghe,
He gafe his childe at ete y-noghe,   365
  His hert thane was fulle sare;
In his mantille of skarlet rede
Y-mange his golde he did his brede,
  And with hyme he it bare.

XXXII.

The knyghte come to a banke fulle drye,   370
And thare byhoves hym al nyghte to lye,
  For ferrere myghte noghte he;
There come in the mournynge an egle flyande,
And sone the knyghtes mantille he fande,
  And awaye therwith gane flye.   375

The knyghte folowed that egle to the see;
And that same tyde come an unycorne,
His ʒongeste sone away hase he borne,
  Swylke sorowe that knyghte gane dree!

XXXIII.

Ofte was that knyghte bothe wele and woo, 380
Bot never ʒitt als he was thoo;
f. 112.] He sett hym one a stone.
With carefulle mode and drery stevene,
Unto the heghe kyng of hevene
  Made he thane his mone. 385
"A! Lorde," he saide, "fulle wo es me,
So faire childir als I hafede thre,
  And nowe ame I lefte allone!
Now Gode, that beres the heghe crowne,
The waye he wysse me to some towne, 390
  For fulle wille I ame of wone!"

XXXIV.

Bot als the knyghte went thorow a lawe,
Smethymene thore herde he blawe,
  And fyres thore bryne and glewe;
He askede tham mete for charyté, 395
And thay bade hym swynke, "And swa do we,
  Hafe we none other ploghe."
"For mete," he sayde, "I wold wyrke fayne,"
The knyghte ansuerde fulle sone agayne,
  "Bathe bere and drawe y-noghe." 400

Thane mete thay gafe hym fulle gud wone,
And thay garte hym bere iryne and stone
  Owte of a sory sloghe.

XXXV.

And thus bare the knyght iryne and stone
Unto the sevene wyntter were alle gone, 405
  And wroghte hym-selvene fulle woo;
And untille that he couthe make a fyre,
And than thay gafe hym ȝomans hyre,
  Wele more he wroghte thane twoo!
A smethymane thus was he thore 410
Fully sevene ȝere or more,
  And blewe thaire belyes bloo;
And by that he hade hym-selfene dyghte
Alle the atyre that felle to a knyghte,
Bot that he was noghte horsed ryghte 415
  To batelle whenne he solde goo.

XXXVI.

Alle those sevene ȝere, I undirstande,
The sowdane werreyede in Cristene lande,
  And wakkenede woo fulle wyde;
The Crystene kynges hase fledde so lange, 420
To thay hafe getyne tham powere strange,
  Those Sarazenes for to byde.
A daye of batelle than was sett,
That Cristyne and haythene samene solde mete
  A littylle ther besyde. 425
Sir Ysambrace hym umbithoghte

Appone a horse that coles broghte
  That he wolde thedir ryde.

XXXVII.

Bemes thane herde he blowe fulle lowde,
[And sawe knyghtes and beryns prowdе,] 430
  And swerdes drawene one lofte.
He sett hym downe appone his kne,
To Jhesu Criste than prayes he,
  And enterely hym bysoghte:
"Nowe, Lorde," he saide, "thou lene me grace
 in this felde,   435
ȝone heythene sowdane that I may ȝelde
  The woo he hase me wroghte!"

XXXVIII.

The knyghttes herte it was fulle gude,
And forthe he went with hardy mode,
  And thryse he gonne hym sayne 440
For no wapene wolde he stynt;
There lyffede none that hent his dynt,
  Tille that his horse was slayne.
Than the knyghte to the grownde soughte,
A Crystyne erle hym helpede one lofte, 445
And owte of the batelle he hym broghte
  Untille an heghe mountayne;
And stoppede his wondis that gunne blede,
And sythene he horsede hym one a stede,
  And thane he soghte agayne. 450

XXXIX.

Bot whenne he was horsede on a stede,
He sprange als any sparke one glede
   With grymly growndyne gare;
The beryns he hitt appone the hode,
Thorowe the breste-bane it wode,   455
And ȝit es sene whare his horse stode,
   And salle be evermare!
Thane rode he up at ane heghe mountayne,
And thare the sowdane hase he slayne,
   And many that with hym were; 460
Thre dayes and thre nyghttes
Agaynes the Sarazenes helde he fyghttes,
   And the batelle ve[n]queste he thare.

XL.

And whenne the Sarazenes were alle slayne,
The Crystene kynges were fulle fayne, 465
   Thay made thame gamene and glee.
The kyng thane askede after that mekille knyght,
That hase done so doghetyly in this fyghte,
   That I may never hym see:
Erles and baronns thay hafe hym soghte, 470
And byfore the kynge thay hafe hym broghte,
   A fulle sare wondide mane was hee!
The kyng his name faste fraynes thane,
"Sir," he saide "I am a smethymane,
   Whate es ȝour wille with me?" 475

XLI.

The kyng ansuerde the knyghte thane,
" Wondir I hafe that any smethymane
    In werre was ever so wyghte."
The kynge bad that he solde hafe mete and drynke,
And alle that he wolde after thynke,   480
    Tille he hade coverde his myghte;
And thane by his crowne the kyng sware,
That whenne he were coverde of his care,
    That he wolde dubbe hym knyghte.
And at a nunrye the knyght was levede,   485
To hele the wondes in his hevede,
    That he had in the fyghte.

XLII.

The nonnes of hym thay were fulle fayne,
For that he hade the Sarazenes slayne,
    And those haythene houndes;   490
And of his paynnes sare gunne thame rewe,
Ilke a daye thay made salves newe,
    And laid thame tille his wondes.
Thay gafe hym metis and drynkis lythe,
And helid the knyghte wondir swythe;   495
    And within a lyttille stownde,

XLIII.

The knyghte purvayed bothe slavyne and pyke,
And made hymselfe a palmere lyke,
    And thoghte that he wolde wende.

His leve he tuke, withowttyne lesse, 500
And thankede mekille the pryores,
    And alle hir nunnes hende.
The righte waye thane takes he
To a havene of the Grekkes see,
    Als Jhesu Cryste hym sende. 505
A schippe he fonde alle redy ȝare,
With a marynere alle bowne to fare,
    In Acris gunne thay lende.

XLIV.

Whenne thay in that havene lenede,
With wery bones the knyghte up-wenede 510
    In to that haythene stede;
And sevene ȝere he was fully thore,
With hungre, and thriste, and bones sore,
    In storye thus als we rede.
Fulle weryly thane ȝode he thore aye, 515
And wrechidly one nyghttis he laye
    In his povre wede,
Goddes werkkes for to wyrke,
To serve Gode and haly kyrke,
    And to mende hir are mysdede. 520

XLV.

So it by-felle hym sonne onone,
That alle a syde of a cunntré he hase thurgh gone,
Bot mete ne drynke couthe he gete none,
    Ne house to herbere hyme inne;
Withowttene the burghe of Bedeleme, 525

> He layde hym downe by a welle streme,
>> Fulle sore wepande for pyne.
> And als he laye, abowte mydnyghte
> Thare come an angelle faire and bryghte,
>> And broghte hym brede and wyne. 530
> "Palmere," he sayse, "welcome thou bee,
> [f. 113] The kynge of hevene wele gretis the,
>> Forgyffene erre synnes thyne!

XLVI.

> "And welecome," he sais, "Syr Ysambrace!
> Forgeffene es the alle thi tryspase,   535
>> For sothe als I the sayne!
> And wele the gretis now oure hevens kynge,
> And grauntes the nowe his dere blyssynge,
>> And byddes the torne agayne."
> The knyghte knelide thane appone his knee, 540
> Jhesu Criste thane thankede hee,
>> He wepide so was he fayne:
> Bot wyste he never whedirwarde to gonne,
> For had he nowre no wonnynge wone,
>> Bot aye to walke in payne.   545

XLVII.

> Sevene kynges landes hase he gone thurgh,
> Untille he come tille a riche burgh,
>> Thare als a castelle inne stode;
> Thenne herde he telle ther wonned a qwene,
> That was a lady fayre and schene,   550
>> And grete worde of hir ȝode,

XLVIII.

That everylke a daye scho gyffes at hir ȝate,
To povre mene that golde wille take,
   Fulle many fand scho there;
Ilkone hade a florence, noghte to layne; 555
Sir Ysambrace was never so fayne,
   Hym hungrede never so sare!
Of povre mene that myghte ille goo,
Thay tuke inne welle a sexty or moo,
   Of thame that sekeste were; 560
And in thay tuke syr Ysambrace,
At myschefe thay sawe wele that he was,
   And of hym thame rewede sare.

XLIX.

The riche qwene in haulle was sett,
Knyghttes hir serves to handes and fete, 565
   Were clede in robis of palle;
In the floure a clothe was layde,
"This povre palmere," the stewarde sayde,
   "Salle sytt abowene ȝow alle."
Mete and drynke was forthe broghte, 570
Sir Ysambrace sett and ete noghte,
   Bot luked abowte in the haulle.
So mekille he sawe of gamene and glee,
And thoghte what he was wonnt to be,
   And terys lete he falle. 575

L.

So lange he satt and ete noghte,
That the lady grete wondir thoghte,
    And tille a knyghte gane saye,
" Bryng a chayere and a qwyschene,
And sett ȝone povre palmere ther-in,   580
    That he to me telle maye
What tydans that he hase herde and sene
In haythynenes, whare he hase bene
    In many a wilfulle waye."
A riche chayere than was ther fett,   585
This povre palmere ther-in was sett,
    He tolde hir of his laye.

LI.

And so nobilly he hase hir tolde,
That scho myghte frayne hym what scho wolde,
    To whils that he there sett;   590
" Now, palmere," scho said, " I salle the gyffe
Evermare whils I may lyfe,
    Thou salle hafe clothe and mete,

LII.

" And a mane to serve the daye and nyghte,
And a chambir faire and bryghte   595
    Withinne the castelle walle."
The palmere thankes that lady free,
And in hir courte thare thus duellys he,
    And thankes God of alle.
He duellid there fulle many a ȝere,   600

Tille that he was bothe hale and fere,
    And servede in that haulle;
He was mane bothe fayre and heghe,
Alle had wondir that hym see,
    So stylle he was with-alle.   605
And when knyghtes went to put the stane,
Twelve fote over thaym everylke ane,
    He keste it als a balle;
Therefore at hym thay hade envy;
A tornament than did thay crye,   610
Thay thoghte to do hym quede,
    And schames dede with-alle.
That daye the tournament solde be stede,
Thay horsede hym on ane olde crokede stede,
    And ȝitt for-thoghte thame alle.   615

LIII.

Bot by syr Ysambrace hade redyne thurgh the felde,
There was none that undir schilde
    Durste mete his crokede stede,
That he ne gafe hym swylke a clowte,
That bothe his eghne stode one strowte;   620
    Wele a sevene score garte he blede!
And some he keste into a slake,
That bothe braste neke and bakke,
    And many flede for drede:
The qwene hirselfe at hym faste loghe,   625
And sayd, "My palmere es styffe enoghe,
    He es wele worthi to fede!"

LIV.

And so it byfelle ones appone a daye,
The palmere wente to the wode to playe,
  Als it was are his kynde; 630
The palmere sawe a neste one heghe,
A rede clothe therinne he seghe
  Owte-wappande with the wynde;
And to the neste thane gane he wynne,
His awene golde he sawe therinne, 635
  His mantille thare gane he fynde.
With eghne whenne that he sawe the golde,
That his wyfe was fore solde,
  His sorowe bygane to mene.

LV.

The golde unto his chambir he bare, 640
And hyd it fulle prevaly thare,
  And wepande he went awaye;
And aye whenne he gunne the golde see,
He grette fulle sare for his lady,
  And to pyne tornes alle his playe! 645
So lange the palmere lede that lyffe,
That with knyghtes it wexe fulle ryffe,
  And to the lady thay gane it saye.

LVI.

And so it felle appone a daye,
The palmere went to the wode to playe, 650
  His myrthis for to mene;

The knyghtes brake up his chambir dore,
And fande the golde right in the flore,
   And bare it unto the qwene;
And als sone als scho saw it with syghte, 655
In swonyng than felle that swete wyghte,
   For scho had are it sene!
Scho kyssede it, and sayde, "Allas!
This golde aughte syr Ysambrace,
   My lorde was wonte to bene!" 660

LVII.

Than scho to the knyghtes tolde,
How scho was for that golde solde,
   And hir lorde was wondide sore;
"Bot faste whenne ȝe the palmere see,
Dose hyme swythe to speke with me, 665
   Aftir hym me langes fulle sore."
The knyghtes gane brynge hym to the haulle,
The lady gane hym to concelle calle,
   And fraystes at hym there,
"Was thou ever gentylle mane? 670
Whare and howe that thou this golde wanne?"
   His sorowe thane wexe the mare!

LVIII.

With dulefulle mode and herte fulle sare,
He gafe the lady ane ansuare,
   And one his knee hym sett; 675

And a fulle nobille tale ther tille hir he tolde,
"My wyfe was for this golde solde,
  Myselfe was fulle sare bett!"
And downe than knelide the lady byfore his face,
And sayde, "Welecome, my lorde syr Ysam-
 brace!"   680
  Fulle grete joye scho hade in herte.

LIX.

Thane aythir of other were so fayne,
That thay myghte no lengere layne,
  Bot to the knyghtes it tolde;
f. 114] Thane crownnede he was with riche gyfte, 685
And made hym kynge, that are was knyghte,
  Over alle those knyghttes bolde.

LX.

And whenne he was kynge and bare the crowne,
He sent his sande fra towne to towne,
  Tille ylke a ryche ceté,   690
And he gerte krye in borowes bolde,
Riche and povre, bothe ȝonge and olde,
  That alle solde crystende bee;
And thay that wolde noghte do swaa,
He wolde thame bathe brynne and slaa, 695
Solde nothynge for thaire lyfe gaa,
  Silvere, golde, nor fee!

LXI.

A riche kynge was syr Ysambrace,
In mare welthe thane ever he was
   Of haythene landes thare; 700
Crystene lawes to kepe in that tyde,
Sandes he sente fulle ferly wyde
   To thame that haythene ware.
Bot thay turnede alle tille ane assent,
That schortly there-to thay ne wolde conscent, 705
   Bot to a batelle fare.
Thay sayde, and thay myghte hym hent,
That he solde come to thaire perlement,
And there be bothe hangede and brynt,
   And alle that with hym were. 710

LXII.

A daye of batelle thus was ther sett,
And alle the haythene ther was mett
   Sir Ysambrace to slaa;
Fele Sarazenes semblede that tyde,
Fra fele ferre costes to that batelle thay ryde 715
   With knyghtes many and maa.
Sir Ysambrace was fulle of care,
He hade no mene with hym to fare,
   His mene awaye gane gaa:
The Sarazenes faylede hym at that nede, 720
Be he was horsede one his stede
   Thay were alle flede hym fraa.

LXIII.

Sir Ysambrace was thane fulle waa,
He kyssede his lady and wolde furthe gaa
   With sorow and hert fulle sare; 725
A dolefulle worde thane gunne he saye,
"Nowe, certis, lady, hafe now gud daye,
   For nowe and evermare!"
"A! lorde," scho sayd, "helpe that I were dyghte
In armours, als I were a knyghte, 730
   And with the wille I fare;
And God that made bothe see and lande,
My saule I wyte into thy hande,
   For I kepe to lyffe no mare!"

LXIV.

Sone was the lady dyghte 735
In armours, als thofe scho were a knyghte,
   And had bothe spere and schelde;
Agaynes thrytty thowsandez and maa
Come there nane bot thay twaa,
   Nyne hundrethe sone hafe thay slayne! 740
And righte als thay solde hafe takene bee,
There come rydande knyghttes three
   Appone thre bestes wylde;
One on a lebarde, another on a unycorne,
And one on a lyone he come by-forne, 745
   That was thair eldeste childe!

LXV.

In angells wede were thay alle clede,
An angelle thame to the batelle lede,
  That semely was to sene:
Thay slewe the haythene knyghttes swa,   750
And of the Sarazenes many alswa,
  ȝa twentty thowsandez and thre.
Sir Ysambrace prayed the knyghtes swaa,
Hame with hym that thay walde gaa,
  And be of his menȝé;   755
Thay ansuerde, als the angelle tham kende,
" For the were we to the batelle sende,
  Thyne awenne sonnes are wee!"

LXVI.

Ofte was syr Ysambrace wele and woo,
Bot never ȝitt als he was tho,   760
  One knees than he hym sett;
He grett, and sayde wyth mylde stevene,
"Thankede be the heghe kyng of hevene,
  My bale thane hase he bett!"
Sir Ysambrace and that lady free   765
Kyssed alle thaire childir three,
  Ilkane for joye thay grett;
Mare joye myghte never no mane see,
Thane men myghte one thame see,
  In armes whenne thay were mett. 770

LXVII.

A ryche ceté was there besyde,
And syr Ysambrace byfore gane ryde
  His sonnes hame for to lede;
Chambirs fande thay faire and bryghte,
Robys faire and redy dyghte,   775
  And thare thay chaunged thaire wede;
Riche metis wantted thame nane,
Nowther of wylde nor of tame,
  Nor no riche brede.
Fyve landis thus gunne thay wynne,   780
And stabylde Crystyndome thame inne,
  In storyes thus als we rede.

LXVIII.

A fulle riche kynge thane was syr Ysambrace,
And coverde he hase alle his myscas,
  He lyffes nowe fulle richely;   785
Ilkane of his sonnes he gafe a lande,
Durste na mane agayne thame stande,
  Whare so that thay solde fare.
Thay lyffede and dyed with gud entent,
And sythene alle tille hevene thay went,   790
  Whenne that thay dede ware.
Praye we now to hevenes kynge,
He gyffe us alle his dere blyssynge
  Nowe and evermare!
  Amene. Amene.
 Explicit Syr Ysambrace.

THE ROMANCE

OF

SIR EGLAMOUR OF ARTOIS.

I.

f. 63] Jhesu Lorde oure hevyn kynge,
Graunt us alle thy dere blessynge,
    And bylde us in thy bowre!
And yf ye ony yoye wylle here
Of them that beforne us were,   5
    That leved in grete honowre,
Y schalle telle yow of a knyght,
That was bothe hardy and wyght,
    And stronge in eche a stowre;
Of dedes of armys there ye may here,   10
He wynnyth the gree with yurney clere,
    And in the fylde the flowre.

II.

In Artas he was geton and borne,
And thus he holdyth hym beforne,
    Lystenyth, y schalle yow say.   15
To dedes of armes he ys wente,
Wyth the Erle of Artas he ys lente,
    He faylyth hym not nyght nor daye.

Syr Prynsamowre the erle hyght,
Syr Egyllamowre men calle the kny3t, 20
    That was evyr and aye;
Whylle the erle had hym in holde,
Of dedes of armes he was bolde,
    For no man seyde he naye.

III.

The erle had never chylde but oon, 25
That was a maydyn as whyte as fome,
    That hys ryght heyre schulde bee;
The maydenys name was Crystyabelle,
A feyre thynge of flesche and felle,
    Ther was none soche in Crystyanté. 30
Syr Egyllamowre so hym bare,
That above alle erthely thynges sche lovyd hym mare,
    That lady bryght of blee;
Certenly bothe day and nyght,
So dud he hur that nobylle knyght, 35
    That was the more peté!

IV.

The knyght was bothe bolde and stronge,
Therfore the lady lovyd hym longe,
    Lystenyth, y schalle yow telle.
Ther come lordys of ferre londe, 40
For to assay hur, y undurstonde,
    Wyth ferse folke and felle.

Syr Egyllamowre he dud to crye
Of dedes of armys utturly,
  For the love of Crystyabelle. 45
What maner of man that hur wolde have,
So sore strokes he them gave,
  For evyr he dud them to dwelle!

V.

Tylle hyt befelle upon a day,
The knyght to hys squyer can say, 50
  Yn hys chaumbur there he was at reste,
"Belamye, and thou cowdyst hyt layne,
A cownselle y wolde to the sayne,
  Thou walkyst bothe est and weste."
"ʒys, syr, permafay, 55
What some ever that ye to me say,
  Y schalle hyt nevyr owte caste."
"The erlys doghtyr, so God me save!
The love of hur but y have,
  My lyfe dayes be at the laste!" 60

VI.

The squyer seyde, "So muste y the,
Ye have tolde me yowre prevyté,
  Y schalle gyf yow an answere;
Ye are a knyght of lytylle londe,
Take hyt not at evelle, y undurstonde, 65
  For mekylle wolde have mare.

Yf y to that lady thys telle for thy sake,
Peraventour on-henely sche wolde hyt take,
  And lyghtly let me fare."
"Dere frende, y prey the that thou me behete, 70
That thou wylt that lady in thys maner grete,
  What some ever happe to be hur answere."

VII.

" Syr, than umbe-thenke on thys thyng,
Ther woweth hur emperours and kynges,
  Erlys and barons done alsoo ;   75
ȝyt wylle sche not have of thoo,
But in godenes hur holdyth so,
  The whych y trowe ys for thy love and no mo.
Sche wolde never a kynge forsake,
And soche a sympulle knyght to take,   80
  But yf thy love were in hur herte wroght ;
Y swere be God, heven kynge,
Wyste hur fadur of soche a thynge,
  Fulle dere hyt schulde be boght !"

VIII.

The knyȝt answeryd with wordes mylde,   85
" My squyer, evyr syth thou were a chylde,
  Thou haste byn lente wyth me ;
At dedes of armes in many a stowre,
Where wyste me ever have dyshonoure ?
  Say on, so God save thee !"   90

" Nay, syr, be Jhesu Cryste bryght,
Ye are a nobylle knyght
  As any ys knowyn in Crystyanté!
Yn dedes of armes, be God on lyve!
Ye are countyd worthe odur v.,   95
  God a mercy, syr!" seyde hee.

IX.

The knyȝt answeryd and seyde, " Allas!"
Mornyng to hys bedd he gays,
  That rychely was y-wroght.
Bothe hys handys he caste up sone,   100
To Jhesu Cryste he made a boone,
  That Lorde that us hath boght;
" The erlys doghtyr, that swete thynge,
So mote hyt be at my ȝernynge,
  On hur ys alle my thoght,   105
That y myȝt wedde hur to my wyfe,
And sethen reches in my lyfe,
  Owt of care then were y broght!"

X.

Upon the morowe the maydyn smalle,
Sche wente before hur fadur in halle, 110
  Amonge hur byrdys bryght;
Of alle gentyls semyth none to hur but he,
The lady seyde, " For Goddys peté,
  Where ys myn owne knyght?"

Hys squyer answeryd with sympulle chere, 115
" He ys syke and dedd fulle nere,
  He preyeth yow of a syght,
For he ys caste in soche a care,
But ye hym helpe he wylle forfare,
  He levyth not oon sevenyght!" 120

XI.

The erle to hys doghtyr spake,
" Doghtur," he seyde, "for hys sake,
  Lystenyth, y schalle yow say;
Aftur mete do ye as hynde,
To hys chaumbur loke ye wynde, 125
  He hath servyd us many a day
Fulle trewly in hys entente;
Yn yustynge ne in turnament
  He seyde us nevyr nay.
Alle dedes of armes that he may of here, 130
He wynnyth the gree with jurney clere,
  And my worschypp aye."

XII.

Aftur mete the lady gente
Dede hur fadurs commaw[n]demente,
  Scho takyth hur wey to wynde; 135
Tylle hys chaumbur can sche goo,
With hur sche toke but maydenys two,
  There the knyght can lende.

Then seyde that lady whyte as flowre,
" How faryth my knyght syr Egyllamowre,   140
 That doghty was evyr and hende ?"
His squyer seyde, " Make gode chere,
Here comyth the erlys doghtyr dere,
 Y pray God that ye parte gode frende !"

XIII.

Then seyde thys lady whyte as lely flowre,   145
" How faryth my knyght syr Egyllamowre,
 That doghty ys ever and ware ?"
" Damycelle," he seyde, " as ye may see,
Thus y am caste in care for love of the,
 In anger and yn care."   150
" Syr," the maydyn seyde, " so mote y thee,
And ye had ony care for me,
 Myn herte wolde be fulle sore !"
" And y myght turne to my lyfe,
Y wolde wedde yow to my wyfe,   155
 Yf that yowre wylle were."

XIV.

The lady sweryd be Crystys myght,
" Syr, ye are a nobylle knyght,
 And comyn of gentylle blode ;
And ever trewly undur the schylde,   160
Thou wynnyst the gre in ylke a felde
 Worschypfully, be the rode !

Y wylle avyse me as tyte,
And at my fadur wylle y wete,
    Gyf that hys wylle be goode;   165
[f. 64.] As y am lady feyre and gente,
When my fadur and y be at assente,
    Y wylle not fayle the, be the rode!"

XV.

The knyght kepte no more blys,
When he had geton graunt of thys,   170
    But made hur fulle gode chere;
He commawndyd a squyer for to go,
And take an hundurd pownd or two,
    And gyf hur maydenys clere.
"Damycelle," he seyde, "so God me save! 175
Thys to yowre maryage schalle ye have,
    Thys ys the fyrste tyme that ever ye come here."
Sche thanked hym anon-ryght,
Sche toke hur leve and kyssyd the knyght,
    And seyde, "Farewelle, my fere."   180

XVI.

Crystyabelle hath takyn hur way
To hur fadurs chaumbur there he lay,
    Was made of lyme and stone;
And he seyde, "Welcome, as whyte as flowre!
How faryth thy knyȝt, syr Egyllamowre?" 185
    Sche answeryd hym anone,

" Grete othys to me he sware,
That he was botyd of mekylle care,
  And gode comfort to hym hath tane;
He tolde me and my maydenys hynde,   190
To-morowe he wolde over the rever wynde
  Wyth hys hawkys ylke a oon."

XVII.

The erle seyde, " As mote y the,
Doghtyr, y schalle ryde to see them flee,
  For comforte of that knyght."   195
The erle buskyd and made hym yare
For to ryde ovyr the revere,
  To see that semely syght.
Alle the day he made gode chere;
A wrath felle, as ye may here,   200
  Anone betwene them twoo,
Or hyt nyghed the nyʒt fulle nere,
That made them of stryvys were,
  And afturward dud them woo!

XVIII.

As he rode homeward be the way,   205
The knyght can to the erle say,
  " Gode lorde, wylle ye me here?"
" Ye," he seyde, " so mote y the,
What some ever thou seyst to me,
  Hyt ys to me leve and dere;   210

For oon the beste knyghtes art thou,
That in thys londe ys levyd now,
    Awnturs ferre or nere."
" Gode lorde, for charyté,
Crystyabelle, yowre doghtur fre,   215
    When schalle sche have a fere ?"

XIX.

The erle seyde, " So God me save,
Y knowe no man that hur schalle have,
    Sche ys so bryght of blee !"
The knyght can to the erle pray,   220
" Lorde, y have servyd yow many a day,
    Vowche-safe ye hur on mee !"
" Ye," he seyde, " be Crystys payne,
Yf thou wynne hur, as y schalle ye sayne,
    In dedes of armes three,   225
Broke hur wele, my doghtyr dere,
And alle Artas ferre and nere,
    Y holde ther-to," seyde hee.

XX.

The knyght sweryd, " As mote y thee,
At my jurney wolde y bee,   230
    And y wyste evyr whare."
The erle seyde, " Here be weste
Ther dwellyth a yeaunt in a foreste,
    Soche oon thou nevyr sayste are ;

Cypur treys there growe owte longe, 235
Grete hertys there walke them amonge,
  The fayreste that on fote may fare:
Go thedur and fett me oon away;
Syr knyght, than dare y hardely say
  That thou haste byn thare." 240

XXI.

Be Jhesu swere the knyght than,
" Yf he be ony Crystyn-man,
  Y schalle hym nevyr forsake.
Holde wele my lady and my londe."
" ȝys," seyde the erle, " here myn honde!" 245
  Hys trowthe to hym he strake.

XXII.

Aftur mete, os y yow telle,
He takyth hys leve of Crystyabelle,
  Hys leve then takyth hee.
" Damycelle," he seyde anon than, 250
" For thy love y have undurtane
  Dedes of armys thre."
" Syr," sche seyde, " make yow gladd,
For an hardere fytt never ye had,
  Be God in no cuntré! 255
Or that yurney be over passyd,
For my love ye schalle sey fulle ofte allas!
  And so schalle y for thee.

XXIII.

"Syr knyght, when thou an-huntyng fowndes,
Y schalle gyf the two greyhowndys,   260
    As wyght as any roo;
As y am trewe gentylwoman,
Ther was never beste that on fote ran
    Awey fro them myght goo.
A fulle gode swerde y schalle geve the,   265
Seynt Poule fonde hyt in the Grekes see,
    Of soche knowe y no moo.
Ther was never helme of yron nor stele,
And thou have to hytte hyt wele,
    But hyt wylle thorow hyt goo!"   270

XXIV.

He seyde, "God ȝylde yow, lady gente!"
He takyth hys leve and forthe he wente,
    Hys way now hath he tane;
A brode wey he helde forthe faste
Tylle he come to a foreste,   275
    Soche oon sawe he nevyr none;
Cypur treys were growyn owte,
The wode was wallyd abowte,
    And wele corvyn wyth ryche ston.
Forthe he wente, y undurstonde,   280
Tylle a brode yate that he fonde,
    Ther-ynne the knyght ys gone.

XXV.

He blewe hys horne in that tyde;
Hertys reson on eche a syde,
    Wythowtyn any lesynge: 285
Then hys howndys began to baye,
That harde the jeant there he laye,
    And he rysyth fro hys restynge.
" Me thynkyth howndys that y here,
Yondur ys a thefe to stele my dere,   290
    He were welle bettur to be at the see!
Be hym that lett me be geton and borne,
Yn werse tyme blewe he never hys horne,
    Neythur hys bowe bende in no manys fee."

XXVI.

Anon the jeant hath take hys way   295
To the ȝate there he lay,
    Hys bakk he sett ther tylle.
Then had syr Egyllamowre don to dedd
A grete herte, and tan the hedd,
    The pryce he blewe fulle schylle!   300
He come where the yeant was,
And seyde, " Gode syr, let me passe,
    Yf hyt be yowre wylle."
" Nay, thefe traytur, thou art tan!
My chefe herte thou haste slayn,   305
    That schalt thou lyke fulle ylle!"

XXVII.

The yeant to the kny3t ys gon,
A clobb of yron in honde hathe tan,
  That was mekylle and fulle unwelde;
Grete strokys the yeant gafe, 310
And to the erthe fley hys stafe
  Two fote on every syde.
"Thefe traytur, what dost thou here
Yn my foreste to stele my dere?
  Here, thefe, thou schalt abyde!" 315
Syr Egyllamowre hys swerde owt drowe,
And to the yeant he gafe a sowe,
  And blyndyd hym in that tyde!

XXVIII.

That lorelle had loste hys syght,
3yt he fyghtyth with that knyght 320
  Alle that day fulle yare;
Tylle on the todur day abowte prime,
Syr Egyllamowre waytyd hys tyme,
  And to herte hym bare!
He thanked God that weldyth thys worlde, 325
And at the yeant he smote harde,
  The thefe began to rore!
[f. 65.] Sythen he mett hym, os y say,
Upon the grownde there he lay,
  He was xl. fote and more. 330

XXIX.

He thankyd God and hys knyfe,
Therwith he berevyd the jeaunt hys lyfe;
    He thanked God hylye!
Syr Egyllamowre wente hys way
Wyth the yeauntes hedd, os y yow say,   335
    To a castelle of stone there-by.

XXX.

The contré come hym abowte,
To see the hedd that was grete and stowte,
    Soche a hedd sawe they never none.
Before the erle he hyt bare,   340
" Lo! lorde, y have byn thare,
    And that bare ye wytnesse echon."
Make we mery, so have we blys,
Thys ys the furste fytt of thys
    That we have undurtane.   345

XXXI.

" What!" seyde the erle, " Yf thys be done,
Thou getyst anodur jeaunt sone,
    Buske the forthe to fare;
In Sydon, in that ryche cuntré,
There dar no man abyde nor bee   350
    For drede of a wylde bare.

Beste and man alle sleyth hee,
That ever he may wyth eye see,
 And grevyth them wondur sore;
Hys toschys passen a fote longe,   355
The flesche that fastenyth them amonge
 They kever hyt nevyr more."

XXXII.

That nobylle kny3t he seyde not naye;
Upon the morowe, when hyt was day,
 Hys leve then takyth hee.   360
Forthe he wendyth, y understonde,
A fowrtenyght jurney on the londe,
 And also mekylle on the see,
Tylle ageynys the none-tyde,
Yn a foreste there he can ryde   365
 Where the bore had wonte to bee;
Tydyngys of hym sone he fonde,
Slayne men on every honde,
 That grymly was to see!

XXXIII.

Syr Egyllamowre restyd hym undur an oke; 370
Tylle on the morowe that he can wake,
 The sonne rose hye and schon;
Swythe further in the foreste he drowe,
On the see he harde a sowe,
 And thedurward the knyght ys gon.   375

Bryght helmes he fonde strawed wyde,
As men of armys had loste ther pryde,
 That wyckyd bore had them slayne!
To a clyfe of ston than rydyth hee,
And say the bore come fro the see,   380
 Hys morne-drynke he had tane.

XXXIV.

The bore say hym there as he stode,
And whettyd hys tuschys as he were wode,
 And to hym come asyde;
Syr Egyllamowre wened welle to do,   385
And wyth a spere rode hym too
 As faste as he myght ryde.
Gyf he rode nevyr so faste,
Hys gode spere in sonder braste,
 The hedd wolde not in hym glyde;   390
He come to hym wyth a swowe,
Hys gode stede undur hym he slowe,
 On fote the knyght muste abyde.

XXXV.

Tylle a banke he sett hys syde,
Was undur a roche large and wyde,   395
 Hys herte hyt was fulle sore.
Hys nobylle swerde he drowe owte tho,
And fyghtyth with the wylde swyne with woo
 Thre dayes and more;

Tylle on the iiij^{the} day abowte noon, 400
He thoght hys lyfe dayes were y-done,
 For fyght wyth that wylde bore.
The knyght cowde no bettur redd,
But stroke faste on the swynes hedd,
 Hys tuschys he brake thore. 405

XXXVI.

He thankyd God that ylke stownde,
And gaf the bore hys dethys wound,
 The boke of Rome thus can telle.
The kyng of Sydon an-huntyng ys gon
Wyth men of armys mony oon, 410
 The bore then harde he ʒelle.
He comawnded a squyer for to fare,
" Some man ys fyghtyng with that bore,
 Y trowe fulle wele there he schalle dwelle."
The squyer rydyth to a clefe of ston, 415
And say a knyght ley hym on
 Wyth a swerde scharpe and felle.

XXXVII.

The squyer hovyd and behelde them two,
And ageyne to the kyng he can go,
 And seyde, "Lorde, the bore ys slayne!" 420
" Seynt Mary!" seyde the kyng, "who myʒt
 hyt bee?"
" ʒys, syr, a knyght y see,
 To God y trowe be fulle bayne!

He beryth of golde a fulle feyre syght,
A stede of aser and a knyght, 425
    Alle armyd for to gone.
That bryght upon hys hedd hyt ys
A lady of golde in hur ryches,
    Hys sperys of sabulle everychone."

XXXVIII.

The kyng swere, " So mote y thee, 430
Hys gentylle armys wylle y see."
    And thedur he takyth hys way.
Be that had syr Egyllamowre
Ovyr-come alle hys styffe stowre,
    And to reste hym down he lay. 435
The kyng seyde, " God reste with the!"
" Lorde, welcome mote yow bee,
    Of pese y yow pray;
Y have so foghtyn with the bore,
That be my feyth y may no more, 440
    Thys ys the fourthe day!"

XXXIX.

The kynge seyde, " Be Goddys myght,
Here schalle no man with the fyght,
    Grete synne hyt were the to tene!
Thou haste ben ferre and wyde-where, 445
And now haste slayn the wylde bore,
    That many a mannys bane hath bene.

Worschypfully undur the schylde,
Thou haste slayn thy foo and wonne the fylde,
  That we alle have seyn.   450
Y have wetyn, syth y was man of aray,
He hath slayne syxty on a day,
  Welle armyd men and clene!"

XL.

Ryche metys forthe he broght,
The ryche wyne forgetyth he noght, 455
  And clothys there were spradd.
The kynge swere, " So mote y thee,
Y wylle dyne for love of thee,
  Thou haste byn strongly stadd."
" Ye," he seyde, " permafay, 460
Now hyt ys the fyrste day
  That evyr oon fote y fledd."
The kynge preyd that gentylle knyght
For to be wyth hym alle nyght,
  And reste hym in a ryche bedd. 465

XLI.

Aftur mete, as y yow say,
The kynge can to the knyght pray
  Of what londe that he was.
He seyde, " My name ys syr Awntour,
Y dwelle with syr Prynsamowre, 470
  The erle of Artas."

Knyghtys nere the kynge they drowe,
" Yondur ys he that Arrok slowee,
    The yeauntys brodur Maras!"
The kynge preyed the knyght so free,   475
Two dayes wyth hym to be,
    Or that he schoulde forthe passe.

XLII.

" Ther ys a jeaunt here besyde,
That sorowe doyth ferre and wyde
    On us and odur moo,   480
That y dar no way ryde owt,
But men of armys me abowte,
    Fulle seldone have y thus sene soo.
[f. 66.] Thys wylde bore that thou haste slayne here,
He hath fedd hym xv. yere,   485
    Crystyn men for to sloo!
Now ys he wente with care ynogh
To berye hys brodur that thou slogh,
    That evyrmore be hym woo!"

XLIII.

To splatt the bore they wente fulle tyte,   490
Ther was no knyfe that wolde hym byte,
    So harde of hyde was hee.
" Syr Awntour," seyde the kynge, " thou hym slowe,
Y trowe thy knyfe be gode y-nogh,
    Gyf that thy wylle bee."   495

The knyght to the bore ys gon,
And clevyth hym be the rugge-bone,
    That grete yoye hyt was to see.
" Lorde," seyde the knyght, " y dud hym falle,
Gyf me the hedd and take thou alle,   500
    Thou wottyst wele hyt ys my fee."

XLIV.

Aftur cartys can they sende,
Ageyn none home with that they wende,
    The cyté was them nere;
Alle the cuntré was fulle fayne   505
That the wekyd bore was slayne,
    They made hym fulle gode chere.
The quene seyde, " God schylde us fro schame,
When the jeaunt ys comyn home,
    Newe tydyngys gete we sone;   510
For he ys stronge and stowte,
And therof y have mekylle dowte
    That he wylle do us grete dere or we have done."

XLV.

Syr Egyllamowre, that nobylle kny3t,
Was sett with the kynges doghtyr bryght,   515
    For that he schoulde be blythe;
The maydenys name was Organata so fre,
Sche preyeth hym of gode chere to bee,
    And besechyd hym so many a sythe.

Aftur mete sche can hym telle 520
How that geant wolde them quelle :
 The knyght began to lagh anone.
" Damyselle," he seyde, " so mote y thee,
And he come whylle y here bee,
 Y schalle hym assay sone ! " 525

XLVI.

Ageyne the evyn the kyng can dyȝt
A bath for that nobylle knyght,
 Of ȝerbys that were fulle gode ;
And alle the nyght ther-in he lay
Tyl on the morowe that hyt was day, 530
 That men to mete yode.
Be the kynge he herde hys masse,
The wekyd geant comyn was,
 And cryed as he were wode.
" Syr kynge," he seyde, " sende thou to me 535
Organata thy doghtur free,
 Or thou schalt spylle thy blode ! "

XLVII.

Syr Egyllamowre, that nobylle knyght,
Armyd hym anon-ryght,
 And to the wallys wendyth hee. 540
The borys hedd he made forthe to bere,
And sett hyt upon a spere,
 That Maras myght hym see.

The jeant lokyd upon the hedd,
"Allas! my bore, art thou dedd? 545
 My tryste was mekylle on the!
Be that lay that y leve ynne,
My lytylle spote hoglyn,
 Dere boght thy dethe schalle bee!"

XLVIII.

The yeant on the walle dange, 550
At eche stroke the fyre owt sprange,
 For nothyng wolde he spare!
Yn-to the cyté he caste a crye,
"Thevys, trayturs, ye schalle abye
 For sleyng of my bore! 555
Thys stone walle y schalle down dynge,
And with myn hondys y schalle yow hynge
 Or that y hens fare!"
With the grace of God, or hyt were nyght
The yeant had hys fulle of fyght, 560
 The boke seythe some dele more!

XLIX.

"Syr Awntur," seyde the kynge than,
"Y rede we arme us ylke-oon,
 Thys fende wylle felly fyght."
The knyght swere be the rode, 565
"Y schalle assay hym, thogh he were wode,
 Fulle mekylle ys Goddys myght!"

Syr Egyllamowre was not agaste,
Of the helpe of God was alle hys tryste,
    And of hys swerde so bryght;   570
He rode a course to assay hys stede,
He toke hys leve and forthe he yede,
    And alle prayed for that knyght.

L.

Syr Egyllamowre the felde hath tane;
The geant say and tylle hym came,   575
    And seyde, " Art thou comyn, my fere?
Y trowe thou halpe to sle my bore,
Thou schalt abye trewly therfore,
    Hyt schalle be boght fulle dere!"
Syr Egyllamowre wened welle to do,   580
And wyth a spere rode hym too,
    As man of armes clere;
The yeant buskyd and made hym bowne,
Hors and man he stroke alle downe,
    The knyght was dede fulle nere.   585

LI.

The knyght cowde no bettur redd,
When hys nowbylle stede was dedd,
    But to hys fote he hath hym tane;
Sethen so nere he can hym goo,
Hys ryght arme he stroke hym froo,   590
    Faste be the schouldur-bone,

Thowe the lorelle had loste hys hande,
Alle day stondyth he faste fyghtande
 Tylle the sonne to reste was goon;
Then was he so wery he myȝt not stonde,   595
The blode ran so faste fro hym on every honde,
 That lyfe dayes hadd he nevyr oon.

LII.

When the thefe began to rore,
Alle that in that cyté wore
 For yoye the bellus can rynge.   600
Edmonde was the kynges name,
" Awnturs," he seyde, " be seynt Jame,
 Here schalt thou be kynge!
To-morowe schalle y crowne the,
And thou schalt wedd Organata, my doghtur fre,
 Wyth a fulle ryche rynge."   606
The knyȝt answeryd with wordes mylde,
" Syr, yf you yoye of yowre chylde,
 For here may y not lende."

LIII.

" Syr knyght, for thy nobylle dede,   610
Y schalle geve the a nobylle stede,
 Also redd as ony roone;
Yn yustyng ne in turnement,
Thou schalt never soffur dethys wound,
 Whylle thou syttyst hym upon."   615

Seyde Organata that swete thynge,
" Y schalle geve the a gode golde rynge,
    Wyth a fulle ryche stone;
Whedur that ye be on water or on londe,
And that rynge be upon yowre honde,   620
    Ther schalle nothyng yow slon."

LIV.

He seyde, " God ȝylde yow, lady clere."
" Syr, y schalle abyde yow thys xv. yere,
    Yf that ye wylle me wedd.
Worschypfully, so God me save,   625
Kyng nor dewke schalle me not have,
    Thowe he be comely cladd."
The knyght answeryd, " Permafay,
Withyn thys xv. yere ye schalle here say
    How that y have spedde."   630
The knyght takyth hys leve and farys,
Wyth the geauntys hedd and the borys,
    The weyes owre Lord wylle hym lede.
Thys ys the seconde fytt of thys,
Make we mery, so have we blys,   635
    For ferre have we to rede.

LV.

Into the londe of Artas
Syr Egyllamowre can passe,
    There the erlys were;
Alle that cuntrey was fulle fayne,   640
That he homeward was comyn ageyne,
    Alle tho that he fonde there.

f. 67] Crystyabelle herde telle of hys comyng home,
Ageyne the knyght then ys sche gone,
    Sche buskyd and made hur ȝare.   645
" Syr," sche seyde, " how have ye faryn ?"
" Damycelle, wele, and in travelle byn
    To brynge us bothe owt of care."

LVI.

There he kyssyd the lady gente,
And to halle they wente,   650
    The erle there-wyth to tene.
The hedys to hym there he down layde,
" Lo ! lorde," the knyght sayde,
    " In Sydon have y bene."
Therfore was the erle fulle woo,   655
" Y trowe ther wylle no develle the sloo,
    Be Cryste, syr, so y wene ;
Thou art abowteward, y undurstonde,
To wynne alle Artas of myn honde,
    And wynne my doghtyr schene."   660

LVII.

The knyght seyde, " So mote y the,
Noght but y worthy bee,
    Helpe God that ys beste !"
The erle seyde, " ȝyt hyt schalle falle,
That oon schalle come and pay for alle,   665
    Thowe thou be nevyr so preste."

The knyght preyed the erle so free,
"xij. wekys that ye wylle geve me,
    My boonys for to reste."

LVIII.

Aftur soper, as y yow telle,   670
He wendyd to chaumbur with Crystyabelle,
    There laumpus were brennyng bryght;
That lady was not for to hyde,
Sche sett hym on hur beddys syde,
    And welcomyd home that knyght.   675
" Damycelle," he seyde, " so have y spede,
With the grace of God y schalle the wedd;"
    Therto ther trowthys they plyght.
So gracyously he come hur tylle,
Of poyntes of armys he schewyd hur hys fylle,
    That there they dwellyd alle ny3t.   681

LIX.

Be xij. wekys were comyn and gone,
Crystyabelle as whyte as fome,
    Alle pale was hur hewe!
Sche prayed hur gentylle women so fre,   685
That they wolde layne hur privyté,
    " To me that ye be trewe !"
The erle brennyth for sorow and care,
" Have doo, syr kny3t, and make the yare,
    Thy jurnay comyth alle newe."   690

When Crystyabelle herde ther-of say,
Scho mornyd for hym bothe nyʒt and day,
   That sone myght hur rewe.

LX.

" Syr, at grete Rome, as y the telle,
Ther lythe a dragon ferse and felle;   695
   Herkenyth, y schalle yow say.
The fende ys of so grete renowne,
Ther dar no man come nere the town
   Be xv. myle of way.
Arme the, syr knyʒt, and thedur wende,   700
And loke thou slee hym with thyn honde,
   Or ellys thou sey me nay."
" Syr, that was never my purpos
For to leve oon soche a trase,
   Be nyght nor be day.   705

LXI.

" With the grace of God Almyght,
Wyth the worme ʒyt schalle y fyght,
   Thowe he be nevyr so wylde."
Afturward, as y yow telle,
He takyth hys leve of Crystyabelle,   710
   As fayre as floure in felde:
" Damycelle," he seyde, " a poynt of armys ys
   ondone,
Me be-hovyth to wende and come fulle sone,
   Wyth the helpe of Mary mylde!

A golde rynge y schalle geve the, 715
Kepe hyt wele, my lady free,
  Yf Cryste sende the a chylde."

LXII.

Forthe he wendyth, as y yow say,
To grete Rome he takyth the way
  To seke the worme so bolde; 720
Tokenynges sone of hym he fonde,
Slayne men on every honde,
  Be hunderdes he them tolde.
Yf he were never so bolde a knyght,
Of that worme when he had a syght 725
  Hys herte began to folde;
Hyt was no wondur thoghe he were wrothe,
He stroke hym and hys stede bothe
  To the grounde so colde!

LXIII.

The kny3t rose and hys schylde up sett, 730
That wyckyd worme ther-with mett
  Wyth byttur dynte and felle;
He schett fyre ryght sore,
Evyr nere the nyght the more,
  As the develle of helle. 735
Syr Egyllamowre, for sothe to say,
Halfe the tonge he stroke away,
  That fende began to 3elle!

And with the stompe that hym was levyd,
He stroke the knyght in the hedd   740
 A depe wounde and a felle.

LXIV.

The knyght seyde, "Now am y schente!"
Nere that wyckyd worme he wente,
 Hys hedd he stroke away;
And sythen so nere ys he gone,   745
He clevyd hym by the rugge-bone,
 The felde he wan that day.
The emperoure stode in hys towre,
And say the fyght of syr Egyllamowre,
 And to hys men can say,   750
"Do to crye in Rome the worme ys slayne,
That hathe a kny3t done hym selfe allone,
 Pertly be my fay!"

LXV.

Yn grete Rome they dyd to crye,
Every offycer in hys bayly,   755
 "The dragon hath tan hys 3ynde."
The emperoure hath tan the way
To the knyght, there as he lay
 Besyde the dylfulle thynge;
And alle that ever myght ryde or goo   760
Come syr Egyllamowre unto,
 And wyth blysse home can hym brynge.

They were so fayne the worme was slayn,
Wyth procescions hym comyng ageyn,
 They dydd the bellus to rynge.   765

LXVI.

The emperoure hath a doghtyr bryght,
Hath undurtane to hele that knyght,
 Hur name ys Dawntowre;
Scho savys hym fro the dedd,
And with hur handys sche helyth hys hedd   770
 A twelmonyth in hur bowre.

LXVII.

The ryche emperoure of Rome,
He sende aftur the dragon sone
 That in the felde was leyde;
Hys syde was herde as any bras,   775
Hys whyngus grene as any gras,
 Hys hedd as fyre was redd.
Hys body gretter then a tunne;
The nobylle kny3t the felde hath wonne,
 And slayn hym in that tyde;   780
The emperoure was mekylle of pryde,
And made to bete hym bak and syde,
 Ryght thorowe hys owne rede.

LXVIII.

When they sye that grete beste,
Mony a man was of hym agaste,   785
 And fro hym flewe fulle sone;

Ther mett hym thre hundurd and moo,
The emperoure badd they schulde hym take tho,
 Hys wylle to be done.
f. 68.] To seynt Laurens kyrke they hym bare,   790
There schalle he lye for evyrmare,
 That fowle worme withowten wone.
When they remevyd that fowle thynge,
Mony a man felle in dede swownyng,
 For stynke that fro hym come.   795

LXIX.

Then come letturs to Artas,
That the worme in Rome slayn was,
 A knyght then hath hym sloon.
So longe at leche-crafte can he dwelle,
A man-chylde had Crystyabelle,   800
 As whyte as whallys boon.
The erle had made to God a vowe,
" Doghtur, in-to the see schalt thou
 Yn a schypp allone;
And that bastard that to the ys dere,   805
Crystyndome schalle he non have here!"
 Hyr maydenys wepte everychon.

LXX.

Thowe sche were never so feyre a wyght,
ȝyt was a schypp fulle redy dyght,
 That sche in forthe schulde fare.   810

Sche lokyd on hur sone with hur eye,
" Sone," sche seyde, " now schalle we dye,
  Thy fadur schalle see us no mare!"
Hur chaumbur women that be hur can stonde,
They weptyn faste and wrang ther hande, 815
  They had fulle mekylle care.
When they wyste that sche schoulde forthe passe,
Then they cryed and seyde, " Allas!
  Now are we lafte fulle bare."

LXXI.

Thys lady was in care cladd, 820
To a schypp they have hur ladd,
  Alle and hur frely fode.
Sche seyde, " Feyre fadur, y yow pray,
Let a preste me a gospelle saye
  For fendys on the flode." 825
Sche preyd hur gentylwomen so free,
" Grete wele my lorde, whan ye hym see."
  They weptyn as they were wode.
Hur chaumbur women in swownyng dud falle,
And so dud hur frendys alle, 830
  That wolde hur ony gode.

LXXII.

The lady syghed with herte so sore,
A wynde rose and to a roche hur bare,
  And there-up can sche londe.

Sche was fulle fayne, y undurstonde, 835
Sche wende there had be a kende londe,
    And thedurward can sche wende.
Nothyng ellys fonde sche thare,
But fowlys mony that wylde ware,
    Faght faste on every honde; 840
A grype come in alle hur care,
Hur yonge sone awey he bare
    Yn-to a cuntré unkende.

LXXIII.

Than that lady seyde, " Allas!
That ever y woman borne was, 845
    My chylde ys thus rafte me froo!"
Yn the londe of Ysraelle can he lyght,
A gryffon seythe the boke he hyght
    That wroght the lady woo.
The kyng of Israelle an-huntyng ys wente, 850
And say where the grype was lente,
    And thedurward can he goo;
He stroke on the chylde with hys bylle,
And the chylde cryed lowde and schylle,
    And he rose and levyd the chylde soo. 855

LXXIV.

A squyer to the chylde can passe,
Yn a scarlet mantelle fowndyn he was
    Wyth a fulle a ryche pane;

Yn a scarlet mantelle woundyn,
And with a goldyn gyrdylle bowndyn, 860
 Hys eyen grey as crystalle stone.
Alle they sweryn be the rode,
"Thys chylde ys comyn of gentylle blode,
 Where that ever that he was tane."
For that he fro the gryffon felle, 865
They namyd the chylde syr Degrabelle,
 That welsome was of wone.

LXXV.

The kyng lafte huntyng at that tyde,
And home with the chylde can he ryde,
 That fro the grype was hente. 870
"Dame," he seyde to the qwene,
"Mekylle of solas have we sene,
 To day God hath me sente."
Therof he was bothe glad and blythe,
He sende aftur a norse swythe, 875
 Hys sydes were bothe large and gente.
Kepe we thys chylde of mekylle honowre,
And speke we of hys modur whyte as flowre,
 What weyes oure Lord hath hur lente.

LXXVI.

Alle nyght in the roche sche laye, 880
A wynde rose ageynys day,
 And fro the londe hur dryvys.

Sche had neydur reste then odur,
But eche storme gretter then odur,
   On God fulle faste scho cryes.   885
As the boke of Rome says,
Sche was meteles vj. dayes,
   For care hur herte clevyth.
Be the vij. day abowte none,
Jhesu sende hur socowre sone,   890
   Yn Egypt forthe sche ryvyth.

LXXVII.

The kyng of Egyp stode in a towre,
He say that lady whyte as flowre,
   Was wrekyd on the sonde;
He comawndyd a squyer for to go to the see,   895
And loke what in the yondur schyp may be,
   The wynde hath drevyn hur to the londe.
To that schypp he come fulle tyte,
Upon the syde then can he smyte,
   Than sche up can stonde.   900
For feyntnes sche myght not speke a worde,
The lady leynyd hur on the borde,
   And made sygnys wyth hur hande.
Make we mery for Goddys est,
Thys ys the thrydd fytt of owre geste,   905
   That dar y take an hande.

LXXVIII.

The squyer wyste not what she mente,
Ageyne to the kyng he went,
 And knelyd downe on hys kne.
" Lorde, in the yondur schyp nothyng ys,   910
But a woman in lyknes,
 Sche rose and lokyd on me.
A fayrer thyng say y never none,
That ever was made of flesche and bone,
 But hyt were Mary free!   915
Sche makyth me sygnes with hur honde,
As sche were of an unknowen londe
 Beyonde the Grekys see."

LXXIX.

Be Jhesu swere that gentylle kynge,
" Y wylle se that gentylle thynge,"   920
 And thedur he goyth apase.
To the schyp he come anon;
Ageyne the kyng sche rose sone,
 That lady that was so feyre of face:
That damycelle that was so mylde,   925
So sore had gret for hur chylde,
 Sche was wexyn alle horse.
To a chaumbur they hur ladd,
Dylycyus metys they hur badd,
 Wyth gode wylle sche them tase.   930

LXXX.

Aftur mete hur frayneth the kyng,
" Of whens art thou, my swete thyng,
    For thou art bryght of blee?"
Sche seyde, " Y was borne in Artas,
Syr Prynsamowre my fadur was,   935
    The lorde of that cuntré.
Sythen hyt befelle upon a day,
Y and my maydenys went to play
    Be the syde of the see.
There was a lytylle bote stode,   940
Y and my squyer ther in yode,
    Un-Crystynman was hee.

LXXXI.

" On londe y lafte my maydenys alle,
My squyer on slepyng can falle,
[f. 69.]   A mantelle y ovyr hym drewe."   945
The kyng seyde, " Make gode chere,
Thou art my brothurs doghtyr dere."
    For yoye on hym sche logh.
Kepe we thys lady whyte as flowre,
And speke we of syr Egyllamowre,   950
    Now comyth to hym care y-nogh.

LXXXII.

When syr Egyllamowre was hole and sounde,
And wele recovyrd on hys wounde,
    He buskyd and made hym yare;

He thankyth the emperoure of thys, 955
Hys doghtur and the emperes,
    And alle that evyr ware thare.
Crystyabelle was in hys thoght,
The dragonys hedd forgeteth he noȝt,
    Upon hys spere he hyt up bare; 960
Be xij. wekys were comyn to ȝende,
Yn the londe of Artas can he londe,
    And to hym come letturs of care.

LXXXIII.

The cuntré herde telle, y undurstonde,
That syr Egyllamowre was come to londe; 965
    Grete yoye they made in dede.
A squyer wente ageyne hym sone,
" Lo! lorde, what the erle hath done!
    Fayre Crystyabelle ys dedd!
A man-chylde had sche with hur borne, 970
The erle hath hys lyfe forlorne,
    He was bothe whyte and rede;
Yn a schypp on the see he dud them two,
And wyth wyndys let them goo!"
    The knyght swownyd in that tyde. 975

LXXXIV.

" Lorde God!" seyde the knyght so free,
" Where ever the gentylle women bee,
    Yn chaumbur that wyth hur was?"

The squyer answeryd hym fulle sone,
"Lorde, when sche to the see was done,   980
    Ylke oon toke ther wey to passe."
Unto the halle than can he fare,
Among the lordys that were thare
    Be the erle of Artas:
"Have thou here thy dragonys hedd,   985
Alle ys myn that here ys levydd,
    Thou syttyst in my place."

LXXXV.

A grete rewthe hyt was to here,
How he callyd Crystyabelle hys fere,
    And seyde, "Art thou gone to the see?   990
God that dyed on crosse verye,
On thy soule have mercy,
    And on thy yong sone so free!"
And for fere of syr Egyllamowre,
The erle rose up and toke a towre,   995
    There evyr more wo hym bee!
"Gentylle men, so God me save,
Alle that ordre of knyght wylle have,
    Ryse up and take hyt at me."

LXXXVI.

The gentyls that come hym tylle,   1000
Then they were fulle fayne to do hys wylle,
    He gave them ordurs sone;

Yn the halle that he there hadd,
V. and thretty knyghtys he madd,
    Be that odur day abowte none;   1005
And he that was the porest of them alle,
He gaf for Crystyabellys soule
    Londys to leve upon.
A thousand, as y undurstonde,
He toke with hym, and went into the Holy
    Londe,   1010
    There God on cros was done.

LXXXVII.

Syr Egyllamowre, as ye may here,
He dwellyd in the Holy Londe xv. yere,
    The hethen men amonge;
Fulle doghtyly he hym bare,   1015
There ony dedes of armys ware,
    Ageyne them that levedd wronge.
Be the xv. yerys were comyn and gone,
The chylde that the grype hath tane
    Waxe bothe bolde and stronge;   1020
Yn yustyng ne yn turnament,
Ther myȝt no man with-sytt hys dynte,
    But he to the erthe them thronge.

LXXXVIII.

Syr Degrabelle was wyse and wyght,
The kyng of Ysraelle hath made hym knyȝt   1025
    And prynce wyth hys honde.

Lystenyth, lordyngys, leve and dere,
What armys that thys chylde bere,
   And ye wylle undurstonde.

LXXXIX.

He bare, Aserre, a grype of golde,   1030
Rychely beton on the molde,
   Yn hys clothys hangyng
A chylde in a skarlet mantelle bounde,
As he was broght to londe
   Thorowe that grype, withowt lesynge. 1035

XC.

The kyng of Ysraelle waxe fulle olde,
To Syr Degrabelle hys sone he tolde,
   " Y wolde thou haddyst a wyfe;
For y trowe thou art me dere,
When y am dedd, thou getyst no pere,   1040
   Of ryches thou art so ryfe."
A messengere come before the kyng,
" Yn Egypt wonnyth a swete thyng,
   The feyrest that evyr bare lyfe;
The kyng hath soche othys sworne,   1045
No man schalle have hur that ys borne,
   But he wynne hur wyth stryfe."

XCI.

The kynge swere, " And sche be gode,
Therfore we wylle not let be the rode,
   Have done sone and buske the swvthe." 1050

And he comawndyd a messengere to gon,
To bydd hys knyghtys everychon
    That they were there belyve.
They buskyd them wyth ryalle fare,
And to the see they went fulle yare,   1055
    And passyd the watur lythe;
Be th[r]e wekys were comyn to ȝende,
Yn the londe of Egypt can they wende,
    Ther forsus for to knowe swythe.

XCII.

A messengere wente before to telle,   1060
" Here comyth the kyng of Ysraelle
    Wyth mony a man semelé;
The prynce hys sone with many a knyȝt,
For to wowe yowre doghtur bryght,
    Yf that yowre wylle bee."   1065
He seyde, " Be God, y hope y schalle
Fynde redy yustyng for them alle,
    They be welcome to me;
And yf they come on gode array,
To ther mete y schalle them pray,   1070
    As mote y thryve or the."

XCIII.

Trumpus in the topp-castelle rose,
The ryche kyng to the londe gose
    Wyth hys knyghtys clad in palle;

The chylde, that was of xv. yere, 1075
Gothe them among, as ye may here,
   A fote above them alle;
The kyng of Egypt ageyn hym wente,
And sythen be the honde hym hente,
   And bad hym to the halle. 1080
" Y prey the thou gyf me a syght
Of Crystyabelle, yowre doghtur bryght,
   As whyte as bone of whalle."

XCIV.

Owt of a chaumbur was sche broght,
With mannys hondes as sche were wroght, 1085
   Or corvyn on a tree;
By rome some stode and hur behelde,
" Wele were hym that hur myght welde,"
   To hym-selfe seyde hee.
The kyng of Ysraelle that lady can asche, 1090
Yf she myght the see ovyr-passe,
   Hys sonnys wyfe for to bee.
Tho seyde sche, " Yf he may
Gete me with hys schafte to-morowe at day,
   Thy askyng grawnte y the." 1095

XCV.

Grete lordys were at the assent;
Waytys blewe, to mete they wente
   Wyth a fulle ryalle chere.

Two kynges the deyse began,
Syr Degrabelle and Crystyabelle than, 1100
 Thowe they were sybbe fulle nere.
Kynges wente to sytt y-wys,
Ylke squyer in hys offyce
 To serve hys lorde fulle dere;
Aftur mete than seyde they 1105
Deus pacis, clerkys cunne seye
f. 70.] Yn the halle there men may hyt here.

XCVI.

At morne when day sprange,
Gentyl men to haruds thrange,
 Syr Degrabelle was dyght; 1110
Trumpus in the felde rose,
Eche lorde to odur goys,
 That was a semely syght.
Grete lordys made to crye,
" What maner of man ys hee, 1115
 That beryth the grype so bryght?"
Harowdes of armes conne them telle,
" That ys the prynce of Ysraelle,
 Be war, for he ys wyght!"

XCVII.

The kyng of Egypt hath take a schafte, 1120
The chylde satt and nere hym raght,
 Thogh he be nevyr so kene;

Ageyn the kyng the chylde can fare,
Hors and man he bare downe thare
  Strongely on the grene. 1125
The kynge seyde, " So God me save,
Thou art beste worthy hur to have."
  Thus seyn they alle-be-dene.
Lordys they justyd there that day,
The squyers on the morne, withowt nay, 1130
  Doghty men and kene.

XCVIII.

Two kynges have there trowthe plyght
To Crystyabelle that was so bryght,
  To the churche they conne hur lede.
Thus gracyously he hath spedd, 1135
Hys owne modur he hath wedd,
  Thus harde y a clerke rede.

XCIX.

Hys armes they bere hym beforne,
Sche thenkyth how hur chylde was awey borne,
  And grete sorow she made in thoght. 1140
" Lorde, in thyn armes a fowle y see,
That sometyme rafte a chylde fro me,
  A knyght fulle dere hym boght."
The kynge swere be Goddys myght,
" In my foreste can he lyght, 1145
  A grype to londe hym broght."

He comawndyd a squyer for to wende,
And aftur hys cofur he hym sende,
 Ther in hyt was leyde so softe;
There y wot he toke owte thare   1150
The mantelle and the gyrdylle bothe,
 That rychely was be-wroght.

C.

The lady seyde, "Fulle wo ys me,
They were rafte fro me in the see!"
 On-swownyng downe sche brayde.   1155
"How longe sethen?" the kyng can say.
"xv. yere, syr, permafay!"
 They grauntyd alle that sche sayde.

CI.

"Gode Lorde, we alle thou wys and rede,
A sybbe maryage thys day have we made 1160
 In the spryngyng of the mone;
Y rede ye loke, so God me save,
What maner of man that hur schalle have,
 That hyt were done full sone."
"Ye, ffadur, y trowe, hyt be gode,   1165
And so dothe my modur, be the rode!
 But y weddyd hur before none;
Therfore ther schalle no man have hur, be seynt
  Mary,
But he hur wynne os doghtyly,
 As y myselfe have done."   1170

CII.

Grete lordys conne to odur saye,
" For hur love we wylle turnay,
    Wyth swerdus in owre honde;
He that wynnyth that lady clere,
He schalle wedd hur to hys fere,   1175
    There hym lovyth beste to lende."
Harowdes of armes than they wente,
For to dyscrye thys turnayment
    In eche londys ȝende;
Syr Egyllamowre was in that cuntré sone,   1180
And herde telle of thys grete renowne,
    And thedurward can he wende.

CIII.

For Crystyabelle was put in-to the see,
Now soche armes beryth he,
    Lystenyth, y wylle yow dyscrye.   1185
He bare of Aser, a schyp of golde,
A lady as sche dye schoulde,
    And a chylde lay hur bye;
Hys maste of sylvyr and of golde,
The chylde was but of oon nyght olde,   1190
    And evyr in poynte to dye;
And of redd golde was hys fane,
Hys gabulle and hys ropys everechone
    Was portrayed verely.

CIV.

Gentylmen that herde of thys crye,   1195
Thedur come they redylye,
    Tho that doghty were;
The kyng of Sydone came fulle sone
Wyth mony knyghtys herde of bone,
    That yoly colourys bare.   1200
Schaftys they made in the felde,
That grete lordys myght them welde,
    Fulle faste they turnayed thare;
Syr Egyllamowre, thogh he come laste,
ȝyt was he not awey caste,   1205
    The knyght was cladd in care.

CV.

Crystyabelle, that lady smalle,
Was broght to a corner of the walle,
    There the crye was made.
The chylde that was of xv. yere elde,   1210
Was aventurs in the felde,
    And yn a stowre he rode;
When he began to smyte,
Fro hys handys they went not that tyde,
    Ther wolde none hys dyntys abyde;   1215
He sende a knyght anon fulle stylle
Unto syr Egyllamowre, to wyt hys wylle,
    And seyde, "Wylle ye not ryde?"

CVI.

He seyde, " Syr recreawntes,
I am fer comyn owt of hethennes, 1220
    Grete synne hyt were me to tene!"
Hys owne sone seyde, " So mote y the,
Than schulde ye not have armyd be,
    More worschyp had hyt bene."

CVII.

The knyght answeryd, and on hym logh, 1225
" Haste thou not ȝyt askyd me y-nogh,
    But thou on me more praye?"
" Syr, y am aventurs in thys stowre
For a lady whyte as flowre,
    To wynne hur yf y may." 1230
" Be Jhesu," seyde the knyght then,
" Y wylle loke yf y can
    For hur love onythyng turnay;
Be God, sometyme have y sene,
In as herde aventurs have y bene, 1235
    And wonne fulle wele away."

CVIII.

Grete lordys with weponys longe,
Gentylmen to horsus spronge,
    Doghty men echone;
And syr Egyllamowre turnyd hys swerde flatt,
And gafe hys sone soche a patte, 1241
    That to the erthe he ys gone.

Alle they sweryd upon the molde,
" He that beryth the schylde of golde
 Hath wonne hur hymselfe allone." 1245
The lady seyde, " Be Goddys peté,
My sone ys dedd! fulle wo ys me!
 That kene knyght hath hym slone! "

CIX.

Harowdes of armes swore owt than,
" Yf ther be ony gentylman, 1250
 To make hys body gode."
These grete lordys seyde now,
" Beste worthy, syr knyght, art thou
 To wedd thys frely fode."
To onarme hym the knyght goys, 1255
In cortyls, sorcatys and schorte clothys,
 That doghty weryn of dede.
Two kyngys the deyse began,
Syr Egyllamowre and Crystyabelle than,
 Jhesu us alle spede! 1260

CX.

Sche askyth be what chesone he bare
A schyp of golde, bothe maste and ore;
 He tolde hur, as he was hynde.
He seyde, " For in the see was done
f. 71.] My lemman and my yongest sone, 1265
 And there they made ther ȝende."

That lady lettyd for no schame,
" Gode syr, what ys yowre name?"
 He tolde hur in that stownde,
" Men calle me, there y borne was, 1270
Syr Egyllamowre of Artas,
 That with the worme was woundyd."

CXI.

There was many a robe of palle,
The chylde servyd in the halle
 At the fyrste mete that day. 1275
Prevély scho to hym spake,
" ȝondur ys thy fadur that the gate!"
 A grete yoye hyt was to see ay!
When he knelyd downe on hys kne,
There was mony an herte soré, 1280
 Be God that dyed on a tree!
Hyt ys sothe seyde, be God of heven,
Mony metyn at on-sett stevyn;
 And so befelle hyt there!

CXII.

The kyng of Israelle can hym telle 1285
How he fonde syr Degrabelle,
 Knyghtys lystenyd ther-to than.
Syr Egyllamowre knelyd on hys kne,
" A! Lorde God, ȝylde hyt the,
 Thou haste made hym a man!" 1290

The kynge seyde, "Y hym geve
Halfe my kyngdome whylle y leve,
 My sone as whyte os swan."
The kynge of Sydon seyde also,
" And my doghtur Organata y gyf hym to,   1295
 For my londys hys fadur wan."

CXIII.

Syr Egyllamowre prayed these lordys hynde,
Home to Artas that they wolde wynde,
 At hys weddyng to bee.
They grauntyd alle that there ware;   1300
They buskyd them with ryalle fare,
 And sone come ovyr the see.

CXIV.

Schyppus lay wrekyd on the sonde,
Eche lorde toke odur be the honde,
 Pagys ther horsys conne dryve;   1305
Thys behelde syr Prynsamowre,
He felle bakward ovyr a towre,
 And brake hys nekk belyve!
A messengere come before to telle,
What maner aventurs there befelle: 1310
 Wyth God may no man stryve!
Alle the nyght there they laye,
Tylle on the morowe that hyt was day,
 To wedd that lady whyte belyve.

CXV.

Ther was many a lorde of pryde,   1315
A kynge ladde hur on eche a syde,
 Hyt was a semely syght;

Sythen a byschop can them wedde,
Than thanked they God they had so spedd,
 And Mary mekylle of myght!   1320
Sethen to wedde them can they goo,
Syr Degrabelle and Organata tho,
 He was a fulle feyre knyght.
There was throwyn golde in that stounde,
The mowntans of a thousand pounde,   1325
 Gete hyt who so myght.
The mynstrels that were of ferre londe,
They had mony robys, y undurstonde,
 And mony a ryche gyfte.
Sythen to the castelle they wente,   1330
To holde brydale they hente,
 Hyt lastyd a fourtenyght.

CXVI.

When the brydale was alle y-done,
Eche oon toke ther leve to gone,
 There they were levest to lende.   1335
Mynstrels that there were in that stounde,
Ther gyftys were worthe iij. c. pounde,
 The bettur myght they spende.
In Rome thys geste cronyculd ys;
Jhesu brynge us to that blys,   1340
 That lastyth withowten ende! *Amen.*

Here endyth syr Egyllamowre of
Artas, and begynneth syr Tryamowre.

THE ROMANCE

OF

SIR DEGREVANT.

f. 80.] *Sire Degrevvaunt, and theynke and thanke.*

I.

Lord Gode in Trynité,
Yeff home hevene ffor to se,
That lovethe gamene and gle,
  And gestys to ffede.
Ther ffolke sitis in ffere,   5
Shullde mene herkene and here
Off gode that beffore hem were,
  That levede on arthede;
And y schalle karppe off a knyght,
That was both hardy and wyght,   10
Sire Degrevaunt that hend hyght,
  That dowghty was of dede.
Was nevere kyngh that he ffond,
In ffraunce ne in Englond,
Myght sette a schafft of hys hond   15
  One a stythe stede!

II.

Wyth kyng Arrtor, y wene,
And wyth Gwennor the quene,
He was knowun ffor kene,
    That comelych knyght;   20
In Hethenesse and in Spayne,
In ffraunce and in Bryttayne,
Wyth Persevalle and Gawayne,
    ffor herdy and wyght!
He was dowghty and dere,   25
And ther nevew ffulle nere,
Ther he of dedys myght y-here,
    By days or by nyght.
ffor-thy they name hem that stounde
A knyght of tabulle round,   30
As maked is in the mappe-mound,
    In storye ffull ryght.

III.

He was ffayre mane and ffree,
And gretlech yaff hym to gle,
To harp and to sautré,   35
    And geterne ffull gay;
Well to play in a rote,
Off lewtyng, welle y wote,
And syngyng many suet not,
    He bare the pryes aey.   40

Yet gamenes hade he mere,
Grehoundes ffor hert and hare,
Both ffor bokes and the bare,
  Be nyght and be day;
ffelle ffaukons and ffayre,   45
Haukes of nobulle eyre,
Tylle his perke ganne repeyre,
  By sexxty, y dar say.

IV.

He wold be upp or the day
To honte and to revay,   50
Gretly yaff hem to pley
  Eche day to newe;
Tho here hys mas or he went,
Trewly in gode entaunt,
And seththe to bowe into the bente,   55
  There games inne grewe.
Now to fforest he ffounde,
Both wyt horne and with hound,
To breyng the deere to the grond
  Was hys most glew;   60
Certus wyff wold he none,
Wench ne lemone,
Bot as an anker in a stone
  He lyved evere trew.

V.

There was sesyd in hys hand 65
A thousand poundus worth off land,
Off rentes well settand,
 And muchlle delle more;
An houndered plows in demaynus,
ffayere parkes in-wyth haynus, 70
Grett herdus in the playnus,
 Wyth muchelle tame store.
Castelos wyth heygh wallus,
Chambors wyth noble hallus,
ffayer stedes in the stallus, 75
 Lyard and soore;
Wher he herd of anny cry,
Evere he was redy,
He passede never fforth by
 In lond where they were. 80

VI.

He lovede welle almos-dede,
Powr men to cloth and ffede,
Wyth menske and manhede,
 Offe met he was ffre;
And also gestes to calle, 85
And mensteralus her in halle,
He yaff hem robes off palle,
 Off gold and off ffee.

In ych place whaer he comme,
When he wente ffram heme, 90
They hade halowed hys name
    Wyth gret nobullé;
In ych lond where he wentt,
So many mene he hadd schennt,
In justus and on tornament 95
    He whan evere the gre!

VII.

There wonede an eorl him be-syd,
ȝe a lord off mochelle pryd,
That hadd viij. fforestes fful wyd,
    And bowres ffulle brode; 100
He hade a grete spyt of the knyght,
That was so hardy and wyght,
And thought howe he best myght
    That dowghty to grode.
He was sterne and stoute, 105
And rode in a gay route,
And brak hys parkes about,
    The best that he hade;
Ther-inne he made a sory pley,
The ffattest he ffeld in ffey 110
By sexty one a day,
    Suche maystries he made!

VIII.

    He drowhe reveres with ffysh,
    And slogh hys forsteres y-wys.
    The knyght wyste not of thys,   115
        ffor soth y yow say;
    ffor he was in the holy lond,
    Dede of armes for to ffond,
    The hethenemene with hys hond
        He ffeld hem offten in ffey.   120
    Hys steward hadd a lettre y-sent,
    A mesyngere hath hyt hent,
    And forth hys wey ys y-went,
        As ffast as ever he mey:
    When he tylle hys lord come,   125
    The lettre in hys hand he nome,
    He sey, " Alle ʒoode to schome! "
        And went one hys wey.

IX.

f. 81.] Wyth the knytht was none abad,
    He buskyd hyme fforth and rade   130
    ffram the ffrount of the garnad,
        As ffaste as he myght;
    Sone he pased the see,
    He and hys meney,
    And come in-to hys contré   135
        By the twelthe nyght.

Tyll hys maner he went,
A ffeyre place he fond schent,
Hys husbondus that yaf rent
    Was y-heryȝed dounryght: 140
His tenauntrie was alle done,
The best in every tone;
His ffayre perkes wer comene,
    And lothlych by-dyght!

X.

He closed hys perkes ayene;   145
His husbondus they were ff[a]yene,
He lent hem oxone and wayne
    Of his owne store,
And also sede for [to] sowe,
Wyght horse for to drow,   150
And thought werke be lawe,
    And wyth none other schore.
ffor-thi a lettre has he dyght
To this eorl opo[n] myght,
He preyd hem to do him ryght,   155
    Ar telle hyme whereffore;
And wyth sqwere he him sent,
Off an honderd pond of rent,
And fforth hys wey ys he went
    To wytt hys answere.   160

XI.

The squiere nolde nat downe lyght,
Bot haylis this eorl opone hyght,
And sethes bowrone and knyght,
    With wordes fulle wise;
He held the lettre by the nooke,   165
And to the eorle he hit toke;
And he there-one gane loke,
    And seyde his avys,
And spake to the squiere,
" Ne were thow a messengere,   170
Thow shuld abey ryght here,
    Undere this wode rys!
I wulle ffore thy lordes tene,
Honte hys fforesstus and grene,
And breke his perkes bydene,   175
    Proudeste of prys!"

XII.

Thanne the squiere seyde sone,
" Syre, that is nat well done,
Ye have lefft hyme bot whone
    In herde is nat to hyde: 180
He that seyth that hit is ryght,
Be he squiere othere knyght,
Here my glove one to ffyght,
    What chaunce so be-tyde!

Syr, yeff hit be youre welle, 185
Thenkes that ye han done ylle,
Y rede ye amend to schkylle,
    ffor wothes is ever wyde!"
The eorl answeryd y-wyse,
" Y wolle nat amend that mese, 190
Y counte hyme nat at a cres
    ffor alle hys mechelle pryd!"

XIII.

Than the eorl wax worth,
And swore many a gret owth,
He schold be messaggere lothe 195
    But he hys wey wente!
He toke his leve with-outen nay,
And wendus fforth one his way,
As ffast as ever he may,
    Over the brode bent. 200
He come home at the none,
And told how he hade done;
The knyght asked him as sone,
    What answer he sent.
" Sir, and he may as he ment, 205
His game wolt he never stent,
Thyself and he may the hent,
    I telle the, for y-schent."

XIV.

Than syr Degrevvaunt syght,
And byheld the hevene up-an hyght, 210
" Jhesus, save me in my ryght,
    And Maré me spede!
And y schalle yeff Gode a vow,
Some of us schalle hyt row!
Hyt schalle not be for his prow, 215
    And y may right rede!"
Anone to armus they hom dyght,
As fast as evere they myght,
Both squier and kynyght,
    Wys under wede; 220
Ther was armed one hye
Tene score knythis redy,
And iij. hondred archerus by,
    ffulle goode at here nede.

XV.

Anone to the forest they found, 225
    There they stotede a stound;
They pyght pavelouns round,
    And loggede that nyght.
The eorle purveyede him an ost,
And com in at another cost, 230
Wyth his brag and his bost,
    Wyth many a fferres knyght;

He uncouplede his houndus
With-inne the knyghtus boundus;
Bothe the grene and the groundus   235
    They halowede an hyght:
Thus the forest they fray,
Hertus bade at abey;
One a launde by a ley
    These lordus dounne lyght.   240

XVI.

Sextene hertus wase y-slayne,
And wer brought to a pleyne,
Byfore tho cheff cheventene
    Y-leyd wer y-ffere.
Thane seys the dukes on the land,   245
" Wher ys now sir Degrevvaund?
Why wol not come this gyant
    To rescow his dere?
Hys proud hertes of grese
Bereth no chartur of pes;   250
We schalle have som ar we sese,
    Y wold he wer here!
Trewely, are he went,
He schuld the game repent,
The proud lettre that he sent   255
    By hys sqwere."

XVII.

f. 82.] Syre Degrevvaunt was so nere,
That he the wordes can here;
He seyd, " Avaunt banere,
  And trompes apone hyght!" 260
Hys archerus that were thare,
Both lase and the mare,
As swythe were they thare,
  To shote were they dyght.
Thane the eorle was payd, 265
Sone his batelle was reyde,
He was nothyng afreyd
  Off that feris knyght;
Now ar they met one a feld,
Both with spere and sheld, 270
Wyghtly wepenes they weld,
  And fersly they ffyght!

XVIII.

And whan the batelle enjoined,
With speres ferisly they foynede,
There myght no sege be ensoynd, 275
  That faught in the ffeld;
Wyth bryght swerdus one the bent
Rych hawberkes they rent,
Gleves gleteryng glent
  Opone geldene scheldus. 280

They stykene stedus in stoure,
Knyghtus thorow her armere,
Lordus off honore,
 Opone the hethene heldus;
Thenne ffoughtene so ferisly,
Ther weste non so myghty,
Who schold have the victory,
 Bot He that alle weldus.

XIX.

The doughty knyght sure Degrevaunt
Leys the lordes one the laund,
Thorw jepun and jesseraund,
 And lames the ledes:
Schyre scheldus they schrede,
Many dowghty was dede,
Ryche maylus wexen rede,
 So manye bolde dedus.
Thus they fowghtene one frythe,
Kene kyneghus in-with kyth,
Wo wrekes thare wryth,
 These doughty one dede!
Burnes he hadde y-borne doune,
Gomes wyth gambisoune
Lyes opone bent broune,
 And sterff undere stede.

XX.

Sire Degrevaunt, the gode knyght,　　305
Br[i]ghtenes the basnettus bryght;
Hys fferis ferysly they fyght,
　　And ffelles home to grond:
The knyghtus of the eorlus hous,
That were y-halden so chyvalrous,　　310
And in batelle so bountyveus,
　　They deydene alle that stond!
The eorl hovede and beheld,
Both with spere and with scheld,
How they ffayre in the ffeld,　　315
　　And syght un-sound;
The best mene that he ledde,
He hadd y-lefft home to wedde,
With ffyffty spers is he ffledd,
　　And wodelech was y-wounded.　　320

XXI.

Syr Degrivvant and his mene
ffeld home ffaste in the fene,
As the deere in the dene
　　To dethe he thame denges!
Wyth scharpe exus of stelle　　325
He playtede here basnetus welle,
Many a knygh gart he knelle
　　In the morny[n]g.

Sire Degrevvant was fulle thro,
Deperted her batelle a-two;   330
The eorl sley and was wo,
    One a stede cane he spryng:
He laf slawe in a slak
fforty score on a pak,
Wyd opene one here bake,   335
    Dede in the lyng.

XXII.

Syre Degrevvant gat a sted,
That was gode in ilk a ned;
Many a side grat he bled,
    Thorow dent of his spere,   340
And schased the eorl within a whylle,
More then enleve mele.
Many bold gert he syle,
    That byfore dud hym dere!
He come schygynge ayene,   345
And of hys folk was fyene,
And fond nevere one slayne,
    Ne worse be a pere.
He knelyde doune in that place,
And thankyd God of his grace;   350
And alle wend that there was
    Tylle his feyre manere.

Here endyth the furst fit.
Howe say ye? will ye any more of hit?

XXIII.

Bleve to soper they dyght,
Both squiere and knygh[t];
They daunsed and revelide that nyght, 355
    In hert were they blythe.
And whane the eorl come hame,
He was wonded to schame;
The lady ses he was lame,
    And swouned fulle swyth! 360
Offte she cryed, " Alas!
Have ye nat perkus and chas?
What schuld ye do a this place,
    Swych costus to kythe?"
" Dame," he seys, " y was thare, 365
And me rews now fulle sare,
Y take m[y] leve for evere mare
    Swych wornges to wrythe!"

XXIV.

One the morow sire Degrevva[n]t
Dyght him at is avennaunt, 370
On a sted fferraunt
    Y-armed at ryghtes.
To the castelle he rad,
With folkys that he had;
At the barnekynch he abad, 375
    And lordelych doune lyght,

And axed yef ther eny were,
That wold hyme delyvere him ther
Off thre corses of wer,
  Hym and xij. knythus; 380
He prayd the portere
ffor to bene his mesengere,
And to wit an answere,
  And anone he him hytus.

XXV.

The portere went to the halle, 385
And to the eorl he cane calle,
" Her is comen to thus walle,
  Y-armed apone a sted,
Sire Degrevvant the gode knygt,
With hey helmes bryght, 390
Many bold mene and wyght,
  Wyse undere wede;
He axit justes of were,
And prays the of answere:
He mad me his mesager 395
  To walk one his ned."
[f. 83.] The eorl answerd an hy,
" Here is none redy."
Hit semes as that dowghty
  Sire Degrevaunt drede. 400

XXVI.

The contase wendes to the halle,
And hure doughter withalle;
Sche was jentelle and smalle,
  And lovesome to seyght.
She lokyd one that aunterous, 405
And seygh, " Sire kynghtes,
Thou art a mane marvelus,
  My troth y the plyght!
Yeff Gode hath lent the grace,
That thou hast vencoust thy foos, 410
Ne sekes nat at oure ples
  Be day ne be nynght."
The knyght spekes to that free,
" Maydame, wytes nat me,
Muchelle mawgré have he 415
  That chalangeth unryght!"

XXVII.

He sais, " My perkes ar stroyed,
And reveres endreyde;
Y gretly ame anoyde,
  ffor south as y yow say! 420
Whyle y wared in Spyane,
He made my londes barreyne,
My wodes and my warreyne,
  My wylde ys away!

Y shalle do yow withowtene dred, 425
He that dede me that dede,
Y schalle quite heme his mede,
  Y telle yow in ffay,
Yeff y dey in the pleyne!
That my fosteres hath slayne, 430
He shalle award home eyane,
  As sone as y may!"

XXVIII.

Thane spekes that wis in-with wane,
" Ye have welle good mene y-slayne,
Y rede ye be at ane 435
  Or there dey any moo."
The knyght answeres an hy,
" He schalle that bargayne aby,
That dede me this v[y]lany,
  As evere mote y goo! 440
Madame, yef hit be youre welle,
Y pray yow take hit not to ille,
Y ame holdene ther-tylle
  To fyght on my ffoo;
Y telle yow trewly, 445
Hyt leyves not so lyeghtly,
Many dowghty schalle dey
  Or hyt ende soo!"

XXIX.

The knyth hoves in the feld
Bothe weth ax and with sheld;　　450
The eorlus doughdere beheld
　　That borlich and bolde,
ffor he was armed so clene,
With gold azoure ffule schene,
And with his trewe-loves bytwene,　　455
　　Was joy to behold.
She was comlech y-clade,
To ryche banrettes hur lade,
Alle the beut[é] sche hade
　　That frely to folde;　　460
Wyth love she wendus the kny3t,
In hert trewly he hyeght,
That he shalle love that swet wy3t,
　　Acheve how hit wold.

XXX.

How as evere hit cheve;　　465
The knyght takes his leve,
" Madame, takes not a-greve
　　A thyng that y yow say;
Gret welle the eorl they lord,
And sey we shalle not acord,　　470
Tylle my thyng be restored,
　　That he hath done awey.

Here afore myght he eyth
Sone have made me aseyth;
Nowe schalle he, magré his tyeth, 475
    For alle is grete arey!
Trewly y undertake,
Were hit not for youre sake,
Y schalle hym wynly wake
    Or to-morow it were day! 480

XXXI.

" Y lette ffor my gentriose
To do swych roberyse,
ffor seche ffayre laydés,
    There casteles to ffray;
Sene y mey do no mare, 485
Tylle his freth wyle y fare,
Y wolle no wyld best spare
    ffor soth alle this day!"
Anone to forest they founde,
Both with horne and with hound, 490
To breng the dere to the grond
    Alaund ther they lay:
Thus this games he begane,
Rachis reyally rane;
Sexti bockes, ar he blane, 495
    Hadde he felde in ffay.

XXXII.

Sire Degrevant, ar he reste,
Temede the eorl one the beste,
And hontede his forste
    Wyth bernus fulle bolde;   500
His depe dychys he drowe,
Hys whyght swannes he slow,
Grete luces y-nowe
    He gat home wold.
Now hyme lykys no pley,   505
To honte ne to revey,
ffor mayd Melidore the may
    His care wax alle cold!
As he hounted in a chas,
He told his squier his case,   510
That he loved in a place
    A frely to ffolde.

XXXIII.

" My love is leliche y-lyeght
One a worthly wyeght,
There is no berelle so bryght,   515
    Ne cristalle so clere;
She is waré and wyse,
Rode ronne hit ys,
As the rose in the ris,
    Wyth lylye in lere.   520

She ys precious and palle,
ffere feyrest of alle,
Y say hure ones one a walle,
    Y ney3ed hure so nere;
Y hade leve she were myne   525
Thane alle the gold in the Reyne,
ffausoned one florene,
    She is myne so drere!"

XXXIV.

His squier answered y-wyse,
" Lat me wyte what she is,   530
And y wol syker the this,
    In payne of my lyff,
That y wolle do that y mey,
Both be nyght and be day,
Yef y cane be any way   535
    Wyn hure to youre wyf;
And here y shalle the ensure,
Thi conselle nevere descure,
Whylle my body may endure,
    Wyth swerd and wyth knyef   540
That y shalle faythly fyeght,
Both in worng and in ryght,
Or he be squier or knyght,
    Ayenese the wolle streff."

XXXV.

"Melydore ys hure naume, 545
Whyegh as the seys ffame;
My bolde burnes wold me blame,
What bot is that y ley?
[f. 84.] That I shoulde wow in a stede,
A3eyn alle mene rede, 550
And bothe my lyff and my dede
Ys loken in hur tye;
ffor she is frely and fair,
And the eorlus owne eyer,
I wolde nothing off their, 555
Broche ne bye.
I wolde aske tham na mare
But hyr body all bare,
And we frendes for evermare,
What doel that I drye!" 560

XXXVI.

That sqwyer seyde hys avyse,
"Think that 3e ere enemys;
Lat some wye that ys wys
Walk one thus nede,
ffor I dare saffly swere, 565
Gyff he take the in werre,
Alle Englond here
Wold spek of thi dede,

And say hyt ys a ffolly,
ffor to love thin enemy, 570
Gyf thou gett a vylony,
    But maugré to mede;
Other ladyes wolde say,
My3the no womman the apay
Bete maiede Mylder the may, 575
    Vlonkest on wede?"

XXXVII.

Then saide syr Degrivaunt,
"Thou shal not mak thin avaunt
That I shall be recreaunt,
    ffor frende ne for foo! 580
Thou woldest halde me ful made,
ffor the erle ful rade;
Troust I be so made
    To leve my love so?
At even arme the well 585
Bothe in yren and in stel,
And we shullen to the castel
    Bytwyx us owne two;
Sertenly this ylke ny3th,
I wylle see hyr with sy3th, 590
And spek with that byrde bry3th,
    ffor wel or for wo!"

XXXVIII.

Tow ryche cou[r]sers thei hente,
And forthe here weys thei wente;
Undir a lynd or thei lente,   595
    By a launde syde.
Whyle hyt dawed ly3th day,
The eorle buskede on hys way,
Out at a posterne to play
    With kny3th of pryde.   600
Sir Degrivaunt helde hym styll,
Whyle the eorle passyde the hyll,
And seid hys squier hym tyll
    Pryvaly that tyde,
" I rede we hye us ful 3erne   605
In at the 3ond posterne,
And let us halde us in derne
    The burde tyll abyde."

XXXIX.

Syr Degrivaunt tok non hede;
In at the posterne he 3ede.   610
The porter hade ben in drede,
    Hadd he ben thare.
He that the 3att schulde kepe,
He was go for to slepe;
In at an orcherd thei lepe,   615
    Y-armede as thei ware.

The kny3t and the squiere
Resten in a rosere,
Tylle the day wex clere,
    Undurne and mare;   620
Whyle that hurde thei a bell
Ryng in a chapell;
To chyrche the gay dammisel
    Buskede hyr 3are.

XL.

Sche come in a vyolet,   625
With why3the perl overfret,
And saphyrus therinne i-sett
    On everyche a syde;
All of pall work fyn,
With miche and nevyn,   630
Anerlud with ermyn,
    And overt for pryde.
To tell hure botenus was toore,
Anamelede with azoure;
With topyes and trechoure   635
    Overtrasyd that tyde,
Sche was recevyd a spanne
Of any lyvand manne;
Off rede golde the rybanne
    Glemyd hure syde.   640

XLI.

Hyr here was hy3thtyd on hold
With a coronal of golde;
Was never made upon mold
    A worthelyche wy3th.
Sche was frely and fair,   645
And well hyr semed hyr geyr,
With ryche boses a payr,
    That derely were by-dy3th
With a front endent,
With peyrl of orient,   650
Out of Syprus was sent
    To that burd bry3th;
Hur kerchevus was curyus,
Hyr vyssag ful gracious.
Sir Degrivaunt that amerus   655
    Had joye of that sy3th.

XLII.

By that the masse was i-seid,
The halle was ryaly areyd;
The eorlle hadd i-revayd,
    And in hys 3erd ly3thus: 660
Trompers tromped to the mete,
They weshen and went to sette,
So duden all the grete,
    Ladyes and kny3ttus.

When the lordys were drawin, 665
Ladyes rysen, was not to leyn,
And wentten to chaumbur aȝeyne,
  Anon thei hom dyȝthus;
Dame Mildore and hyr may
Went to the orcherd to play, 670
Ther syr Degrivaunt lay
  Thei com anon-ryȝthus.

XLIII.

Syr Degrivaunt withouten lett
In an aley he hyr mete,
And godlyche he hyr gret, 675
  That worthelyche wyȝth,
f. 85.] And seyd, " Certys, lady and fre,
Jhesu save the and see,
Thi servaunt wold I be,
  My trouȝth I the plyȝth! 680
I wold spek, hadd I space,
Privély in a place;
My lyff ys loken in thi grace,
  Thou worthilyche wyȝth!"
The byrd was gretely affraid, 685
But natheles hoo was wel paid,
He was so ryally arayd,
  That commolyche knyȝth.

XLIV.

The byrd answerus on hy3th,
" Whethur thou be squier or kny3th,   690
Me thenkus thou not dost ry3th,
    Sothely to say;
That thou commyst armid on werre,
To maydenus to afferre,
That walkes in here erbere   695
    Privély to play.
By God and by Sent Jame,
Y know not thi name,
Thou erte gretely to blame,
    I tell the in fay!"   700
The kny3t kneled hyr tyll,
" Medame, yf hit be 3oure wyll,
I graunt I have done yll,
    I may not ageyn-say.

XLV.

" As God save me of synne,   705
I my3th with non other gynne
Tyl 3our spech for to wynne,
    By day ne be ny3the;
ffro I telle the my name,
I am not for to blame,   710
And yf hit turne me to grame,
    I shal anon-ry3th:

Hyt ys I, syre Degryvaunt!
And hit were 3oure avenaunt,
I wold be 3oure servaunt, 715
  As y am trew kny3th!"
Sho seyd, "Tratur, lat be the,
Be Hym that dyed on tre,
My lord hymself shal the see
  Hanged on hy3th!" 720

XLVI.

Than syr Degrivaunt lou3h,
As he stod under the bow,
"Madame, 3e wyteth me with wou3h,
  Gyf hyt be 3oure wyll!
I had never no gylt, 725
Of al that blod that was spylt,
That wyll I prove, as thou wylt,
  Above the 3ondur hyll:
Corteys lady and wyse,
As thou arte pervenke of pryse, 730
I do me on thi gentryse,
  Why wolt thou me spyll?
And I be slayn in this stede,
Thou shalt be cause of my dede;
3et wolt thou rew that rede, 735
  And lyke hyt ful yll!"

XLVII.

Sche said, " Tratur, thou shalt bye!
Why were thou so hardye
To do me this vylanye,
  By day ar by ny3th? 740
For oure folk that thou hast slayn,
Thou shalt be honged and drawyn,
Therof my fadyr wol be fayn
  To see that with sy3th!"
The kny3t spak to this fre, 745
" Seththe hyt may no bettur be,
Go feche all hys many
  With me for to fy3th;
And here my trou3th er I leton,
The geyest of hem shal gron, 750
Gyf ther come fourty for on,
  My trou3th I the ply3th!

XLVIII.

" And her my trou3th I the ply3the,.
Tho that lepeth now ful ly3th
Shal be ffay, and we ffy3th, 755
  ffor all here michel pryde!"
The stout man was astered,
Hys squiere rau3th hym hys swerd;
Thanne the borlych berde
  No lenger durst byde. 760

Tyl hyr chaumbur sche went,
And swore the kny3th shulde be schent.
The mayde hur hood of hoe hent,
    And knelyd that tyde;
"Meydame, oppon 3owlus ny3the   765
My waryson 3e me hy3th;
Y ne axe the bote 3onde kny3th
    To slep by my syde!"

XLIX.

Blyve the burde gat a blame,
But sche ne let for no schame,   770
That sche ne asked the same,
    Sothly to say.
"Damesel, go do thi best,
I pray the let me have my rest;
Go and glad thi gest,   775
    In all the devyl way!
ffor as ever Gode me save,
Haddest thou asked a knave,
The symplust that I have,
    Hadd be more to my pay: 780
I swere the by Goddus grace,
Come he never in this place,
He passed never syche a pace,
    By ny3the ne by day!"

L.

"Maydame," sche seid, " gramercy   785
Of thi gret cortesy."
Blyve a chaumbur ther-by
    Busked was ȝare,
And in sche feches the knyȝth,
Prevaly withouten syȝthe,   790
As wymmen conn mychel slyȝth,
    And ther wylles ware.
Sche dyȝt to hys sopere
The foules of the ryvere,
Ther was no deyntethus to dere,   795
    Ne spyces to spare.
The knyȝt sat at hys avenaunt,
In a gentyl jesseraunt;
The mayd mad hym semblaunt,
    And hys met schare.   800

LI.

Of all the met that she schare,
The knyȝt ete never the mare;
Whan he syȝthe ful sare,
    The mayden gan smyle.
Sone aftyr he seys,   805
" What useth the eorl a-dayes?
Hontes he ar revayes?
    What does he this whyle?"

f. 86.] The burd answerus agayn,
"Seththe hys chyvalry was slayn, 810
He passed never out on the playn
    Halvendel a myle;
Hys hurtus has hym so y-deryd,
He has byn gretely afferyd:
The ȝatus has byn ay y-speryd 815
    ffor dred of thi gyle!"

LII.

"Or hys ȝatis be y-speryd,
I shal mak hym afferyd,
I shal schak hym by the berd
    The nexte tyme we mete! 820
But I let for hur sake,
That I have chosen to my mak,
Sche doys me unwynly to wak,
    With wongus ful wete!
I had levere sche were sauȝthe, 825
Then all the golde in hys auȝthe,
And I in armus hade y-lauȝthe
    That commely and swete.
Thane durste I saffly syng,
Was never emporoure ne kyng 830
More at hys lykyng,
    And honde I the hete."

LIII.

The mayd answerus aȝeyn,
" Me think thou travelus in vayn,
Thou hast oure kunred y-slayn, 835
  How myȝt hit so be?
I swere the by Godus myȝthe,
Com thou ever in hur syȝth,
Thou bes honged on hyȝthe
  Hyie one a tre! 840
Hyr preferrys par-amoure
Both dukes and emperoure;
Hyt were hyr disonowre
  For to taken the:
The duke of Gerle for hir has sent, 845
That he wol have a tornament,
Hyt ys my lordys assent,
  Withynne for to be.

LIV.

" Tho duke comes of so gret arey
To juste and to tornay; 850
Thou comes nat at that play
  By counsayl of me.
Hyt is my lordys ensent,
Come thou to that torniment,
Sertaynly thou be schent 855
  And all thi meynye!"

"Damesele, withouten drede,
Thou hast warnyd me of this dede;
Of this gret gentyl rede
    God for-ȝelde the!   860
And y swere be Sent Luke,
I shal juste with that duke,
Or I gete a rebuke,
    How ever that hyt be!

LV.

"And, damesel, for thi chere,   865
And for my god sopere,
Thou shalt have my squiere,
    Lok yf the paye;
Here i-gyf I ȝow be band
An c. pownd worth of land,   870
To tak hyr by the hond,
    And do as y the saye."
Whan here trouthus were plyȝthe,
Sone torches were i-lyȝthe,
And gaff hym ordyr of knyȝthe,   875
    For sothe as I say.
"Recumaunde, for Godys pyne,
To my lady and thinne,
As thou wolt that I be thin,
    To my dethus day!   880

LVI.

" Recumaund me pryvaly
To that fayre lady,
Or hur thonke ly3therely
    That I am pore;
Ther shal emporoure ne kyng,   885
That shal hyr to bed bryng,
That I shall make a lettyng,
    I sey the tho sothe.
Here my trouth I the ply3the,
Seyn fyrst I see hyr with sy3the,   890
I sleped never o ny3the
    Halvendel an houre!
Pray that corteys and hende
That sche wold be my frend,
And some socoure me send   895
    ffor hyr mychel honowre."

LVII.

The maid seis, " I take on hand,
That I shal do thyn errand,
Or I be flemyd out of lond,
    Y lete for no dred;   900
I shall teche the a gyn
Out of this castel to wyn,
And how thou shal come in
    Thyn erond to spede.

Ther ys a place in the wall, 905
Bytwyne the chaumbur and the hal,
Thor ly3the a mychel watur-wal
 Of fourty feyt brede :
Ther shalt thou come in a ny3the
Prevaly withouten sy3th, 910
And here thi chaumbur shal by dy3t,
 And I can ry3th rede."

LVIII.

" Damesel, for Godus grace,
Teche me to that ylke place."
The maid prevaly apace 915
 Passes byfore,
And ledes hym out at a gate,
In at a watur-3ate,
Ther men vytayled by bate
 That castel with cornes. 920
" At ebbe of the see,
Thou shalt not wad to the kne."
The kny3t kyst that fre.
 Erly at the morow
ffayir thei passed that flode, 925
To tho forest thei 3oud,
And toke here stedus where thei stod
 Undur the hawthrone.

LIX.

Syre Degrivaunt ys whom went
And aftyr hys reten sent; 930
To that gret tornament
    Thei busked hem ȝare.
But leve we now that gentyl knyȝt,
And spek we of that byrd bryȝt;
How thei gestened that nyȝt 935
    Carp wyll we mare.
Erly one the mowroun
The lady louȝh hyr to scorne,
Sche seys, " Thi maydynhed is lorne,
    God gyf the care ! " 940
[f. 87.] " Maydame, gyff hyt so be,
Hyt deres no man but me !
I fouchesaff on that fre,
    And hyt so ware."

LX.

Tho lady louȝhwes uppon hyȝt, 945
" Damesele, for Godys myȝt,
How peyis the that knyȝt,
    As evere mote thou the ? "
" I dare make myn avaunt
ffor my lord syre Degrivaunt, 950
Corteys and avenaunt,
    I know non so fre !

Sertaynly this ylke ny3the,
Hys squier ys mad kny3the,
He and I ys trouthe ply3the 955
 My housbond to be ;
And he hath gyf us by band,
An c. pownd worth of land :
Here the chartur in thi hand,
 Thiself may hyt see !" 960

LXI.

Than that lady was glad
By sche that chartur had rad,
" Had thou syre Degrivaunant had,
 Then had thou wel i-gon."
" Nay, meydame, so mot I thryve, 965
Ther ys now lady on lyve,
That he wol wed to wyff,
 But only the allone.
Y warne the of o thing,
Ther shall be emporoure ne kyng, 970
That shal the to bede bryng,
 I owttake none,
That hee wol make a lettyng ;
He sendys the syche a gretyng,
Lo! here ys a rede gold ryng, 975
 With a ryche stone."

LXII.

The lady loked on that ryng,
Hyt was a gyfte fore a kyng,
"This ys a merveylous thing!
  Wenus thou I be wode 980
To do syche a ffoly,
To love my lordys enemy,
Thow he were to so dowȝty?
  Nay, by the rode!
Y do the wele for to wyte, 985
Y nel non housbond have ȝyte:
Seye the knyȝthe whan ȝe mete,
  I wol hym no gude!
The duk of Gerle hase i-hyȝt
That he wol soupe here this nyȝt, 990
And gyf my chaumbur were i-dyȝt,
  Nothing for-ȝeed."

LXIII.

The duk ys comen over the see
With a ful grete meyné;
The eorl cortays and fre 995
  ffayre hym gan praye
To dwel at hys costage,
At bouche and court and wage,
With knyȝt, squiere, and page,
  Tyl the tent day. 1000

A thousaund hors and thre
Of the dukus meyné
Ylke ny3t tok lyveré
    Off cowrne and off hay;
The ryche duk whan he eet,   1005
The eorle hertely hym hete,
And with mayd Myldore the swet,
    To have hyre for ay.

LXIV.

The k[n]y3thus of the eorles house
Held the duk so chyvalrous,   1010
ffor he was gay and amorous,
    And made hyt so tow.
The eorl tol[d] hym anon,
What armes he hadde cone,
And how hys chyvalré was slone   1015
    Undir the wod bowe.
" The baneret that wonnes here by
Wol asayl the cry,
He wro3the me this vylany,
    And dud me this wou3he!"   1020
The duk answerus on hy3the,
" Here my trouth I the ply3the,
Whedur he wol tornay or fy3the,
    He shal have i-now!"

LXV.

The duk answerus on hy3the, 1025
" Wherby k[n]owus thou the kny3the?"
The eorle tau3th hym ful ry3the,
    With wordys, I wene.
" He beres in cheef of azour,
Engrelyd with a satur, 1030
With doubule tressour,
    And treweloves bytwene;
Hys bagges this blake,
ffor he wol no man forsake,
A lyoun tyed to an ake 1035
    Off gold and of grene:
An helme ryche to behold;
He beres a dolfyn of gold,
With trewelovus in the mold,
    Compasyd ful clene. 1040

LXVI.

" He ys a lyoun in feld,
When he ys spred undur scheld!
Hys helme shal be wel steled,
    That stond shal as stak:
He ys so stalloworth in stoure, 1045
By seynt Martyn of Toure,
Couthe he love paramoure,
    I k[n]ew never hys mak!

All the londes that I welde,
Wold I gyf in my ȝelde, 1050
To se hym falde in the feld,
  Ho wold hyt undurtake."
The duk louȝh hym to scorune,
Hys othe heyly has i-swrun,
" He shal abye to mowrun, 1055
  Syre, for thi sake!"

LXVII.

And on morow the duk hym dyȝthe,
Also fast as he miȝthe,
The eorl hardy and wyȝthe,
  Cruel and kene. 1060
The sonne schonne en clere,
They uschen in with banere,
v. hunderyd knyȝtus in fere,
  I-armed ful clene,
And the servitourus by-syde: 1065
All that contray so wyde
Come thedur that tyde,
  That solas to sene.
Sire [D]egrivaunt out of the west
Brouȝth out of the fforest 1070
Thre hundred knyȝttus of the best,
  Was greythed al on grene.

LXVIII.

 Ther was non so hardy,
 That durst asayl the cry;
 The held this duk so dou3ty,   1075
[f. 88.]   ffor hys mychel pryd.
 But when thei se syre Degrivans
 Com armed up a ferauns,
 Thei thonked Gode of here shaunce,
   All that other syde!   1080
 Then thei drowe hym ful nere,
 Baneret and bachelere,
 To ben undur hys banere,
   To tornay that tyde,
 With trompe and with nakere,   1085
 And the scalmuse clere;
 ffolke frouschen in fere,
   In herd ys not to hyde.

LXIX.

 And when the renkus gane mete,
 ffele was fouled undur fete,   1090
 Kny3thus strewed in the strete,
   Stony3ed with stedys;
 With swerdus smartely thei smyt,
 The temes sadely ful tyte,
 Ther was no lengur delyte,   1095
   These worthely in wedus!

Baronus syttys on the bent
With shuldrys shamly shent;
Bryȝthe browus and bent
  Brodelyche bledus!   1100
Manye harmes has thei hent,
That was never at hore asent,
To come to that tornament,
  To do suche dedus.

LXX.

Syre Degrivaunt, withouten les,   1105
Prykkus fast therow the pres;
To the cheventayn he ches,
  And rauȝth hym a strok:
The duk dotered to the ground,
On erthe swyfftly he swouned,   1110
Syre Degrivaunt, within a stound,
  He wan hys sted blak.
He was stalworȝth in stoure,
ffor he loved paramoure;
The lady lay in the toure   1115
  That shuld be hys mak.
Syre Degrivaunt, are he blan,
This sey many a man,
Syxty stedus he wan,
  And brouȝth to stak.   1120

LXXI.

Syre Degrevaunt every day,
The sertayn soth for to say,
Al the prys of the play
    Was put on that fre;
Sone that dou3ty undur sheld   1125
Had y-venkessyd the feld,
Many a man hym byheld,
    So hardy was he!
Ladyes seyden al-bydene,
Bothe contasse and qwene,   1130
"3ond gentyl kny3t on grene
    Hath deservyd the gre!"
Bry3the burdus in ther boure
Loved that kny3th paramoure,
Gret ladyes of honoure,   1135
    And that hym seyen.

LXXII.

The duk was horsed agayn,
And prycked fast thorw the playne;
The eorl and he with a trayn
    To the castel gan fare: 1140
Thane an heroud gon crye,
And prayd al the chyvalrye
To soupe at the maungerye,
    Gyff ther wyllus ware.

The good kny3t syre Degrivaunce, 1145
He had y-made repurveaunce
ffor al hys retenaunce,
  Fourty days and mare,
In the syde at a fel,
At a wel feyre castel, 1150
Whyle hym was lefte for to dwel,
  ffor to sle care.

LXXIII.

The sterne kny3thus and the stout,
Whylk that tornyment without,
Ryden away in hys rout, 1155
  Thre hundred and mo;
And c. pound and a stede
He send the mynstralus to mede,
Off gyffte was he never gnede,
  ffor wele nor for wo! 1160
Tyl hys castel he rade,
A ryal maungerye he made,
Alle the bold ther abade,
  Ther scapyd non hym fro.
At even seyd syr Degrivauns, 1165
" I wol se the countenauns
Of the chyvalrye of Frauns,
  As ever mote I go!"

LXXIV.

Syr [D]egrivaunt at evyn-ly3thus
Armed hym at al ry3thus,　　　　　　　　1170
And callyd to hym tolly kny3thus,
　　　That pryvest were ay;
" Have dy3t 3ow on stedus
In two damysel wedus,
ffor I wol found in my nedus　　　　　　1175
　　　As fast as I may.
Tak ether of 3ow a spere,
Bothe of pes and of were,
Greyth myn hors on hore gere,
　　　And lok that thei be gay;　　　　1180
That they be trapped a get,
In topteler and in mauntolet,
In a fyn vyolet,
　　　And makes non delay."

LXXV.

And whan here hors were held,　　　　　1185
Thei toke ther sperus and there scheldus,
And prycked fast over the felde,
　　　No lenger wolde thei dwel;
And sy[th]en thei ryden even west
Thorw a fayr forest,　　　　　　　　　　1190
With two trompess of the best,
　　　That range as a bell.

On an hull he gan hym rest,
Thei gaf hym hys helm in hys rest,
He was the sternest gest 1195
    ffro heven to helle!
Syr Degrivaunt, withouten abad,
To the eorlus castel he rade,
He found the ȝat so brad,
    Swyche hap hym felle. 1200

LXXVI.

And rydes up to the des,
As thei were servid of here mes,
To mayd Myldor he ches,
    And chalangys that fre!
The duk sterte up an hyȝt, 1205
" Here my trouthe y the plyȝt,
I shal delyver the this bryȝt,
    To-morow shalt thou se,
Bytwene undurne and prime;
Loke at thou come at that tyme, 1210
Other swowne shal i[n] sweme,
    The lady shall i-se.
[f. 89.] And trewly, withouten les,
Thou shalt be servid, or I sess,
Bothe of werre and of pess, 1215
    Of ayther cours thre."

LXXVII.

The kny3th was so dressé,
Hytt was gret joye to se,
So fayre an hors-man as he
    Seye thei never are;   1220
Some loked one hys stede,
And some on hys rych wede,
And some the resone gan rede
    What the kny3the bare.
He loutes down to them alle,   1225
Bothe to the [riche] and to the smalle,
And rydys out of the halle,
    And buskys hym 3are.
Of all that loked one the kny3t,
Was non that knew hym with sy3t,   1230
Bot mayden Myldor the bry3t,
    Of all that ther ware.

LXXVIII.

Hammard he rydes ry3th,
And as fast as he my3th,
On the mowro he hym dy3th   1235
    Ry3th as he dude are;
And fyndys the duk in the feld,
Bothe with spere and with sche[l]d:
The eorl hoved and byheld,
    Brem as a bare!   1240

Than seid the duke one the land,
" Whare ys now this geand?
He wol hald no covenand,
  ffor alle hys gret fare!"
But when he say syre Degrivaunt 1245
Come armed up a fferauns,
Hys hert wex recreaunt,
  And syȝth ful sare!

LXXIX.

The duke send a squiere
To wytt what hys wyll were, 1250
To juste o pesse or off were,
  So sore he hym dredus!
The knyȝt answerd ther-tyll,
Bothe with resone and with skyll,
" Hyt shal be at hys wyll, 1255
  Tak hap what ledus!"
Then the douȝthy hym dyȝth
As faste as thei myȝth,
Thei set helmus on hyȝth,
  Thes douȝty on dedus: 1260
To gret sperus of pese
Bothe these lordes hem chese,
And prikes fast thorw the prese
  Opon stout stedus.

LXXX.

Ther stedes styrres hom faste, 1265
The kny3thus jusset or thy cast,
Ther good speres al to-brast,
  That weren gode at nede;
Syr Degrivaunt, as he had ment,
And gaf the duk swych a dynt, 1270
That bothe styroppus he tynt,
  And hond I the hete.
The duke rekyvered a3yne,
Hys frenchepys were fayn,
The proford hym payn-mayn, 1275
  Vernage and Crete;
The duk swore by gret God of hevene,
" Wold my hors so evene,
3et wold I sett all one seven
  ffor Myldor the swet!" 1280

LXXXI.

Tow gret sperus ha they ton,
And gerd there stedus whyll the gron!
Wytt 3ow wel that many on
  Lokede on them two;
The dou3ty kny3thus of pryde, 1285
Thorw the renckus gon thei ryde,
Bote they myssede at that tyde,
  Thorw hap hyt fell so.

The good kny3th, syre Auntorus,
Come in at the thryd cours, 1290
ffor he loved paramours,
 In hert that he was thro,
And strykus the duk thorw the scheld,
Wyd opon in the feld;
The eorl hoved and byheld, 1295
 In hert he was wo!

LXXXII.

The damessel toke the stede,
And thorw the renkus gone hym lede,
And seys, " Have this for thi mede,
 Tyl thou gete mo." 1300
3et she spekys a word of pride,
" On this stede wol I ryde
By my lemmanus syde,
 I [n] lond whare I go."
That kny3t dressyd hym in hys gere, 1305
Hys felawe rau3th hym a spere,
A scharpe wepon of were,
 The duk for to slo;
And seis, " Syre duke avenaunt,
I pray the hold couvenaunt, 1310
3ondur ys a kny3the erraunt,
 Why taryest thou hym so?"

LXXXIII.

The duk lay on the grownd,
On erthe swyftely he swound,
He was stonyed that stownd, 1315
    Trewely that tyde;
And ȝit she cryes upone hyȝth,
" ȝondur ys armed a knyȝth,
All redy and y-dyȝth,
    Thi comes for to abyde." 1320
The duke answerd ther-tyle,
Bothe with reson and skyle,
" I am y-hurte ful yle,
    In herd is not to hyde!
Pray hym tak hit nat a-greff, 1325
He ses I am at myscheff,
Y hathe nat y my lyff,
    So sore ys my syde!"

LXXXIV.

Syre Degrivaunt toke hys stede,
And gaff the mynstrallus to mede, 1330
And to forest thei spede
    As faste as the may;
The duke that was this y-dyȝt,
He toke his leve that ylk nyȝt
Bothe with baroun and with knyȝt, 1335
    And went one hys way.

Sire Degrivaunt on the morwoun
Com aȝé to the thorun,
Ther hys stede stod by-forun,
  And lenges all that day; 1340
Privayly at the nyȝth
He come in with hys knyȝth,
To spek with Myldore the bryȝth,
  Spede yf he may.

LXXXV.

The mayde wyst by a gyne, 1345
That the knyȝth was comen in;
The lady of heye kyne
  Perseved the thouȝth.
"Damesele, so have I rest,
Thou hast geton the a gest 1350
Off wylde men of the west,
  Delayne thou hom nouȝth;
Privayly withouten syȝth
Do me carp with that knyȝth,
Here my trouȝth y the plyȝth, 1355
[f. 90.] Hee has dere y-bouȝth!"
Thanne the mayden was glade,
Sche dude as the lady bade,
And up at the grese hoe him lade,
  And to chaumbur hym brouȝth." 1360

LXXXVI.

The lady of honowre
Metes the [kny3t] in the doure,
Knelyd doun in the floure,
    And fel hym to feet;
ffrek as fuyre in the flynt   1365
He in armes had hyre hynt,
And thrytty sythes, are he stynt,
    He kyst that swet!
" Welcome, syre Aunterous,
Me thenkus thou art mervelous;   1370
Wyst my lord of this hous,
    With grame [he] wolde the gret!"
Swythe chayres was i-sete,
And quyschonus of vyolete,
Thus this semely was i-sete   1375
    With mouth for to mete.

LXXXVII.

" Damesele, loke ther be
A ffuyre in the chymené,
ffagattus of fyre tre,
    That fetchyd was 3are."   1380
Sche sett a bourd of yvore,
Trestellus ordeyned therfor,
Clothus keverede that over,
    Swyche seye thei never are!

Towellus of Eylyssham, 1385
Why3th as the seeys fame,
Sanappus of the same,
  Thus servyd thei ware;
With a gyld salere,
Basyn and ewere, 1390
Watyr of everrose clere,
  They wesche ry3th thare.

LXXXVIII.

Paynemayn prevayly
Sche brou3th fram the pantry,
And served that semely, 1395
  Same ther thei seet.
Sche brou3t fram the kychene
A scheld of a wylde swynne,
Hastelettus in galantyne,
  An hand y 3ow hete. 1400
Seththe sche brou3t hom in haste,
Ploverys poudryd in paste,
Ther ware metus with the maste,
  I do 3ow to wytte;
ffatt conyngus and newe, 1405
ffesauntus and corelewe,
Ryche she tham drewe
  Vernage and Crete.

LXXXIX.

To tell here metus was tere,
That was served at here sopere,   1410
Ther was no dentethus to dere,
    Ne spyces to spare;
And evere sche drow hom the wyn,
Bothe the Roche and the Reyn,
And the good Malvesyn   1415
    ffelde sche hom ȝare.
And evere Myldore sche sete
Harpyng notus ful swet,
And other whyle sche et,
    Whan hur leveste ware;   1420
Songe ȝeddyngus above,
Swyche murthus they move,
In the chaumbur of love
    Thus thei sleye care!

XC.

Ther was a ryall rooffe   1425
In the chaumbur of loffe,
Hyt was buskyd above
    With besauntus ful bryȝth
All off ruel bon,
Whyȝth oger and parpon,   1430
Mony a dere wrothe stone,
    Endentyd and dyȝthe.

Ther men myȝth se, ho that wolde,
Arcangelus of rede golde,
ffyfty mad of o molde,   1435
  Lowynge ful lyȝth;
With the Pocalyps of Jon,
The Powlus Pystolus everychon,
The Parabolus of Salamon
  Payntyd ful ryȝth.   1440

XCI.

And the foure gospellorus
Syttyng on pyllorus;
Hend, herkeneth and herus,
  Gyf hyt be ȝoure wyll.
Austyn and Gregory,   1445
Jerome and Ambrose,
Thus the foure doctorus
  Lystened than tylle:
There was purtred in ston
The fylesoferus everychon,   1450
The story of Absolon,
  That lyked ful ylle;
With an orrelegge one hyȝth
To rynge the ours at nyȝth,
To waken Myldore the bryȝth,   1455
  With bellus to knylle.

XCII.

Square wyndowus of glas,
The rechest that ever was,
Tho moynelus was off bras
    Made with menne handus;   1460
Alle the wallus of geete,
With gaye gablettus and grete,
Kynggus syttyng in ther sete
    Out of sure londus.
Grete Charlus with the crounne,   1465
Syre Godfray the Boyloune,
And Arthur the Bretoune,
    With here bry3t broundus.
The floure was paned over-al
With a clere crystal,   1470
And overe keveryd with a pal,
    A-fflore where she stondes.

XCIII.

Hur bede was off aszure,
With testur and celure,
With a bry3t bordure   1475
    Compasyd ful clene;
And all a storye as hit was
Of Ydoyne and Amadas,
Perreye in ylke a plas,
    And papageyes of grene.   1480

The scochenus of many kny3t
Of gold and cyprus was i-dy3t,
Brode besauntus and bry3t,
  And trewelovus bytwene;
Ther was at hur testere   1485
The kyngus owne banere:
Was nevere bede rychere
  Of empryce ne qwene!

XCIV.

ffayre schetus of sylk
Chalk-why3th as the mylk,   1490
Quyltus poyned of that ylk,
  Touseled they ware;
f. 91.] Coddys of sendall,
Knoppus of crystal,
That was mad in Westfal   1495
  With women of lare.
Hyt was a mervelous thing
To se the rydalus hyng,
With mony a rede gold ryng,
  That home up bare;   1500
The cordes that thei one ran,
The duk Betyse hom wan,
Mayd Medyore hom span
  Of meré maydenus hare.

XCV.

Ryȝt abouȝt mydnyȝt,   1505
Seyd syre Degrivaunt the knyȝt,
" When wolt thou, the worthely wyȝt,
    Lysten me tyll?
ffor love my hert wyl to-brest,
When wylt thou bryng me to rest?   1510
Lady, wysse me the [best],
    Gyf hyt be thi wyll."
The burde answered [ffulle ȝa]re,
" Nevene thou that eny mare,
Thou schalt rew hit ful sare,   1515
    And lyke hit ful ylle!
Sertes tho thou were a kyng,
Thou touchest non swych thing,
Or thou wed me with a ryng,
    And maryage fulfylle!   1520

XCVI.

" Leff thou well, withouten lette,
The ferste tyme y the mette,
Myn hert on the was sette,
    And my love on the lyȝth!
I thouȝthe never to have non   1525
Lord nothur lemman,
Bot onely the allon;
    Caysere ne knyȝth,

Kyng ne non conquerour,
Ne no lord of honour, 1530
And gyff hit were the emperour,
    Most proved of my3th!
ffor-thy, syre, hald the stylle,
Whyle thou get my fadyr wylle."
Tho kny3t sentus ther-tylle, 1535
    And trouthus thei ply3th.

XCVII.

And whan here trouthus was ply3t,
Than here hertus were ly3t,
Was never faukons off fly3t
    So fayn as thei ware! 1540
Thai lay doun in ther bede,
In ryche clothus was spred,
Wytte 3e wel, or thei were wed,
    Thei synnyd nat thare.
Than spekus tho burd bry3th 1545
To syre Degrivaunt the kny3th,
" Swet syre, come ylke ny3th,
    And loke how we fare."
And the bold bachylere
Toke the damysele clere; 1550
This thei dured that 3ere,
    Thre [qua]rterus and mare.

XCVIII.

At [mis]somere in a nyȝth,
The [mo]ne schone wondur bryȝt,
S[ire De]grivaunt and hys knyȝt   1555
    [Bu]sked to wend.
[The] douȝty knyȝthus so fre
[L]yȝth doun by a tre;
A prout fostere gane tham se
    A-laund ther thei lende,   1560
And folewes hom thorw the wode,
Alle the weyes that thei ȝode,
And how thei passed the flode,
    The knyȝthus so hende:
So dud the weyt one the walle,   1565
The eorlus owne mynstralle,
Sey tham wende to the halle,
    And wyst nevere what hyt mende.

XCIX.

The pypere haldus hys pays,
Tyl no man he hyt says;   1570
Mynstralus shuld be cortays,
    And skyl that thei ben.
The foster tolde anone-ryȝthus
To the eorle and hys knyȝthus,
How thei come armede a-nyȝthus,   1575
    As he hadde y-sen.

The styward was chyvalrous,
Syre Eymour the kayous,
With offycyrus of that hous,
  Cruel and kene,   1580
A gret buschement hadde he [sette],
Ther the fostere hom mette,
And thou3th syre Degrivaunt lette
  The wayes ful grene.

C.

The stywarde heylé hath swornne,   1585
" And he come be thi[s thor]nne,
We bryng hys he[d on th]e mornne,
  And non othur mede ! "
Dame Myldor w[ist righte no]u3th
What al this folkys [had th]ou3th,   1590
She wende no man that ha[d ben]e wrou3th
  Hadde wyten of hore [dede] ;
And syre Degrivaunt hadde y-[hi3t]h,
Ry3th as he was trew kny3th,
To speke with Myldore that ny3th,   1595
  And lette for no drede.
God, as 3e are muchel of my3t,
Save syre Degrivaunt the kny3t,
And lene hym grace in that fy3t
  Wel for to spede !   1600

CI.

Syre Degrivaunt at evene-ly3th
Armede hym and hys kny3th,
And toke on privayly for sy3th
  Two gownes off grene;
Nothur schelde ne spere,   1605
Ne no wepen of werre,
Bot twey swerdus thei berre
  Off Florence ful kene.
Whan thei come to the slac,
The bolde buschament brac,   1610
......nte opone stedus bac
  [Ar]mede ful clene.
[Si]re Degrivaunt, ys nat to layne,
[B]lyve hys swerde had y-drayne,
He that come formast was slayne 1615
  In the schaw schene!

CII.

Whan thei syre Degrivaunt mett,
Sevene sperus one hym y-sett
Evene in hys bassonett
  Brasten a-two.   1620
Some bare hym thorw the gowne,
Some brast one hys haberjowne;
Hys sqwyere was borne downe,
  Hys swerd cast hym fro!

Then syre Degrivaunt ly3th, 1625
And rescowede hys kny3th,
And cryed to hym an hy3th,
    " Why wolt thou lyen so?"
f. 92.] The beste stedes that thei hade
   By the scholders he them scharde, 1630
He was never so hard y-stade
    ffor wele ne for wo!

CIII.

The styward syre Eymere
Com a lytyl to nere,
Hys hede by the colere 1635
    He kerves away!
The body syttys opon the hors,
Hyt was uncomely to the cors,
The stede stert over a fosse,
    And strykys a-stray; 1640
Y wyst never how hyt ferde.
He betus hom fast to the erthe;
With hys two-honde swerde
    He made swyche paye,
That syxty lay one the feld, 1645
Bothe with spere and with schelde,
That never wepen my3th [welde]
    Sen that ylke day!

CIV.

The panter, the botelere,
The eorlus cheff sqwyere, 1650
They lyes slay y-fere
    In the schawe schene!
Than the remenaunt fles
On the sort that thei sees,
And some lorkus undur tres 1655
    In slowes unshene.
Thonkede be Godes grace,
He has venkest hys face,
And made a chyvalrous chace,
    That crewel and kene! 1660
Nouʒth fourty fot fram the wal,
He slowe the marchal of the hal,
And other gode sqwyers with-al,
    Mo then fyftene!

CV.

By that hyt dawed ney day, 1665
By that he hade endyd this play,
Some scaped away,
    And many one was slayne.
Than sayd syre Degrivaunt the knyʒt,
"Here my trouthe y the plyʒt, 1670
I shal speke with Myldore to nyʒt,
    To dey in the payne."

Thei set here stedus ther thei stode,
And fayre passede the flode,
To the eorlus castel the[i] ȝode 1675
  The gatus ful gayn:
Than the lady so bryȝth,
ffayre she welcomed the knyȝth;
She had nat hard [of] hore fyȝth,
  Therof were thei fayn. 1680

CVI.

She had wondur in hyr wyt,
Why here clothus ware to-slyt,
As thei in holtus had byn hyt
  With dyntus of spere:
[The]re gay gownus of grene 1685
[We]re ful schamely be-sene;
" [Le]ve syre, where have ȝe bene,
  [ȝoure] clothus to tere?"
The knyȝth sat semely,
And seide tyl hyre prevely, 1690
" We sey [never selly]
  That sh[oulde us] auȝth dere;
But as [we came] by a thorne,
Thus [wer ou]re gownus to-torne;
We sh[alle] have new to-morne, 1695
  We [cownt]e hyt not a payre."

CVII.

The kniȝ[th] had fouȝten as a bare,
[Therfore h]ym fersted ful sare;
[The m]ayde brouȝth hym ful ȝare
    [The s]pyces and the wyn.   1700
Dyverse spices thei ete,
And ofte with mowthus thei mete;
Sche brouȝthe hem Vernage and Crete,
    And wyne of the Reyne.
He toke his leve at the day   1705
At mayde Myldore the may,
ȝet wyste ho note of the fray
    That she hard sethȝne.
The knyȝth one wendys his way,
Ther the dede men lay,   1710
And seyde soufft one his play,
    " ȝondur was stout hyne!"

CVIII.

Thei brouȝthe home on bere
The stywarde syre Eymere,
And other gode sqwyere,   1715
    Off fryththus unfayne;
And cryide out over alle,
Both gret and smalle.
The mayde wyndus to the halle
    Tythyngus to frayne.   1720

The ȝorle spekus to that fre,
" Y wytt syr Degrivaunt and the
The slauȝthtur of my mené;
  This is ȝowre false treyne!
By Hym that dyede one tre,   1725
This day shall thou [dede] be!
I wat welle hit [es he]
  That hase the be[layne!]"

CIX.

The mayde answer[d agayne],
And seis, " Peter! I [am f]ayne 1730
And that knyȝth be [not slay]ne;
  What bote is that I lye?
Sene he was chosene my fy[rst] make,
Shall I hym never forsake,
What dethe that I take,   1735
  Or dool that I drye!"
Thane the ȝorle wax wode,
And swore be bonus and blode,
" Mete ne drynk shall do me gode,
  Ar I se the dye!"   1740
The contasse knelyd tho anone,
" Gode schylde, syr, that he be slone,
We hade never chyl[d] but hyr one!"
  And cryid ful hye.

CX.

The contasse cryed, " Alas ! 1745
ʒe have ben to longe foas ;
Wycked tonge hit mas,
  God ʒif them shame !
I dare savely say,
The knyʒth went one his way, 1750
[O]wre men by-sett hym the way,
  [He] was not to blame.
[W]as not his fosteres slayne
While he werred in Spayne?
Hys woddys and hys waryne, 1755
  ʒe made hem alle tame !
Y rede ʒe sauʒthle with the knyʒt,
That is so hardy and wyʒth,
And graunte hym Myldore the bryʒt,
  By hyr ryʒth name !" 1760

CXI.

Than spekus Myldore the bryʒth,
" Ther was but he and a knyʒth,
I spake with hym this nyʒth,
  Why shulde I spare?
He is my love and my lorde, 1765
Myne hele and my counforde,
Hyt is gode ʒe be a-corde,
  And ʒowre wyllus ware :

f. 93.] And giff ȝe holde us a-gret,
　　　　Shall I never ete mete." 1770
　　　　The ȝorl for angur gane swet,
　　　　　　And syȝthe ful sare;
　　　　" Damesele, ar thou be spylte,
　　　　I forgiff the the gylte,
　　　　Hit is alle as thou wylte; 1775
　　　　　　I cane say na mare!"

CXII.

Bylyve a lettur ho sent,
Thorw the ȝorlus comandment;
A messengere has hit hent,
　　With tythingus ful newe. 1780
She bad hym cume prively
With hys best chyvalry,
As he was gode and douȝty,
　　And holdene for trewe;
And hoe shuld make swych acord 1785
Bytwene hym and hur lorde,
That shulde be a coumforde
　　Tyl alle that hym ever knewe.
ȝet syr Degrivant hym drade,
Syxty knyȝthus he clade, 1790
Tyl the ȝorlus castel he spede
　　By the day dewe.

CXIII.

The ȝorle metus hym withoute,
With sterne knyȝthus and stoute,
Wonder low gane he loute,   1795
      And haylus that hende;
And says, " Syr, by Goddys grace,
Welcome to this place,
We have ben to longe fase,
      Now wyl I be thi frende."   1800
Prively that no man wyste,
Alle wrongus was redressyde,
The ȝorle and he hade keste,
      And to chaumbur thei wende.
Withoutyne more rehersynge   1805
Made was the sauȝthlynge,
And grauntyd hym Myldore the ȝinge
      Tille hys lyves ende.

CXIV.

Was never sych a purvyaunce
In Englond ne in Fraunce,   1810
As was at sir Degrivaunce
      And Myldore the schene;
Ther com tyl hir weddyng
An emperoure and a kyng,
Erchebyschopbz with ryng   1815
      Mo then fyftene!

The mayster of hospitalle
Come over with a cardinalle,
The gret kyng of Portyngalle,
  With kny3thus ful kene; 1820
Alle the lordys of that lond
War holy at that offorand,
And ladyes, y undyrstond,
  Emperyce and qwene!

CXV.

One the Trinité day, 1825
Thus in romance herd y say,
He toke hyr in Godus lay
  Tylle hys lyvys ende.
Solempnely a cardinal,
Revescyd with a pontifical, 1830
Sang the masse ryal,
  And wedded that hend.
And the ryche Emperoure
Gaff [hyre] at the kyrke dore,
With w[orschy]p and honoure, 1835
  As f[or hi]s owne frend;
And [sa]w gold in that stonde,
W[elle] a thowsand pounde,
Lay glyterynge in the gronde,
  By the way as thei wende! 1840

CXVI.

Thane the semelede the sale,
Kyng and cardynale,
And the emperoure ryale,
    With barnus ful bolde;
So dud ladies bydene,   1845
Both contasse and qwene,
Bry3th burdys and schene,
    Was joye to beholde!
ffro the mangery bygane,
Wyne in condyt rane   1850
Redy tyll ylke mane,
    Take ho so wolde.
Ther com in a daunse
ix. doseperus of Fraunce,
Methow3th syche a countynaunce   1855
    Was joye to beholde!

CXVII.

I knewe never mane so wys,
That couth telle the servise,
Ne scrye the metys of prys
    Was servyd in that sale;   1860
Mynstrallus hade in halle
Grete gyftys withalle,
Ryche robus of palle,
    With garnementus hale.

Ylke day that fourtyny3th 1865
Justyng of seryd kny3thus,
To revele ho best my3th,
      With wyne and with ale;
And one the fyftethe day,
Thus in romaunce h[erd I] say, 1870
They toke here leve and [wen]t here way,
      Thys worthely to w......

CXVIII.

Al thei maketh ther avaunt
Off the lord syre Degrivaunt,
Cortays and avenaunt, 1875
      Ladyes and kny3thus.
He gaff stedus that stound
Worth a thousand pound,
Withouten haukes and hound,
      And faukun of fly3thus! 1880
The 3orle dyede that same 3ere,
And the contasse clere;
Bothe hore beryelus y-ffere
      Was gayly bydy3th.
Syr Degrivaunt bylefte ther eyre, 1885
With brod londus and faire,
Was never perus my3th hym peyre
      By resone ne ry3th.

CXIX.

Thrytty wyntur and mare
Thei lyvede to-gydur without care,   1890
And sevene chyldur she hym bare,
    That worthly in wede;
And sene sche dyed, y undurstond,
He seysed hys eyre with hys hond,
And went into the Holy Lond,   1895
    Hevene be hys mede!
At Port-gaff was he slone,
ffor-justyd with a Soudone:
Thus to Gode is he gone,
    Thus douȝty in dede!   1900
Lord Gode in Trinité
Gyff hem Heven for to see,
That loves gamene and gle,
    And gestus to fede!

NOTES.

SIR PERCEVAL OF GALLES.

L. 1. *Lef, lythes to me.*—A curious short poetical tale in MS. Porkington 10, commences with the same two lines. Lady C. Guest, in her abstract of this romance in the Mabinogion, p. 398, prints *gef* instead of *lef*, although there is a facsimile from the original MS. on the opposite page.

L. 7. *He dranke water of the welle.*—Compare l. 2208. Chaucer probably had these lines, or at all events an English translation of Perceval, in his mind, when in Sire Thopas he says,

> " Himself *dronke watir of the well*,
> As did the knight sir Persivell,
> So worthy undir wede."—ed. Urry, p. 146.

the last line possibly alluding to the rough dress of young Perceval, but the phrase is common in the old romances.

L. 11. *Miche wirchippe he wane.*—" And as for syr Percyvale, he was called that tyme of his tyme one of the best knyghtes of the world, and the best assured." *Morte d'Arthur,* ii. 89.

L. 18. *He was doughty of dede.*—Compare Mr. Robson's Romances, p. 75,—

> He is duȝti of dede,
> A blithe burne on a stede.

L. 21. *Thare-fore kyng Arthoure.*—Dr. Forman, in a curious paper on giants, gives the following minute account of King Arthur :—

" King Arthur was fifteen foote longe in the prime of his yers. His

berd was somwhat flaxen, but gray in his age, and longe and very brod;
his hair gray and longe, a brod full face, somwhat ruddy, a gren juell in
his right eare ; a thick body, well made, and a full breste ; a ringe on the
lyttel finger on his right hand set with rubies. He slue fifty knightes with
his own handes that dai he was slaine. He had five thousand and more
men in his last battell, and Murdred had four thousand, and all were slaine
ner Glassenbury. And he was buried by Morgan le Fay in the valle of
Avalen. He was buried fifteen foote depe." *MS. Ashmole*, 802, f. 56.

To this we may add the annexed account of the pretended moving of the
bones of Arthur and his queen. A similar narrative is given in Robinson's translation of Leland, 4to. Lond. 1582; and this may be taken from
the last mentioned writer, or perhaps from Giraldus Cambrensis.

" Memorandum quod anno Domini millesimo trecentesimo sexagesimo
octavo, et regni regis Edwardi tertii post conquestum quadragesimo secundo,
tempore reverendi in Christo patris dompni Walteri de Moncton, Dei
gratia tunc abbatis monasterii beatæ Mariæ Glastoniæ, qui novum opus
chori feliciter consummavit, nono Maii amotus fuit tumulus incliti regis
Arthuri ab inferiore parte chori versus magnum altare, propter ampliationem
chori et honorem regis ejusdem ; in cujus tumulo inventæ fuerunt duæ
cistæ, ossa regis ejusdem et Gwinaveræ uxoris suæ continentes, sigillis regis
Edwardi, avi regis Edwardi tertii post conquestum, et Alienoris uxoris suæ,
filiæ domini Ferandi regis Hispaniæ, consignatæ, cedula testimoniali supposita super cistam regis Arthuri, cujus tenor sequitur in hac forma ;

" Hæc sunt ossa nobilissimi regis Arthuri et Gwenaveræ reginæ uxoris
ejusdem, quæ anno Incarnationis Dominicæ millesimo ducentesimo septuagesimo octavo, xiij. kalendis Maii, per dominum Edwardum regem Angliæ
illustrem, hic fuerunt sic locata, præsentibus domina Alienora ejusdem
domini regis consorte et filia domini Ferandi regis Hispaniæ, domino Amadeo
comite Sabaudiæ, domino Henrico de Lacye comite Lincolniæ, domino
Willelmo de Midilton, Thoma Norwicensi electo, magistro Thoma Beck
tunc archidiacono Dorsetiæ et prædicti regis thesaurario, et multis aliis
magnatibus Angliæ." *MS. Ashmole*, 826, f. 107.

L. 24. *To have and to holde.*—The same phrase still remains in our
prayer-book, in the order for the Solemnization of Matrimony.

L. 77.   *Thay gaffe syr Percyvelle the gree,*
              Beste worthy was he.—

Compare the following lines, which are spoken of Chaucer :—

> Off poetes ever hase he the gree,
> For of alle moste worthy is hee.
>
> *MS. Fairfax* 16.

L. 83.   *Knyghte.*—In MS. *kynghte,* an irregular form for the Lincoln MS., but we find it frequently in Sir Degrevant, and later transcripts.

L. 85.   *And therfore gyffes he a gyfte.*—That is, makes a resolution. See l. 163. So Gower,

> " My fader god, y ȝeve a ȝyffte,
> Alle ydelle was y never ȝytt,
> Ne never schalle wyle y may go."

L. 249.   *By grete Godd.*—The writer here forgets that Perceval was then ignorant of the very name of the Almighty, and could not consistently make such an oath.

L. 261.   *One was Ewayne fytz Asoure.*—See the note on l. 264, and and Syr Gawayne, p. 312. It is not improbable that *vytt* in Syr Gawayne, p. 188, may be a corruption of *fitz,* rather than of *wytt,* somewhat boldly conjectured by Sir F. Madden.

L. 262-3. *Gawayne with honour, and Kay.*—The courtesy of the first of these knights, and the malice of the other, are frequently alluded to by the old romance writers, as we shall presently have occasion to notice more particularly. They are mentioned together in the prologue to the *Cursor Mundi,* which contains a curious and well-known enumeration of the old romances. In a fragment of a MS. of the 15th century in the Ashmolean Museum, these same lines, with several curious alterations and additions, are introduced; and the reader may not be displeased to have the opportunity of comparing the variations. The writer, however, does not extend his censure to the Gesta,—*Non reprehendo eos qui Gesta Imperatorum.* It is as follows:—

> But alle meschef in this werld here
> Is for-thi that men willen nouȝt lere

To kepe the sevene sacramentis,
Ne be obedient to the comandementis;
Ful litil pris sette thei therby,
But suwen evere her owen foly.
Hem is levere for to here
Romaunces, many and sere,
Of Alisaundre the Conquerour;
Of Julius Cesar the Emperour;
Of Grece and Troie the stronge stryve,
Ther many a thowsand lesten her lyve;
Of Bruyt, that barn bald of hand,
The firste conquerour of Engeland;
Of kyng Arthurgh that was so riche,
To whom in hys tyme was non liche;
Of ferlies that to his kny3ttis felle,
And adventuris, as 3e han herd telle,
As of Gawayn and Kay, and othere stable,
Whiche that weren of the rounde table;
How kyng Charlis and Rouland fau3t,
With Sarasyns wolde thei nou3t sau3t;
Of Tristem and of his lief Isot,
How he for hire bicom a sot;*
Of Odan and of Amadas,
How Dydan di3ed for Ennyas;
Of Felice and of Dymmafon,
That litil profit hangeth uppon;
Of Pirremus and Tysbese,
Ther was gret sorwe, withoute lese;
Of Paris and of Elyna,
Achilles and Pollexina.
Storis also of serkyn thyngis,
Of prince, prelatis, and of kyngis;
Sangis faire of selcouth ryme,
Englisch, Frensch, and Latyne,
To rede and here ilk man is prest,
Thise thyngis that hem liketh best,

* *i. e.* a fool. The incident here alluded to does not occur in the metrical romance of Tristrem, printed by Sir Walter Scott from the Auchinleck MS., but it is found in the Anglo-Norman version in the Douce MS. Curious pictures illustrating this romance are contained in MS. Addit. 11,619.

> As ȝeddyngis, japis, and folies,
> And alle harlotries and ribaudies;
> But to here of Cristis Passioun,
> To many a man it is ful laytsom.
> *MS. Ashmole* 60, f. 4, 5.

L. 264.—*Alle were of his kynne.*—If the prose Merlin can be depended upon, the Ewayne just alluded to may have been the natural son of King Leodagan, for, according to that authority, Ywain, the natural son of King Urien, had the seneschal's wife for his mother, and consequently was not related to Arthur. In the Mabinogion, p. 299, however, he is mentioned as the son of Urien, who, by-the-bye, had two sons of that name. Gawayne was the eldest son of Loth, sovereign of the province of Lothian and the adjacent territories, by Anna, half-sister of Arthur; and Kay was Arthur's foster-brother. It ought to be added that the various authorities frequently differ in some of these particulars.

L. 281. *Wilke of ȝow alle three.*—The following corresponding passage is given from the French romance, and I regret that space has not permitted more illustrations from the same source :—

> Fait li valetz, en qui jeo croi,
> N'estes-vus Deus ? Nenil, parfoi.
> Qui estes donc ? chevaler sui.
> Onc mès chevaler ne conui,
> Fait li valetz, ne nul ne vi,
> N'onques mais parler n'en oi;
> Mais vus estes plus beals que Deus;
> Car susse-jeo ore autre tiels,
> Ausi luisanz e ausi faitz.
> A cest mot près de li s'est traitz
> E li chevalers li demande,
> Veis-tu hui en ceste lande
> Cink chevalers e treis puceles ?
> Li valetz à altres noveles
> Enquere e demander entent,
> E à sa lance sa main tent,
> Si la prent, e dit, Beals sire chiers,
> Vus qui avez non chevalers,
> Que est çeo que vus tenez ?
> Ore sui-jeo mult mal asenez,

> Fait li chevaler, çeo m'est vis,
> Jeo quidoe, beal douz amis,
> Noveles aprendre de toi,
> E tu les viels oir de moi.
> Jeo le te dirrai, çeo est ma lance.
> Dites-vus, fait-il, que hom lance,
> Si com jeo faz mon gaveloz?
> Nenil, valetz, tu ies tut sotz,
> Eins en fiert l'en tut demanois.
> Donc valt mielz li uns de ces trois
> Gaveloz que vus veez çi,
> Que quant que jeo voil jeo en occi
> Oiseals e bestes al bosoign,
> E si les occi de si loign
> Cum l'em porreit un boson traire.
> Valet, de ce n'ai-jeo que faire;
> Mais des chevaliers me respont :
> Di moi si tu siez où il sont,
> E les puceles veis-tu.
> Li valetz al pié de l'escu
> Le prent, e dit tut en apert,
> Ceo que est, e de quei vus sert?
> Valet, fait-il, est-çeo gabez,
> Que en autres noveles me menez,
> Que jeo ne te quier ne demand ?
> Jeo quidoe, si Deus m'amend,
> Que tu noveles me deisses,
> Einz que de moi les apreisses;
> E tu viels que jeo t'en apreigne.
> Jeo le te dirrai coment que preigne,
> Car à toi volentiers m'acord.
> Escuz ad non çeo que jeo port.
> Escuz ad non ? voir, fait-il,
> Ne l' doi mie tenir vil,
> Car il m'est tant de bone foi
> Que si nuls lance on trait à moi,
> Encontre tost l'escuz se trait,
> Ceo est li servises quil me fait.
>
> *Perceval, MS. Arundel, Coll. Arm.* 14, f. 151.

L. 291.   *To Gawayne that was meke and mylde.*—Gawayne's constant character in the old romances, of course not including Malory's "Morte d'Arthur." See Rom. of the Rose, 2209, and Tyrwhitt's Glossary, in v. *Gawain.* Sir F. Madden has given a complete history of this hero, drawn up with great care. It is curious to observe the conflicting accounts of the place of his death and burial. Aubrey, in his "Naturall History of Wilts," MS. in the Library of the Royal Society, p. 356, says, "On the south-downe of the farme of Broad-Chalke is a little barrow called Gawen's barrow." This does not seem to have been yet quoted, and may be thought worthy of notice. The following account of him is given by Dr. Forman:—

"Sir Gawine was twelve foote and a half in height, more slender made then Sir Tristram, and had longe leges, a red head and a red berde, a taunie face, longe hair on his head, and his berd was longe and thine, many wrinkells in his forhed and aboute his eyes. He drawed in his nether lip, that his teath were seen over yt; a full round black ey, a long straight nose, a peace of flesh cut awai on the ball of his right chek. The top of the lyttell finger of his lefte hand was cut away; a great voice, a mild countenance."—*MS. Ashmole*, 802.—(Cf. Sir F. Madden's Introduction to Syr Gawayne, pp. xviii. xix.)

L. 306. *Thi prowde wordes pares ay.*—According to the prose Merlin, Kay "was a strong, and a puissant, and a good knight, and, if it had not been that his mode of speech was annoying and displeasing to other knights, they would have esteemed and praised him still more than they did; but his companions forsook him because of his language, which misbecame him. This blot Keux took from the nurse who suckled him, for he had it not from the nature of his mother, who was a good dame and a wise." See Southey's notes to Malory, p. 459.

L. 346. *Bot stert up one the mere.*—It was considered a disgrace in the days of chivalry to ride on a mare, which is no doubt the reason young Perceval is here represented as riding on one, to add to the absurdity of his appearance. See the Mabinogion, p. 401. There is a curious passage to this effect in Bede's Hist. Eccl. lib. ii. c. 13, in the account of the Pagan priest Coifi destroying the temple at Godmundingham, when he was converted to Christianity,—" Statimque, abjecta superstitione vanitatis, rogavit sibi regem arma dare et equum emissarium, quem ascendens ad idola destruenda veniret; non enim licuerat pontificem sacrorum vel arma ferre vel præter in equa equitare." The carrying arms and riding on a *horse* are here distinctly pointed out as the characteristic of a soldier early in the seventh century. It is probably for this reason that in drawings and illuminations of the Middle Ages, where knights are represented mounted, even in tapestry worked by ladies, the sex of the animal is generally made very apparent. In the romance of Richard I. the Sultan of Damascus rides on a mare when he encounters that sovereign. See Warton's Hist. Engl. Poet., ed. 1840, i. 167.

L. 397. *Lyttille thou cane of nurtoure.*—It may be worth noticing that in the original MS. at the bottom of this folio, the scribe (probably Thornton) has written, " Here is ix. qwayers."

L. 471. *A tokyne to wedde.*—Compare l. 2150. A ring was sometimes a betrothing present. Compare the following passage in the Erle of Tolous, 394—405; after the Empress had given the Earl a ring,—

> The erle wente home to hys ynnys,
> And grete yoye he begynnys,
>   When he founde the rynge;
> Yn hys herte he waxe blythe,
> And kyssyd hyt fele sythe,
>   And seyde, " My dere derlynge,
> On thy fyngyr thys was,
> Wele ys me y have thy grace
>   Of the to have thys rynge;
> Yf evyr y gete grace of the quene,
> That any love betwene us bene,
>   *Thys may be oure tokenyng.*"

L. 495. *Kyste the forhevede of the kynge.*—A similar occurrence, as Dunlop observes, is mentioned in the old ballad of King Estmere,—

> Then they pulled out a ryng of gold,
>   Layd itt on the porters arme;
> " And ever we will thee, proud porter,
>   Thow wilt saye us no harme."
>
> Sore he looked on Kyng Estmere,
>   And sore he handled the ryng,

> Then opened to them the fayre hall yates,
> He lett for no kind of thyng.
>
> Kyng Estmere he stabled his steede
> Soe fayre att the hall bord;
> The froth that came from his brydle bitte,
> Light in King Bremor's beard.
>
> Saies, "Stable thy steed, thou proud harper,"
> Saies, "Stable him in the stalle;
> It doth not beseeme a proud harper
> To stable him in a kyng's halle."
>
> *Percy's Reliques*, ed. 1840, p. 18.

So also Sir Degrevant rides up " to the des" of the Duke Betyse. See the present volume, p. 227.

L. 512. *Thi mete or thou schere.*—This line by mistake is repeated in the original MS.

L. 626. *Als he says that this made.*—That is, wrote. To *make*, to write poetry, as in Piers Ploughman, p. 229. See Mr. Wright's note, and Jamieson, in v. *Makar*.

L. 688. *Whose browes schalle blakke.*—That is, who shall be slain, or vanquished. The same phrase occurs again at l. 1056.

L. 853. *Than wist Percyvelle by thatt.*—That is, he then knew her to be a witch, not *intuitively*, as Lady C. Guest says in her abstract of this romance in the " Mabinogion," p. 404; for l. 826 does not necessarily imply that knowledge on the part of Perceval.

L. 855. *Wylde fyre.*—Not the destructive element formerly so called, but merely a fire rudely made in the open air.

L. 895. *In his armes.*—That is, in the arms of the red knight.

L. 1017. *For thenne.*—Perceval here begins speaking. These two speeches are so arranged, that it is not very easily seen where the first ends and the second begins.

L. 1024. *He nykkes hyme with nay.*—A common phrase of denial in old poetry. Compare Wright's Lyric Poetry, p. 32; Audelay's Poems, p. 28; Sir Gawayne, gloss. in v. *Nikked*; Percy's Reliques, ed. 1840, p. 17.

L. 1409. *Mekyl.*—This word is defaced in the manuscript, but compare l. 1131.

L. 1698. *Then.*—" The," MS.

L. 1705. *His awnne wille.*—Perhaps the word *at* ought to be inserted before this passage. The reverse of f. 172 is very pale.

L. 1775. *Lesse.*—This word is partly defaced in the manuscript.

L. 1802. *Lemmane.*—In Shakespeare's time the word is generally used in a bad sense, as in Twelfth Night, Act. ii. Sc. 3, and other places. See Dyce's Remarks, p. 75, where a wrong reference is given. The following extract from a very rare tract will give a good illustration of the word :—

"One demanded of his friend what was the reason that when a man meets a light wench, the first word he speaks to her is, Gentlewoman, will you goe to the taverne? O, saies the other, a *leman* is never good without wine."—*Jests to Make you Merie*, 1607, p. 4.

Mr. Collier, in his Shakespeare, vol. iii. p. 353, gives another apposite quotation of similar import. At p. 240 the term is applied to a man.

L. 1803. *The heghe dayes of ȝole.*—The feast of Christmas was generally celebrated with great splendour. See Sir F. Madden's notes to Gawayne, p. 310 ; Sir Amadas, 141.

> Hit wes at Cristemasse,
> Nouther more ne lasse,
> The kyng made feste
> Of his knyhtes beste.
> *Kyng Horn*, 805-8.

L. 1864. *Ne to.*—" Ne the to," MS.

L. 1884. *His hede one hir kne.*—By no means an unusual position in the old romances. See an extract from Syr Gawayne at p. 302. So in the ballad of Thomas and the Elf Queen,—

> She seid, " Thomas, I the hight,
>   Come *lay thy hed on my kne,*
> And thou shalle se the feyrest sight
>   That ever saw men of the cuntré."
> *MS. Bibl. Publ. Cantab.* Ff. v. 48, f. 118.

L. 1946. *He swere.*—Here, and in a few other places, it is difficult to mark the speeches precisely, the narrative being confused with them. See also Isumbras, 469.

L. 2041. *That.*—This word, although in the manuscript, does not appear to be necessary to the construction of the sentence.

L. 2044. *Whenne he.*—These words are repeated in the manuscript.

L. 2064. *Hys.*—" He," MS.

L. 2189. *Ne I ne salle.*—So in the MS. though the first two words appear to be redundant.

L. 2275. *Certenly.*—The MS. erroneously reads " centenly."

L. 2284. *Thus gatis endis hee.*—The epitaph of our hero, as given in the French romance, recommends him to posterity for his achievement of the San Graal, in which he is said to have been assisted by two other knights. No mention of the circumstance occurs in this abridgement. The epitaph is as follows,—

>Cy gist Parceval le Gallois,
>Qui du saint Graal depieça
>Les avantures acheva.
>
>*Hist. Lit. de France,* tom. xv. p. 250.

L. 2285. *Now Jhesu Criste.*—The third romance in Mr. Robson's collection, p. 93, concludes in a similar manner.

SIR ISUMBRAS.

L. 1.—There are several early copies of this romance, differing considerably from each other. It would take too much space to point out all the numerous variations, but the commencing lines of each are here given.

>Hynd in halle, yf ye wylle here
>Of elders that befor hus were,
> That gud were at nede;
>Jhesu Cryst, Heven kyng,
>Grant us alle thi blessyng,
> And heven tylle owre mede.
>I wylle yow telle of a kny3t,
>That was bothe hardé and wy3th,
> And du3ty in every dede;

His name was callyd Ysumbras,
For seche a kny3th as he was
  Non levys now in lede.
      MS. Advocates' Library, Edinburgh, 19. 3. 1.

[H]ende in halle, and 3e schalle here
Of elders that be-forne us were,
  There lyves how thei dyde lede,
I schall 3ow telle a wonder case,
Frendes, herkyns how it was,
  3e schalle have heven to mede.
I wylle 3ou telle of a knyght,
That was both herdy and wyght,
  A dughty mone he was;
Syre Isombras was his name,
A nobulle knyght of ryalle fame,
  And stronge in every cas.
      MS. Ashmole 61, f. 9.

Hic incipit de milite Ysumbras.

Hende in halle, and 3e wole here
Off eldres that before us were,
  [There lyves how thei dyde lede.]
Jhesu Cryst, hevene kyng,
Geve hem alle hys blessyng,
  [And heven tille theire mede.]
I wole 3ow telle off a kny3t,
That was bothe hardy and wy3t,
  And doughty man of dede;
Hys name was callyd sere Ysumbras,
So dou3ty a kny3t as he was,
  Ther levyd non in lede.
      MS. Coll. Caii Cantab. 175.

Here begynneth the hystorye of the valyaunte knyght syr Isenbras.

Lordynges, lysten and youe shall heare
Of elders that before us weare,
  That lyved in lande and deede;
Jesu Chryste, heaven kynge,
Graunte them all hys dere blessinge,
  And heaven to theyr meede.

SIR ISUMBRAS.

Ye shall well heare of a knyght,
That was in warres full wight,
    And doughtye of hys deede;
Hys name was syr Isenbras,
Manne nobler than he was
    Lyved none with brede.
        MS. Douce 261, f. 1.

God that made both erthe and hevene,
And alle this worlde in deyes sevene,
    That is fulle of myʒthe;
Lende us alle his blessynge,
Lasse and more, olde and ʒynge,
    And kepe us day and nyʒte!
I wylle ʒou telle of a knyʒte,
That dowʒty was in eche a fyʒte,
    In towne and eke in felde;
Ther durste no man his dynte abyde,
Ne no man aʒeyn hym ryde
    With spere ne with schelde.
        MS. Cotton. Calig. A. II. f. 128.

He that made both erthe and heven,
And al this worlde in daies sevyn,
    That is ful of myghth;
Send us alle his blessyng,
Las and more, olde and yong,
    And kepe us day and nyght!
Y wol you telle of a knyght,
That was douʒty in ilke fight,
    In towne and eke in fielde,
Ther durst no man his dynt abide,
    With spere ne with schilde.
Man he was riche y-nowe,
Ox to drawe in his plowe,
    And stedis in his stalle;
Man he was curteyse and hynde,
Every man was his frende,
    He was lord of alle.
Curteis and hynde he was,
His name was clepid sir Isombras.
        MS. in the Royal Library at Naples.

The MS. last mentioned is described by Mr. Laing in the Reliq. Antiq. vol. ii. p. 67, and was apparently transcribed in the year 1457. To the same gentleman I am indebted for the account of the Edinburgh manuscript, and to the Rev. J. J. Smith for the extract from the copy in Caius College library. The copy in MS. Douce 261, was written as late as 1564, and probably copied from one of the early printed editions. Copland printed an edition of Isumbras, in 4to. no date, a copy of which is in Garrick's collection of old plays in the British Museum; and one leaf of another early edition is preserved in Douce's library. Copland's edition has been reprinted by Mr. Utterson, in his " Select Pieces of Early Popular Poetry," 8vo. Lond. 1817, i. 77–112.

L. 16. *So was he bothe faire and heghe.*—The Caius College MS. reads,—

> " He was long man and heye,
> The fayreste that evere man seye,
> A gret lord was he."

L. 19. *He luffede glewmene.*—In the romance of Sir Degrevant are several curious notices of gifts to minstrels. See the present volume, pp. 180, 225, 254, and Sir Eglamour, p. 176. In " Manners and Household Expenses," p. 141, is printed a curious roll containing the names of the minstrels who played before Edward I. at Whitsuntide in 1306. They were divided into ranks, five of them being styled kings, each of whom had five marks. At p. 110 of that work mention is made of a valuable gold cup being given to a minstrel; but robes and garments were the more usual presents. See Piers Ploughman, ed. Wright, pp. 259, 274. The title of king * was merely a popular dignity, and does not necessarily imply a greater degree of " dignity" than Ritson allowed the old " glewmene." Like all professors of music and the light arts, the majority of them were always a wandering class of persons, whose manner of living must generally have excluded them from any rank in society. They were, however, of " great admittance" in the houses of the nobility. We have a curious

---

* Percy, in the notes to his Essay, has collected much curious information relative to this title of the ancient minstrels.

instance of this in the romance of Orpheo, who, when he is questioned by the king of the fairies how he had the audacity to enter his palace, replies,—

> "Syre," he seyd, "I trow wele
> I ame bot a pore mynstrelle,
> And ȝit it ys the maner off us,
> For to seke to gret lordes hous;
> And thoff we not welcome be,
> ȝit we behovyth to profere our gle."
>
> *Sir Orfeo, MS. Ashmole* 61.

The reader will find a curious passage concerning the courtesy of the minstrels in the present volume, p. 242. For further information on the subject, see the dissertations of Percy and Ritson, Warton's Hist. Engl. Poet. ed. 1840, ii. 309, &c. In the sixteenth century, the order had fallen altogether into disrepute. See Northbrooke's Treatise, ed. Collier, p. 114.

L. 28. *Knave.*—" Gentylle," Edinburgh MS.

L. 47. *Werldes wele.*—This line is omitted in the Cottonian MS.

L. 71. *Whate wondir was thofe hym ware wo.*—This line occurs in other romances, as in Octavian, MS. Cantab. Ff. ii. 38, f. 84.

L. 79. *His bestes werene alle slayne.*—The Cottonian MS. reads, " Thy menne be manye sleyne ;" and Copland's edition, " With venyme are they blowe," *i. e.* swelled. See Malone's Shakespeare, ed. 1821, xii. 425.

L. 102. *Alle als nakede als thay were borne.*—That is, they jumped out of their beds to avoid the fire. See l. 104. The custom of sleeping without night linen has been so frequently illustrated, that a passing remark is all that is necessary. From the Norman Conquest to the time of Elizabeth night-gowns were scarcely known, both sexes sleeping quite naked. The Saxons, however, appear to have worn close shirts at night. See Wright's notes to Piers Ploughman, p. 557; Sir F. Madden's notes to Havelok, p. 198; Strutt's Dress and Habits of the People of England, ed. Planché, ii. 224; Reynard the Foxe, ed. Thoms, p. 175.

L. 107. *He levyde so.*—" That erste were," MS. Cott.

L. 110. *That.*—MS. Cott. has " be," which seems a better reading.

L. 123. *Offe.*—Perhaps we should read " tooke offe."

L. 126. *His.*—" Hir," MS.

L. 137. *I ȝowe.*—" Clerkes," Cott. MS.

L. 143. *And made thaire, &c.*—The Cottonian MS. reads, " And forth they wente her waye."

L. 152. *For saynte charité.*—That is, " for holy charity." Later writers made a kind of allegorical saint of Charity. Ophelia sings, " By Gis and by Saint Charity," in Hamlet, Act iv. Sc. 5; and Spenser writes,—

> " Ah ! dear Lord, and sweet Saint Charity !
> That some good body once would pity me."

L. 185. This line, which is wanting in the original, has been supplied from the Cottonian MS. For *went* read *wente*.

L. 298. *Hir to.*—Perhaps we should read " to hir."

L. 300. *Schortly naye.*—So, in an inedited tale,—

> When they come in hys presence, they seyde hym *schortly nay*,
> For they knewe full wele hys lyfe, how he had levyd many a day.
> MS. Cantab. Ff. ii. 38, f. 52.

L. 343. *Mete and drynke.*—This and the next triplet are transposed in the MS., but their present arrangement is necessary to the sense.

L. 347. " The kny3te was kalled a3eyne," Cott. MS.

L. 376. *The knyghte folowed, &c.*—The Cottonian MS. reads,—

> " The kny3te was both hende and fre,
> And folowed hym to the Grekes see,
> Ther over the gryffyn he fly3e."

L. 380. *Ofte was that, &c.*—A kind of proverbial phrase occurring in other romances. It is repeated at p. 119.

> Ofte hade Horn be wo,
> Ah never wors then him wes tho.
> *Kyng Horn*, 119–20.

L. 398. *For mete, he sayde.*—Perhaps it would be better to transpose this and the next line.

L. 498. *A palmere lyke.*—Compare the romance of Octavian, l. 1357.

> Pyk and palm, schryppe and slaveyn,
> He dyghte hym as palmer, queynt of gyn.
> *Weber's Met. Rom.* iii. 214.

L. 520. *Hir.*—So in the MS., but probably an error for *his*.

L. 548. *Inne stode.*—The MS. reads "stode inne," but the metre requires our arrangement.

L. 606. *To put the stane.*—A game of considerable antiquity. Fitzstephen mentions casting of stones among the amusements of the young Londoners in the twelfth century. See Langtoft's Chronicle, p. 26; Octavian, 895; Strutt's Sports and Pastimes, ed. 1830, p. 75; Sir F. Madden's notes to Havelok, p. 192.

L. 786. *He gafe a lande.*—In Copland's version, the distribution to the three sons is more particularly described. See Mr. Utterson's reprint, p. 112.

SIR EGLAMOUR OF ARTOIS.

L. 1. *Jhesu Lorde.*—Copland's edition of this romance commences as follows:—

> Jesu Christe, heaven king,
> Graunt us all his deer blessing,
>   And build us in his bower;
> And give them joy that wil here
> Of elders that before us were,
>   That lived in great honour.
> I will tel you of a knight,
> That was bothe bolde, hardy and wight,
>   And stife in every stoure;
> Where any deedes of armes were,
> The price he wan with sheeld [and spere],
>   And ever he was the flower.

L. 54. *Thou walkyst, &c.*—The Lincoln MS. reads, "In the es alle my trayste." The Cotton. MS. agrees with our text.

L. 70. *Dere frende, &c.*—The Lincoln MS. reads,

> Mayster, the mane that hewes over hey,
> The chyppis fallis in his eye,
> Thus fallis it now and ay was.

L. 73. *Than umbe-thenke.*—" Umbe than thenke," MS.

L. 96. *God a mercy.*—" Gramercy," Lincoln and Cott. MSS.

L. 97. *Answeryd.*—" Sykud," Cott. MS.

L. 107. *And sethen reches in my lyfe.*—The Lincoln MS. reads, "And rejoyse hir alle my lyfe."

L. 111. *Hur byrdys.*—The Lincoln MS. has " the beryns," a much better reading.

L. 120. " He lyves not tylle ny3th," Cott. MS.

L. 122. *Hys.*—" Goddis," Linc. and Cott. MSS.

L. 128. *Yustynge.*—" Batelle," Linc. MS.

L. 139. *Then seyde that, &c.*—This and the next line are repeated shortly afterwards. The Lincoln MS. gets rid of the repetition by the following reading,—

> For na man ne wald scho spare,
> Tille his chambir for to fare,
> Whare that he gane lende.

L. 141. *That doghty was evyr.*—Six lines are here omitted in the Cottonian MS.

L. 153. *Sore.*—The Lincoln MS. reads " sare," which agrees better with the rhythm.

L. 177. *Thys ys the fyrste tyme, &c.*—The Lincoln MS. with more elegance reads, " For 3e come never are here."

L. 191. *Over the rever wynde.*—Compare Sir Thopas,

> He couthe hunt at the wilde dere,
> And ride *an-hawkyng by the rivere.*—ed. Urry, p. 145.

L. 195. After this line the Lincoln MS. reads,—

> Appone the morne whenne it was daye,
> Syr Eglamour tase the waye
> Tille a revere fulle ryght.

L. 201. *Anone betwene them twoo.*—Instead of this and the three following lines the Lincoln MS. reads, " Be that it neghede to nyghte."

L. 211. *Oon.*—Perhaps we should read " oon of."

L. 213. *Awnturs.*—The Lincoln and Cotton. MSS. read " owther," which is probably correct.

L. 222.   Read, "Vowche ye hur safe on mee."
L. 239.   *Hardely.*—"Savely," Cott. MS.
L. 247.   *Aftur mete, &c.*—The Lincoln MS. reads,

>After mete, als I ȝow saye,
>Syr Eglamour he tase the waye
>   To telle that lady free.

L. 256.   "Or thy jurnay shalle alle passe," Cott. MS.
L. 266.   *Seynt Poule.*—Omitted in Lincoln MS.
L. 285.   "A nobille dere he chese," Linc. and Cott. MSS.
L. 288.   "And repid hym of his resse," Lincoln MS.
L. 300.   *The pryce he blewe fulle schylle.*—The note blown at the death of a hert, or rather "three notes or more," as in Sir Tristrem, p. 280,

>He blewe priis as he can,
>Thre mot other mare.

According to another authority, the *pryce* consisted of "two longe notes and the rechate." See notes to Syr Gawayne, p. 322.

L. 312.   *Two.*—"A," Lincoln MS.
L. 330.   *He was xl.*—The Lincoln MS. reads "feftene," and the Cottonian MS. "fyfty."
L. 337.   *Contré.*—"Courte," Lincoln MS.
L. 343.   *Make we mery, &c.*—These three lines are omitted in the Lincoln MS.
L. 345.   "Of syr Eglamour that he has tane," Cott. MS.
L. 347.   *Jeaunt.*—The Lincoln and Cotton. MSS. read "journaye," which is clearly right.
L. 355.   *Passen a fote longe.*—The Lincoln MS. reads "are halfe a ȝerde lange."
L. 362.   *A fowrtenyght.*—"A monethe," Lincoln MS.
L. 364.   *None.*—"Evyne," Lincoln MS.
L. 381.   *Morne-drynke.*—Ellis makes excellent use of this incident. These old romancers had the practice of investing all their characters with habits of every-day life. The present passage may be illustrated by the notes of the commentators on Falstaff's "morning draught of sack" in Malone's Shakespeare, ed. 1821, viii. 85.

L. 399. *More.*—" Somdele mare," Lincoln MS.

L. 408. *The boke of Rome thus can telle.*—The Lincoln MS. reads, " Als that the buke us tellis." The Cottonian MS. agrees with our text. The word *Rome* is, perhaps, a corruption of *Roman*, the romance. Compare the following passage :

<blockquote>
And by-japeth the folk
With gestes of Rome.
Piers Ploughman, ed. Wright, p. 453.
</blockquote>

So, in l. 1339, we are told that " In *Rome* thys geste cronyculd ys," while the printed edition reads, " In *romaunce* this chronicle is." A " grete boke of Rome " would therefore be a large volume of pieces written in the French or Romans language. Sir F. Madden seems to think the phrase may refer to a history treating of Roman affairs. See his Gesta Romanorum, Introd. p. iv. But then we find it in pieces that have no reference whatever to either the genuine or fabulous history of Rome.

L. 427. *That bryght.*—" The crest," Cott. MS.

L. 445. *Thou haste ben, &c.*—The Lincoln MS. reads,

<blockquote>
For thou hase foghttene with a bare,
That hase walked fulle wyde-whare.
</blockquote>

L. 452. *Syxty.*—" Fourty," Lincoln MS.

L. 455. *Ryche.*—" Renyche," Linc. and Cott. MSS.

L. 460. *Ye, he seyde.*—The Cotton. MS. here omits six lines. The Lincoln MS. reads,

<blockquote>
" ȝa, so helpe me God," the knyght says,
" I hafe foghetyne foure dayes,
And never a fote I flede."
</blockquote>

L. 469. *Awntour.*—According to this copy Eglamour, for some reason not explained, thinks proper to conceal his name from the king. See also ll. 493, 562, 602. This is not, however, the case in all the copies, nor does Ellis allude to it in his abstract of this romance. Sir Awntour is probably one form of the generic title *Sir Aunterous* applied to an adventurous knight, as in Sir Degrevant, 1369, and other places. One of Arthur's knights, however, was so called. See Ellis's Met. Rom., ed. 1805, i. 268.

L. 479.   *That sorowe doyth,* &c.—The Lincoln MS., which here agrees with the Cottonian copy, reads,

> My dogheter that es of mekille pryde,
> He wolde hir hafe me fra."

L. 501.   *Hyt ys my fee.*—After this line the Lincoln MS. reads,

> The kyng said, " So God me save,
> Of the bare what thou wille have,
> Thou hase it boghte fulle dere."

L. 510.   *Sone.*—" Here," Lincoln MS.   The three lines following are omitted in the Lincoln and Cotton. MSS.

L. 531.   *Mete.*—" Matens," Cotton. MS.

L. 532.   *He.*—We should probably read " had."

L. 548.   *Spote.*—" Spotted," Cotton. MS.

L. 555.   *Bore.*—" Bare," Cotton. MS.

L. 568.   *Syr Egyllamowre.*—This and the two next lines follow l. 561 in the Lincoln MS.

L. 572.   *Leve.*—" Helme," Lincoln and Cott. MSS.

L. 605.   *Organata.*—Omitted in Lincoln MS.

L. 608.   *Yf you yoye of yowre chylde.*—So in the play of the Shepherds,

> No, so God me blys, and *gyf me joy of my chylde.*
> *Towneley Mysteries,* p. 113.

L. 614.   *Wound.*—The Lincoln and Cotton. MSS. read " dynt," which is clearly necessary for the rhyme.

L. 634.   *Thys ys the,* &c.—This triplet is omitted in the Lincoln MS.

L. 637.   *Into the londe of Artas.*—This and the eight following lines are somewhat different in the Lincoln MS.—

> By the sevene wekes were comene to ende,
> In the lande of Artas gunne he lende,
>   Whare that the erle was;
> Alle bot the erle were fulle fayne
> That he in qwerte was commene agayne,
>   In trouthe* bathe mare and lesse.

---

* In a somewhat later hand "the cowrt" is written above these words, apparently an altered reading.

> Cristabelle, whytt als fame,
> Herde telle that he was comene hame;
> Tille his chambir scho mad hir ȝare.

L. 655. *The.*—The Lincoln MS. reads, "The erle was thane fulle wondir wa." The Cott. MS. agrees with our text.

L. 664. *The erle seyde.*—This triplet is omitted in the Lincoln MS.

L. 668. *xij.*—The Lincoln MS. reads " feftene," which does not agree with l. 682 ; the Cotton. MS. reading " twenty " in the latter place.

L. 669. *My boonys for to reste.*—The Lincoln and Cotton. MSS. here insert three lines,—

> Thorowe prayere of those gentylle-mene,
> Twelve wokes he gaffe hym thane,
> No langere wold he freste.

L. 680. *He schewyd hur hys fylle.*—The Lincoln and Cotton. MSS. read, " that hym byfelle."

L. 687. " And to her for to be trewe," Cott. MS.

L. 699. *xv.*—" Seven," Cotton. MS.

L. 703. *Syr, that was never.*—Instead of this and the five following lines the Lincoln and Cotton. MSS. read,

> The knyght says, " I hafe donne poyntes twa,
> Thorow the myght of God I salle do ma,
> Or elles ende ther for aye."

L. 709. *Afturward.*—" Aftyr mete," Cotton. MS.

L. 715. *Golde.*—" Good," Cotton. MS.

L. 718. " And als the buke of Rome says," Lincoln MS.

L. 720. *Bolde.*—" Wylde," Lincoln MS. After this line the three following occur in the Lincoln MS.

> The knyght wendis on his waye,
> Herkyns now I salle ȝow saye,
> To seke that dragone bolde.

L. 723. " Knyghttis lay fulle colde," Lincoln MS.

L. 734. *Nyght.*—I had thought we might read *knight,* but the Lincoln MS. has, " Ever agayne *evyne* mare and mare."

L. 737. *The tonge.*—" His tayle," Lincoln MS.

L. 740. *Hedd.*—The Lincoln MS. reads " hevede," which agrees better with the rhyme. In later copies of these romances the change of the language frequently causes injudicious alterations.

L. 756. " The worme has evylle endyng," Cott. MS.

L. 765. *They dydd the bellus to rynge.*—The following lines are here inserted in the Lincoln MS., which complete our imperfect stanza:—

> The emperour with hym tuke hym hame,
> Octoveane was his name,
>   A lord of gret honour;
> Bot alle that ever saw his hede,
> Thay sayd that he was bot dede,
>   This knyght syr Eglamour.

L. 768. *Dawntowre.*—" Dyature," Lincoln MS.

L. 772. *The ryche emperoure.*—Line 772 to l. 795 inclusively are wanting in the Lincoln MS., and l. 778 to l. 783 in the Cotton. MS.

L. 787. *Thre hundurd.*—" Forty fote," Cotton. MS.

L. 792. " To the day of dome," Cotton. MS.

L. 801. *As whyte as whallys boon.*—That is, as white as the bone or tooth of the walrus. Compare the note on l. 922. Numerous instances of this phrase might be quoted from the old poets; *e. g.*

> Lady, *as whyte as whales bone,*
> There are thyrty agaynst me one.
>   *Squyr of Lowe Degré*, 537.

> This is the flower that smiles on every one,
> To show his teeth *as white as whales bone.*
>   *Love's Labour's Lost*, v. 2.

L. 808. *A wyght.*—" Ne whyte," Cotton. MS. The Lincoln MS. differs somewhat in the subsequent lines. See f. 143, v°.

L. 822. *Alle.*—" Sche," Cotton. MS.

L. 825. *For fendys on the flode.*—The nickers of Beqwulf and Layamon. In a well-known passage of the latter poet, a lake in Scotland is thus described:—

> That is a seolcuth mere
> I-set a middel-ærde,
> Mid fenne and mid ræode,
> Mid watere swithe bræde,
> Mid fiscen and mid feoȝelen,
> Mid univele thingen.
> That water is unimete brade,
> Nikeres ther bathieth inne;
> Ther is alvene ploȝe
> In atteliche pole.

L. 829. *Hur chaumbur women.*—This triplet is placed after l. 813 in the Lincoln MS.

L. 832. *The lady syghed*, &c.—Instead of this triplet, the Lincoln MS. reads as follows,—

> Now leve this knyght syr Eglamour,
> And speke we of this lady whytt als flour,
>   So wilsome wayes scho ȝode;
> The lady dryves nyght and daye
> Tille an ile, als I ȝowe saye,
>   Thare wilde bestis gane lende.

L. 836. *A kende.*—" Byggyd," Cotton. MS.

L. 848. *A gryffon seythe*, &c.—The Cotton. MS. reads,—

> That wroȝte the ladé both day and nyȝt
> Sorow and mykylle wo.

L. 853. *He stroke on*, &c.—This triplet is omitted in the Lincoln MS.

L. 857. *Fowndyn.*—" Wonden," Cotton. MS.

L. 858. *A ryche.*—The article here seems redundant, and it is omitted in the Cotton. and Lincoln MSS.

L. 861. *Hys eyen grey as crystalle stone.*—Grey eyes were formerly considered a great mark of beauty, though perhaps from the comparisons "grey as glass," and "grey as a cristal stone," Malone may be right when he says the term meant what we now call a blue eye. See Malone's Shakespeare, ed. 1821, iv. 118. Thus in Venus and Adonis,—

> Her two *blue* windows faintly she upheaveth:

and in the same poem the eyes of Venus are termed *grey*,—" Mine eyes are *grey* and bright." This may, however, be merely accidental, and when we find Chaucer writing, " Her eyen graie as is a faucon," there cannot be much doubt which colour is intended. See Romaunt of the Rose, 546, the original French being *vers*. So in the romance of Launfal,—

> Alle yn fere they made proferynge
> That Launfal schuld hys lemman brynge:
>   Hys heed he gan to laye.
> Than seyde the quene, " Wythout lesynge,
> Yyf he bryngeth a fayrer thynge,
>   Put out my eeyn gray."
>   *Ritson's Met. Rom.* i. 205.

L. 865. *For that he fro the gryffon felle.*—" It must be left," says Ellis, " to the sagacity of the reader to find out the language in which the word Degrabell has this meaning." See his Met. Rom., ed. 1805, iii. 275.

L. 873. *To day.*—" Thys chyld," Cotton. MS.

L. 876. *Large.*—" Long," Cotton. MS.

L. 877. *Kepe we.*—" Leve ȝe," Cotton. MS.

L. 883. *Reste then odur.*—The Lincoln MS. reads, " maste ne rothir," which is evidently correct, and reminds one of the account of Prospero's " rotten carcase of a boat" in the Tempest, Act i. sc. 2. It is possible, however, that the original reading may have come nearer the following line,—

> The chylde had nodur reste ne ro.
>   *Octavian, Camb. MS.* 1192.

L. 884. *Storme.*—The Lincoln MS. has " wawe," a better reading.

L. 885. " That sterynly on hir chippe gunne stryfe," Lincoln MS.

L. 888. " Agayne those carefulle clevys," Lincoln MS.

L. 895. *To the see.*—" And se," Cotton. MS.

L. 904. *Make we mery*, &c.—This triplet is omitted in the Lincoln MS. The Cotton. MS. reads as follows,—

> Makes mery, for yt ys beste,
> For this ys the laste geste
> That I now take in honde.

L. 913. *A fayrer thyng say y never none.*—The Virgin is often re-

CAMD. SOC.   2 o

presented of extreme beauty. So when Thomas of Erceldoun first beheld the fairy queen,—

> He seid, " Yonde is Mary of myght,
> That bare the childe that died for me ;
> But I speke with that lady bright,
> I hope my hert wille breke in thre !"
> *MS. Cantab.* Ff. v. 48, f. 116.

L. 920.   *Gentylle.*—" Swete," Cott. MS.

L. 922.   *To the schyp*, &c.—The Lincoln MS. reads,—

> The lady whytte als wallis bone,
> He bade hir speke in Goddis name ;
> Agaynes hym up scho rase.

L. 925.   From this line to l. 937 inclusive, the Lincoln MS. is imperfect, the leaf being torn.

L. 930.   *Sche them tase.*—" Sche with hem gose," Cott. MS.

L. 945.   *A mantelle y ovyr hym drewe.*—The following lines are here inserted in the Lincoln MS.—

> The wynde rase and to a roche us bare,
> A fowle tuke my sqwyere thare,
> Sothe-weste with hym he droghe.

The Cott. MS. reads the third line thus,—

> " And swyftly away hym threwe."

L. 953.   *On.*—" Of," Cott. MS.

L. 961.   *xij.*—" Seven," Cott. MS. The Lincoln MS. is here torn, by which ll. 961 to 964 are partially wanting, and ll. 965 to 974 are altogether lost.

L. 965.   *Come to londe.*" Comand," Cott. MS.

L. 966.   " With the dragons hede," Cott. MS.

L. 975.   *Tyde.*—" Stede," Cott. MS. So also in the similar tale of Torrent of Portugal,—

> Whan he herd telle of Desonelle,
> Swith on sownyng there he felle
> To the ground so cold.—p. 88.

L. 985.   *Hedd.*—" Hevede," Lincoln MS.

L. 986. " And whare es myne that I here levede," Lincoln MS.

L. 990. *Gone to the see.*—" In the see," Cott. MS. When Eglamour implores mercy on his wife's soul, he seems to have forgotten the virtue of the magical ring he had presented to her previously to his last journey. See l. 715.

L. 1000. *The gentyls that.*—" Gentylle men," Cott. MS.

L. 1006. *And he that was,* &c.—Instead of this triplet, the Lincoln MS. reads as follows,—

> Alle that were sembled ylke one,
> He gafe thame for to lyfe appone,
> For Cristabelle saule to mone.

L. 1020. *Bolde.*—" Stren," Cott. MS. The next triplet is omitted in the Lincoln MS.

L. 1025. *Kyng.*—" Knyg," MS.

L. 1059. " Therfore for to kythe," Cott. MS.

L. 1065. In Lincoln MS. ll. 1069—71 are omitted, and the following lines are here inserted,—

> The messangere spake with blythe chere,
> The kynge of Israelle comes here
> With a fulle faire semblee.

L. 1081. *Y prey the,* &c.—The Lincoln MS. reads,—

> " Gud syr, we pray, gyf that we myghte,
> Of ȝowre nece [to] hafe a syghte."

L. 1087. *By rome some stode.*—" Hys sone stode stylle," Cott. MS. The Lincoln MS. agrees with the one quoted, omitting " stylle."

L. 1096. *The.*—" On," Cott. MS.

L. 1100. *Crystyabelle.*—" His modir," Lincoln MS.

L. 1102. *Kynges.*—" Knighttis," Lincoln and Cott. MSS.

L. 1104. *Fulle dere.*—" There," Cott. MS.

L. 1105. *Seyde.*—" Weschen," Cott. MS.

L. 1111. *Trumpus in the felde rose.*—In the Lincoln MS. this triplet is inserted after l. 1119, and in place of it we read,—

> The kyng of Egippe gunne hym hy
> Into a faire felde witterly,
> With many a doghety knyghte.

L. 1136. *Hys owne modur he hath wedd.*—A similar incident occurs in one of the stories in the Gesta Romanorum, and in the romance of Sir Degoré. See Sir F. Madden's Gesta Romanorum, p. 520.

L. 1140. After this line, the Cotton MS. has the following,—

> Sche grette, therfore, and sorow gan make,
> And alle was for hyr sones sake,
> A grett swonyng sche made;
> " What now ?" sayde he, " my lady clere,
> Why makes thou so sympulle chere ?
> Methynkes thou art not glade."

And the Lincoln MS. inserts the following,—

> He sayd, " Qwair now, my lady dere ?
> Why makis thou thus febille chere ?
> Methynke als thou had thoghte."

L. 1143. After this line, the Lincoln MS. inserts the following,—

> In a skarelett mantille was he wondene,
> And with a gold girdille bowndene,
> That fulle richely was wroghte.

L. 1150. " I wote he toke hem out fulle rathe," Cott. MS., a reading which is preferable to that in our text, " there" and "thare" being unnecessary to the construction of the sentence, besides destroying the rhyme. The Lincoln MS. reads,—

> Thay tuk thame owte thane fulle rathe,
> The mantille and the gyrdille bathe.

L. 1159. " Lo, sone, alle that we done hade," Cott. MS.

L. 1189. *Hys maste of.*—This and the next line are transposed in the MS. The Lincoln MS. reads,—

> In the see so gryme and balde,
> Purtrayede of a nyghte alde.

L. 1191. " In every poynte to the ye," Cott. MS.

L. 1201. *Schaftys.*—" Renges," Cott. MS.

L. 1203. " Thaire-selvene made tham ȝare," Lincoln MS. The Cotton. MS. agrees with our text.

L. 1206. After this line, the Lincoln MS. reads,—

    Haurauds of armes bygane to crye,
    Grete lordis fulle rathely
     Into a felde so brade.

L. 1211. *Aventurs.*—" Aunterus," Cott. MS.

L. 1216. *He sende a knyght*, &c.—Instead of this triplet the Lincoln MS. reads,—

    His fadir hovede and byhelde
    How he fellid in the felde
     The knyghtis alle bydene.
    His sonne hym sawe and rade hym tille,
    Said, " Syr, why hovys thou sa stille
     Amange thir knyghtis kene ?"

L. 1219. *He seyde, syr recreawntes.*—The Lincoln MS. reads, " Syr, he said, atrayed I es ;" and the Cotton. MS., " He seyde hit ys for werynesse." Our text seems sufficiently intelligible, and is another instance of the generic appellations before alluded to. See the note on l. 469.

L. 1225. *Answeryd.*—" Smylyd," Cott. MS.

L. 1231. *Be Jhesu.*—" Peter," Lincoln MS. The same variation occurs at ll. 241, 919. This triplet is nearly lost in the Lincoln MS., the leaf being torn.

L. 1245. *Hymselfe allone.*—" Fulle gayne," Cott. MS. This triplet and the next are transposed in the Lincoln MS.

L. 1251. Six lines are here inserted in the Lincoln MS.—

    " Say forthe, whils he was thare,
    That wille juste or turnay any mare,
     He wold be aunterous by the rode !"
    His sone said, " Ne ware his swerd so brighte,
    Alle the day myght I with hym fyght,
     Thofe he were werse thane wode !"

L. 1258. *Two kyngys the deyse began.*—That is, took the principal places at the high table. See l. 1099. Compare the Cokwoldes Daunce, 200,—

" Than seyd thei all at a word,
   That cokwoldes schuld *begynne the bord*,
   And sytt hyest in the halle."

L. 1267.   Instead of ll. 1267 to 1281, the Lincoln MS. has,—

   Knawlege of hym gunne scho taa,
" Swete syr, how felle it swa,
   That thay were broghte to grownde?"
" Dameselle, I was in a ferre contré,
   Hir fadir dide thame to the see,
      With the wawes to confounde!"
In swouny[n]ge thane felle that lady free,
" Welcome, syr Eglamour, to me!
      Dere hase thou boghte me are!"
Grete lordis thane told scho sone,
How that scho to the se was done;
   Thay wepede bothe lesse and mare!
" In the wawes grete and graye,
   A gryffone bare my childe awaye!"
      Gentille-mene thane syghede sare.

L. 1272.   " Tho of a worme had a wonde," Cott. MS.

L. 1297.   Instead of ll. 1297 to 1305, the Lincoln MS. reads as follows :—

   Syr Eglamour prayed the kynges three,
   In Artasse at his weddynge to be,
      His lykynge for to have.
   Thay graunted hym bathe mare and lesse,
   The gret lordis that thare was,
      Thare Jhesu Crist thame save!
   Kynges and dukis, I undirstande,
   And gret lordis of other lande,
      Thaire stremours made thay fulle rathe;
   Trompis in topcastells thay rase,*
   Alle maner of mene to schippe gase,
      A comly wynd thame drave;
   Thorow the myght of God, this fayre navé
   Alle in lykynge passed the see,
      In Artasse up thay raffe.

* Compare l. 1072.

> The erle in his castelle stode,
> Gentille-mene sone to lande ʒode,
> Knyghtis to horse gan dryve.

L. 1312. The Lincoln MS. thus concludes, commencing its principal variations at this line,—

> And thus in Artasse are thay lent,
> Eftir the emperour thay sent
> To that mangery so free;
> And in alle the lande garte thay crye,
> Wha that wolde com to that mangerye,
> Dere welcome solde thay be.
> Sir Eglamour to the kirk gunne ga,
> Sir Degrebelle and Organata,
> The ladys bryghte of blee.
> The kyng of Iraelle sayd, "I ʒow gyffe
> Halfe my kyngdome whils I lyffe,
> Brouke alle wele after me."
> With myrthe that mangery was made,
> Fowrtty dayes it habade
> Amange thase lordis hende;
> And sy[th]ene, for sothe, als I ʒow saye,
> Ilk a mane tuke his awene waye
> Whare hym lyked beste to lende.
> Mynstrales were gyffene gyftis fre,
> That thay myght the better bee,
> The boldlyere for to spende.
> In Rome this romance* crouned es;
> Now Jhesu brynge us to his blysse,
> That lastis withowttyne ende! Amene.

Amen, Amen, par charyté. Amene.

L. 1327. *That were of ferre londe.*—Foreign minstrels were patronised to a large extent by the English and French courts. See Manners and Household Expenses, p. 141.

L. 1329. "In hert they were lyʒt," Cott. MS.

L. 1337. *iij. c.*—"An hondred," Cott. MS.

* Compare the romance of Torrent of Portugal, p. 112.

SIR DEGREVANT.

L. 15. *Myght sette a schafft of hys hond.*—Not an uncommon phrase in the old romances. So in Octavian,—

> Ther was no man yn hethyn londe
> *Myght sytte a dynte of hys honde.*
> MS. *Cantab.* 1064.

> Ther was no knight in Inglond
> That might a dint stond of his hond.
> *Horn Childe*, p. 292.

L. 18. *Gwennor.*—The Lincoln MS. spells her name *Gaynore,* as in various early authorities. So Skelton, i. 70.

> " And dame *Gaynour*, his quene,
> Was somwhat wanton, I wene."

The name of this queen seems to have passed into a kind of proverb in Shakespeare's time. See a passage in Love's Labours Lost, iv. 1, which the commentators might have illustrated by the following extract from Florio's " New World of Words," ed. 1611, p. 224,—" *Guinedra*, a word of mockerie for the Tartares queene or empresse, *as we say, queene Guiniver.*" Dr. Forman thus describes this celebrated sovereign,—

" Quene Guiniver, she was twelve foote longe, and went all in white; a longe lean visage, mixed of red and white, and a crown on her hed; a whitesh flaxen haire, a clear complection, a brod and hie forhed, a round forhed, graie eyes, a full round eye; a lyttle shorte nose and slender; a gren jewell in her lefte eare; a straight bodied gown of whit silk, and a whit mantell; a hie collor in her gowne, and a plain faling band, brod without lace, and her gown buttoned up close before. She had noe hoope, noe fardingalle; a smalle long hand. She lived almost a hundred years."—*MS. Ashmole* 802.

L. 26. *And ther nevew ffulle nere.*—The Lincoln MS. reads, " Ever he drewe hym fulle nere." This line, as given in our text, affords ground for conjecturing that the present romance might originally have concerned

Agravain, who was the son of King Lot, by Belisent, half-sister of Arthur, and consequently his *nevew*. At all events, Agravain, in the list of the Knights of the Round Table, is the only name that approaches *Degrevant*. See the British Bibliographer, i. 116-7. In two places in the Cambridge MS., the knight's name is written without the *d*; and, although I have restored the letter between brackets for the sake of uniformity, it is very possible that the English translator may have mistaken *d'Egrivauns* for the entire name. That it is a translation from the Anglo-Norman seems probable from the name being sometimes written *Degrevauns*, and *Degrewaunce*, as at p. 225, which in that language would be the form of the nominative case, whereas *Degrevaunt* is the accusative.

L. 31. *Mappe-mound.*—It would be difficult to say what authority is here indicated, if, indeed, it is not altogether fanciful. The *Mappa Mundi* mentioned by Maundevile, p. 315, seems to have been literally a map of the world. In Bernard's Catalogus Lib. Man. Bib. Angl. tom. ii. p. 85, mention is made of a MS. called, " *Mappa Mundi;* continet geographicam et historicam descriptionem Europæ, Asiæ, et Africæ; miracula mundi; historias diversorum temporum et locorum."

L. 37. *To play in a rote.*—Compare the following extract from an unpublished poem by Lydgate in MS. Fairfax 16, which contains notices of the musical instruments here mentioned,—

> For they koude the practyke
> Of al maner mynstralcye,
> That any mane kane specifye;
> For ther wer *rotys* of Almanye,
> And eke of Arragone and Spayne:
> Songes, stampes, and eke daunces,
> Dyvers plenté of pleasaunces,
> And many unkouth notys newe
> Of swich folkys as lovde trewe;
> And instrumentys that dyde excelle,
> Many moo thane I kane telle.
> *Harpys*, fythels, and eke *rotys*,
> Wel accordyng with her notys,
> *Lutys*, rubibis, and geterns,
> More for estatys than taverns:

> Orguys, cytolys, monacordys;
> And ther wer founde noo discordys
> Nor variaunce in ther souns,
> Nor lak of noo proporsiouns.

A similar enumeration occurs in the Squyr of Lowe Degré, p. 189-90.

L. 39. *And syngyng many suet not.*—Singing was considered a necessary accomplishment for a young man of rank in the days of chivalry. So in Ipomydon, 53,—

> Tholomew a clerk he toke,
> That taught the chyld uppon the boke,
> Bothe to *synge* and to read.

The acquirements of Horn are described as having been similar to those of Sir Degrevant,—

> Horn was bothe war and wise,
> At hunting oft he wan the priis,
> Loved he nothing mare;
> Harpe and romaunce he radde aright,
> Of al gle he hadde in sight
> That in lond ware.
> *Horn Childe and Maiden Rimnild*, p. 291.

L. 80. *Where they were.*—" Aywhare," Lincoln MS.
L. 91. *Hade halowed.*—" Hafe haldyne up," Lincoln MS.
L. 92. " With mekille melody," Lincoln MS.
L. 95.

> *In justus and on tornament,*
> *He whan evere the gre!*

Compare Horn Childe and Maiden Rimnild, p. 297,—

> At justes and at turnament,
> Whiderward so thai went,
> Ever thai gat the gre.

L. 96. " The knyghte was hardy," Lincoln MS.
L. 99. " Of brade londis and wyde," Lincoln MS.
L. 110. *In ffey.*—" Aye," Lincoln MS.
L. 131. " Fra Flaundres un-to Degranade," Lincoln MS.

SIR DEGREVANT.

L. 142. " The beste innes in ylke towne," Lincoln MS.

L. 149. " Alsua the sothe for to schewe," Lincoln MS.

L. 157. *And wyth sqwere*, &c.—The Lincoln MS. reads,—

> With a sqwyere he it sent,
> Of ten powndis worthe of rent;
> Forthe on his way es he went
> To wret his ansuare.

L. 160. After this line the Lincoln MS. has the following stanza, not found in the Cambridge copy,—

> The sqwyere wold noghte habyd,
> Bot forthe faste gunne he ryde
> Unto the palesse of Pryde,
>   Thare the erle wounde:
> Sone so he of hym had syghte,
> Sir Sere of Cypirs he highte,
> Was buskede with many knyghte
>   In the foreste to hunte;
> He was steryne and stowte,
> With many knyghtes hym abowte.
> The sqwyere thoght gret dowte
>   To byde his firste brount!
> Therefore wold he noghte lett,
> Sone with hym als he mett,
> Evene to hym was he sett
>   With his horse front.

L. 168. " And saide, Art thou wysse ?", Lincoln MS.

L. 180. *In herde is nat to hyde.*—Compare the romance of Octavian, Cambridge MS. l. 1305,—

> The folke seyde they were blythe
> To wynde to the batelle swythe,
> *In herte ys noght to hyde.*

Also, Horn Childe, p. 295,

> Horn, at thi wille schal it be,
> *In herd is nought to hide.*

L. 188. " For wathes walkes wyde," Lincoln MS.

L. 196. "Bothe awaye went," Lincoln MS.

L. 205. *Sir, and he may.*—This and the next three lines are omitted in the Lincoln MS.

L. 234. "Tille his rachis rebundys," Lincoln MS.

L. 241. *Sextene.*—The Lincoln MS. reads "sexty."

L. 244. "Of that contré," Lincoln MS.

L. 245. *Dukes.*—The Lincoln MS. reads "erle," which is no doubt the correct reading.

L. 271. *Wyghtly.*—The Lincoln MS. reads "worthy." The reader may, perhaps, trace in this scene some slight resemblance to the stirring ballad of Chevy Chase.

L. 281. *They stykene stedus in stoure.*—This and the next three lines are omitted in the Lincoln MS.

L. 285. *Ferisly.*—"Frekly," Lincoln MS.

L. 296. "So many doghety bledis," Lincoln MS.

L. 300. "Wyse undire wedis," Lincoln MS.

L. 308. "And stirred thame on thaire stedis," Lincoln MS.

L. 328. "And many worthy wight,' Lincoln MS.

L. 330. *Her.*—So in MS. for "his."

L. 331. *Sley.*—The Lincoln MS. has "fled," which is more likely to be correct.

L. 342. *Enleve.*—"Halfendele," Lincoln MS.

L. 346. *Fyene.*—So in MS., but perhaps an error for "fayne," as in the Lincoln MS.

L. 352. The couplet after this line is not found in the Lincoln MS., and the second line is written in a different and later hand. Compare the Rime of Sire Thopas,—

> Lo, Lordis mine, here is a fit;
> If ye woll any more of it,
> To tell it woll I fond.

L. 360. *Swouned.*—"Syghed," Lincoln MS.

L. 365. *Was.*—The MS. by mistake reads "wys."

L. 368. "Swilk maystrés to dyghte," Lincoln MS.

L. 399. *Hit semes as*, &c.—The Lincoln MS. reads,—

> That schames that ilk doghety
> Sir Degrevaunt dedis.

L. 407. "The semys to be envyous," Lincoln MS.

L. 409. *Yeff.*—"Sir," Lincoln MS.

L. 425. "Dame, I do ʒow owt of drede," Lincoln MS.

L. 428. *Y telle yow in ffay.*—This line and l. 432 are transposed in the Lincoln MS.

L. 456. *Was joy to behold.*—This line and l. 460 are transposed in the Lincoln MS. which is better than the arrangement in our text.

L. 479. *Wynly.*—"Unwynly," Lincoln MS.

L. 504. "Gate he untalde," Lincoln MS.

L. 515. *Berelle so bryght.*—Compare Wright's Lyric Poetry, p. 25,—

> Ichot a burde in a bour *ase beryl so bryht*,
> Ase saphyr in selver semly on syht.

L. 518. *Rode ronne hit ys.*—See the same work, p. 26,—

> Hire rode is ase rose that red is on rys,
> With lilye-white leres lossum he is.

See also King Horn, 15,—

> So whit so eny lylye flour,
> So rose-red wes his colour.

L. 521. *And.*—No doubt a mistake for "in," as the Lincoln MS. reads.

L. 522. *Of alle.*—"In haulle," Lincoln MS.

L. 523. *Y say hure ones one a walle.*—This is love on first sight most completely. The following singular confession from the mouth of a princess occurs in the romance of Sir Ferumbras,—

> Be ye not the duke of Burgoyne, sir Gy,
>   Nevewe unto king Charles so fre?
> Noe, certes, lady, it is not I,
>   It is yonder knight that ye may see.
> *A! him have I loved many a day,*
>   *And yet know I him nought;*
> For his love I do all that I maye,
>   To chere him with dede and thought.

L. 527. "And also in Floreyne," Lincoln MS.

L. 528. *Drere.*—A mistake in the MS. for *dere*.

L. 538. *Descure.*—The Lincoln MS. reads *discover*, which is curious, because the change would reasonably be expected to take place in the later MS. See my notes on Octavian, p. 63.

L. 546. *Whyegh as the seys ffame.*—We have already had this comparison in Sir Eglamour, p. 122. This phrase is by no means unusual in early English poetry.

L. 561. *Hys avyse.*—"Are ȝe wyse," Lincoln MS.

L. 573. *Other.*—"Sertys," Lincoln MS.

L. 595. *Or.*—"Are," Lincoln MS. This is of course the correct reading.

L. 600. *Knyȝth.*—"Knyghtis," Lincoln MS.

L. 625. *Sche come in a vyolet.*—This description of the lady's costume is so curious that the corresponding part of the Lincoln MS., which omits a few lines, and has several variations, is here given,—

>Scho come in a velvet,
>With white perle overfret,
>And faire were thay in sett
>   On everylke a syde;
>Alle of palle-werke fyne,
>Cowchide with newyne,
>Furrede with ermyne,
>   And coverde with pryde.
>To telle hir botonus were dure,
>Thay were anamelde with asure,
>With terepys and with tredoure
>   Glemerand hir syde.
>Hir here hillyd on holde
>With a coroune of golde;
>Was never made on this molde
>   So worthy ne so mylde.
>Scho was frely and fayre,
>Wele semyd hir achayere,
>With riche bosys and fayre,
>   And derely bydyghte

>   With a frountelle endent
>   With perle of the oryent,
>   Owt of Cyprese was it sent
>   To that bird brighte;
>   Her courchefs were curious,
>   Hir face gay and gracyous,
>   Sir Degrevaunt was amorous
>   And had joy of that syghte.

L. 644. *A.*—We should read *so,* as in the Lincoln MS.

L. 662. *They weshen and went to sette.*—It was the ancient custom to wash the hands before and after meals. See again in the present romance, l. 1392, and the note on Syr Eglamour, l. 1105.

>   Then the lordes that wer grete,
>   They wesh and seten doun to mete,
>   And folk hem served swyde.
>   *Emaré,* 218.

>   The wyȝe wesche at his wylle, and went to his mete.
>   *Syr Gawayne, ed. Madden,* p. 34.

L. 665. *Lordys.*—So in the MS., but we should no doubt read *bordys.*

L. 670. *Went to the orcherd to play.*—In the middle ages it was customary for the guests, after dinner was concluded, to amuse themselves in the fields and gardens. See Wright's Anecdota Literaria, p. 74. When the weather did not permit out-door amusements, chess, dancing, and similar pastimes engaged their attention. The following extracts are taken from the romance of Lanfal, in Ritson's Met. Rom. i. 198, 199:

>   And aftyr mete syr Gaweyn,
>   Syr Gyeryes and Agrafayn,
>   And syr Launfal also,
>   Wente to daunce upon the grene,
>   Unther the tour ther lay the quene,
>   Wyth syxty ladyes and mo.
>   *   *   *   *
>   They hadde menstrales of moch honours,
>   Fydelers, sytolyrs, and trompours,
>   And elles hyt were unryght;

> Ther they playde, for sothe to say,
> After mete the somerys day,
> All what hyt was neygh nyght.

L. 675. *And godlyche.*—" Ferly faire," Lincoln MS.

L. 678. *Jhesu save the and see.*—The Lincoln MS. omits the two last words. The phrase is not unusual in early poetry.

> Sire Edward of Carnarvan, *Jhesu him save ant see !*
> Sire Emer de Valence, gentil knyht ant free.
> *Wright's Political Songs,* p. 216.

> Now God you save our queene, madame,
> And *Christ you save and see;*
> Heere you have chosen a newe newe love,
> And you will have none of mee.
> *Percy's Reliques,* ed 1840, p. 102.

L. 683. *Lyff.*—" Lufe," Lincoln MS. In that MS. this and the previous line are transposed.

L. 705. *Of.*—" Fra," Lincoln MS.

L. 728. " On none on ȝone hille," Lincoln MS.

L. 730. *Pervenke of pryse.*—The Lincoln MS. reads " prudeste of pryse," and in the Cambridge MS. the first word is rather obscurely written, as if it were *perveulte*. The phrase corresponds exactly to the more modern one, " the pink of courtesy," as in Romeo and Juliet, Act ii. sc. 4.

> *Parvenke de pris* e sauntz pier,
> Sount femmes sur tote autre rien.
> *Wright's Lyric Poetry,* p. 7.

> The primerole he passeth, *the parvenke of pris.*
> *Ibid.* p. 26.

L. 747. *Hys.*—" ȝour," Lincoln MS.

L. 768. *To slep by my syde.*—For notices of the great laxity of manners among great families in the feudal times, see Wright's Anecdota Literaria, pp. 75-6. In the romance of Kyng Horn, Rimenild makes love in a manner that would not be considered very delicate in these days, and numerous references may be made to our early writers on the same subject.

L. 776. *In all the devyl way!*—A common expression in our early writers, equivalent to " In the name of the devil !"

> Come in, wiffe, *in twentye devilles waye!*
> Or elles stand their all daye.
> *Chester Plays,* i. 53.

> That all the worlde may say,
> Come downe, *in the devyll way!*
> *Skelton's Works,* i. 336.

L. 782. *Never.*—So in MS. but perhaps a mistake for *ever.* The Lincoln MS. reads " evermore."

L. 786. *Of thi gret cortesy.*—A leaf is here wanting in the Lincoln MS., and ll. 786—992 inclusively are lost.

L. 795. *Ther was no,* &c.—This and the next line are repeated at p. 236. We might perhaps read *deynteyus,* but the MS. in both cases has clearly þ.

L. 800. *And hys met schare.*—It was formerly considered a mark of respect or good will to carve a joint for a guest, a task which was often, if not generally, performed by ladies. See a very apposite passage produced by Boswell, in his edition of Malone, vol. viii. p. 38. " Your husband is wondrous discontented.—*Vit.* I did nothing to displease him; *I carved to him at supper time.*" *Vittoria Corombona.*

L. 832. *And honde I the hete.*—The same asseveration occurs at l. 1272, and in other places. See the note on l. 1396.

L. 860. *God for-ʒelde the!*—A common expression, which has even been retained by Shakespeare.

> *Gode the forʒilde,* quod the knyʒte.
> *Robson's Romances,* p. 78.

L. 976. *Stone.*—In case any one may compare the original MS. it may be necessary to observe that the mark over the *n* indicating the final *e* is so very indistinct as to be scarcely discernible.

L. 1005. *The ryche duk whan he eet.*—These four lines and the next are transposed in the Lincoln MS.

L. 1012. " And made so mekille draye," Lincoln MS.

L. 1013. *The eorl,* &c.—This and the next line are transposed in the Lincoln MS.

L. 1021. " The duke ansuerde this knyght," Lincoln MS. This is the better reading, as it avoids the repetition at l. 1025.

L. 1033. " Bot his bagges are blake," Lincoln MS.

L. 1041. The Lincoln MS. reads,—

> He es bowne to the felde
> Bath with spere and with schilde.

L. 1044. " Salle stande hym a strake," Lincoln MS.

L. 1046. *By seynt Martyn of Toure.*—St. Martin, Bishop of Tours, a very popular saint in the middle ages. See note on l. 1114.

L. 1061. *En.*—" Fulle," Lincoln MS. The next two lines are transposed in that MS.

L. 1065. The Lincoln MS. reads,—

> Thay that were aunterous bysyde
> In a cuntré fulle wyde,
> Thay come thedir that tyde
> That semblé to sene.

L. 1079. *Here shaunce.*—" His sant," Lincoln MS.

L. 1094. " Thay teme sadils fulle tyte," Lincoln MS.

L 1101. " Many armys were tynt," Lincoln MS.

L. 1114. " Be sayne Martyne of Towres," Lincoln MS.

L. 1130. *Contasse.*—" Kynge," Lincoln MS. See l. 1846.

L. 1136. *And.*—The Lincoln MS. inserts " alle " after this word, which appears necessary to the sense.

L. 1148. *Fourty.*—" For thre," Lincoln MS.

L. 1150. *At a wel feyre castel.*—This and the next line are transposed in the Lincoln MS.

L. 1154. This line is apparently corrupt. The Lincoln MS. reads,—

> That tournayde that daye withowte.

L. 1173. *Have.*—Perhaps *haw,* an exclamation; but the MS. is somewhat uncertain. This and the three lines following are omitted in the Lincoln MS.

L. 1224. *What the kny3the bare.*—Referring to the motto or legend on his arms, or, perhaps, the devices themselves.

L. 1230. " Nane wyste what he highte," Lincoln MS.

L. 1240. *Brem as a bare !*—A common simile in early poetry.

> Your bragynge bost, your royal aray,
> Your beard *so brym as bore at bay.*
> *Skelton's Works*, i. 187.

L. 1256. " As ever God me spede," Lincoln MS. The lines 1258 and 1259 are transposed in that MS.

L. 1260. " Thir worthily undir wedis," Lincoln MS.

L. 1261. *Sperus of pese.*—That is, spears without heads of iron. Justs were usually conducted with these weapons; but Degrevant promised three courses with " speres of werre," and three with " speres of pese." See l. 1215, and Strutt's Sports and Pastimes, ed. Hone, p. 141.

L. 1268. " On molde whenne thai mett," Lincoln MS.

L. 1285. This and the next line are transposed in the Lincoln MS., and so also are ll. 1294, 1295.

L. 1304. *I go.*—" He fare," Lincoln MS.

L. 1331. " Sythyne hamward he ʒede," Lincoln MS.

L. 1340. " Thare als thay tham levede," Lincoln MS.

L. 1359. *And up at the grese hoe him lade.*—The description of the buildings, food, ornaments, &c. which follow here are exceedingly curious, and might be commented upon at great length. The present passage may be illustrated by the following extract from Lydgate's Troy-Book :—

> Through many a halle, and many a riche toure,
> By many a tourne, and many divers waye,
> By many a gree y-made of marbyll graye.
> And in his chambre, englosed bright and cleare,
> That shone ful shene with gold and with asure,
> Of many image that ther was in picture;
> He hath commaunded to his offycers,
> Only in honour of them that were straungers,
> Spyces and wyne.

L. 1374. *Vyolete.*—The Lincoln MS. has " velvett," which is a better reading. The same variation occurs in other places.

L. 1377. This and the next line are transposed in the Lincoln MS.

L. 1385. *Towellus of Eylyssham.*—The Lincoln MS. reads " Alsame." Compare the following description in Syr Gawayne, p. 34,—

> Sone watz telded up a tapit, on trestez ful fayre,
> Clad wyth a clene clothe, that cler quyt schewed,
> Sanap, and salure, and sylver in sponez.

L. 1396. " On hand I the highte," Lincoln MS.

L. 1399. *Hastelettus.*—This term was applied to part of the inwards of a wild boar. It may, perhaps, bear another signification here. The following receipt is taken from Warner's Antiq. Culin., 1791, p. 33.

Hastletes of fruyt.

Take fyges i-quarterid, raysons hool, dates and almandes hoole; and ryne hem on a spyt, and roost hem; and endore hem as pome dorryes, and serve hem forth.

L. 1399. *Galantyne.*—Numerous meats and fowls were served up in galantine, a term still in use in French cookery. The following receipt is taken from Warner's Antiq. Culin., p. 64.

To make galantyne.

Take crustes of bred, and stepe hom in broken wyn or vynegar, and grinde hit smal, and drawe hit up with vynegur thurgh a streynour, and do therto pouder of galyngale, and of canel, and of ginger, and serve hit forthe.

L. 1405. *And newe.*—The Lincoln MS. reads " y-newe," which is probably correct.

L. 1407.

> *Ryche she tham drewe*
> *Vernage and Crete.*—

That is, she drew them rich Vernage and Crete. It does not appear that they bottled wine in those days. The wines here mentioned, and also those named at p. 236, are enumerated among others in a very curious poem called " Colyn Blowbolles Testament," a piece of an analogous character to " The Testament of Mr. Andro Kennedy " in Dunbar's Poems, i. 137—141.

> And what with gestes and with servauntes eke,
> I trow their shalbe an honeste felowship ;

Sauf first of all they shall have new bake bouns,
With stronge ale bruen in fattes and in tounes,
Pyng, Drangoll, and the Braget fyne,
Methe, Mathebru, and Mathelynge,
Rede wyn, the claret and the white,
With Teynt, and Alycaunt, in whom I delite;
Wyn ryvers and wyn sake also,
Wyne of Langdoke and of Orliaunce therto,
Sengle bere, and othir that is dwobile,
Which causith the brayn of man to trouble;
Spruce beer, and the beer of Hambur,
Whiche makyth oft tymes men to stambur;
Malmasyes, Tires, and Rumneys,
With Caperikis, Campletes, and Osneys,
Vernuge, Crete, and Raspays also,
Whippett and Pyngmedo, that ben lawyers therto;
And I will have also wyne de Ryne,
With new maid Clarye, that is good and fyne,
Muscadell, Terantyne, and Bastard,
With Yporcas and Pyment comyng afterwarde.
And as for mete I will that goo quyte,
For I had never therin grete dylite,
So that I my3t have drynke at my will,
Good ale or wyne my bely for to fille.
MS. Rawl. C. 86.

L. 1412. *Ne spyces to spare.*—Spices were usually offered to guests before they retired to rest.

To daunsyng chambris full of paramentes,
Of riche beddis and of ornamentes,
This Æneas is ledde aftir the mete;
And with the quene whan that he had y-sete,
And spicis partid, and the wine agon,
Unto his chambir was he lad anon.
Legende of Dido, 185.

The miri maiden, also sone
As Hatherof into chamber come,
  Sche wend that it wer Horn;
A riche cheier was undon,
That seiven might sit theron,
  In swiche craft y-corn.

> A baudekin theron was spred,
> Thider the maiden hadde hem led
>   To siten hir biforn;
> Frout and spices sche hem bede,
> Wine to drink, wite and rede,
>   Bothe of coppe and horn.
>
>   *Ritson's Met. Rom.* iii. 293.

L. 1418. *Harpyng notus ful swet.*—This account of the lady playing to her lover is characteristic and curious. There is a description somewhat similar in the " Carle of Carlile,"—

> Downe came a lady faire and free,
> And sett her on the Carles knee;
> One whiles shee harped, another whiles song,
> Both of paramours and lovinge amonge.
>
>   *Syr Gawayne*, ed. Madden, p. 264.

L. 1434. *Arcangelus of rede golde.*—This probably refers to the carved corbels, " ffyfty mad of o molde," as the next line informs us. In 1365, fifty corbels of Maidstone stone were ordered for the clock-tower at Westminster. See Willis's Architectural Nomenclature, p. 70.

L. 1448. " Lystyne tham tille," Lincoln MS.

L. 1452. *Ylle.*—The Lincoln MS. reads " wele," which is doubtlessly correct.

L. 1453. *With an orrelegge one hyʒth.*—A curious early notice of clocks, for illustrations of which the reader may refer to an essay by Barrington, in the Archæologia, vol. v., Ducange, in v. *Horologium*, &c. Perhaps the most ancient and curious clock now existing is that preserved in the Cathedral of Wells, said to have been constructed by Peter Lightfoot about the year 1325. The clock of Richard de Wallingford at St. Alban's is described by Whethamstede, in his *Granarium*, preserved in the Cotton MSS. Bale, who appears to have seen it, says it was made *magno labore, majore sumptu, arte vero maxima*, and it seems to have been considered a great curiosity. I mentioned both in the Rara Mathematica, p. 117, but had not noticed any particulars of the one first mentioned till kindly pointed out to me by Mr. J. G. Nichols.

L. 1457. *Square.*—The Lincoln MS. reads " corvene," referring probably to ornamented mullions. The writer of the romance considers it necessary to say the windows were " of glas," that material not being universally employed in the 14th century for that purpose.

L. 1465. *Grete Charlus with the crounne.*—That is, Charlemagne. A small collection of romances relating to the adventures of this celebrated emperor is in MS. Ashmole 33, a volume very remarkable as containing part of the rough drafts of the author. The editor of the present volume hopes to have the opportunity of publishing it. At Woodstock manor, in the time of Henry VIII., was a tapestrie of Charlemagne. See Warton's Hist. Engl. Poet, ed. 1840, i. 205.

L. 1466. *Syre Godfray the Boyloune.*—A common subject for tapestry. See Warton, i. 204-5.

L. 1469. *Paned.*—" Paynted," Lincoln MS.

L. 1474. " With a chekir seloure," Lincoln MS.

L. 1478. *Of Ydoyne and Amadas.*—A love tale or romance, referred to in the Cursor Mundi, Sir Emaré, and the Confessio Amantis. There is a copy of this Anglo-Norman romance at Paris, MS. No. 6987, consisting of about 7200 lines. See Paulin Paris, Les Manuscrits François de la Bibliothèque du Roi, iii. 224. It does not seem to have been translated into English; at least the tale of Sir Amadas, printed by Weber and Robson, does not answer the description. It was one of the romances bequeathed by Guy Beauchamp, earl of Warwick, to the abbey of Bordesley in Worcestershire. See Todd's Illustrations, p. 161. In the romance of Emaré, the tale is stated to have formed the subject of a tapestry, as in our text.

> And eek in otherwise also,
> Ful ofte tyme it falleth soo
> Myn ere with a good pitaunce
> Is fedde of redynge of romaunce,
> Of Ydoyne and of Amadas,
> That whilom weren in my cas,
> And eek of other many a score,
> That loveden longe er I was bore;
> For whan I of here lovis rede,
> Myn ere with the tale y fede,
> And with the love of here histoyre
> Sumtyme I drawe into memoyre

> How sorow may not ever laste,
> And so cometh hope in at laste,
> Whan I non other foode knowe;
> And that endureth but a throwe,
> Ryȝt as it were a chery-feste.
>
> *Gower, MS. Soc. Antiq.* 134, f. 182.

L. 1481. " The stowt dedis of many a knyght," Lincoln MS.

L. 1496. *With women of lare.*—That is, women who were well taught.

L. 1503. *Medyore.*—The Lincoln MS. reads " Edoyne," the scribe perhaps remembering Idoyne and Amadas just mentioned.

L. 1504. *Meré maydenus.*—The Lincoln MS. reads " mery maydyns," in case any one may think these " cordes " were woven from the yellow tresses of mermaids.

L. 1507. *The.*—This word seems to be redundant.

L. 1510. " Whenne thou gase to thi ryste," Lincoln MS.

L. 1528. " Als I ame trewe wyghte," Lincoln MS.

L. 1531. The Lincoln MS. reads,—

> Of he ware an emperour,
> That mast es of myghte.

L. 1536. *And trouthus thei plyȝth.*—This line is scratched through in the MS.

L. 1544. *Thei synnyd nat thare !*—A Welsh fashion of courting, which is said to be still in vogue in some parts of the Principality. They were betrothed to each other, as appears from l. 1536. See Douce's observations on the subject in his Illustrations of Shakespeare, i. 113-14.

L. 1564. " He sawe wele that tyde," Lincoln MS.

L. 1568. " And thare thay gunne habyde," Lincoln MS.

L. 1572. " Als thay ere kende to be," Lincoln MS. A curious passage in favour of the manners of the old minstrels, which Ritson would have called " a monstrous lie."

L. 1576. " Hymselfe gunne it see," Lincoln MS.

L. 1601. *At evene lyȝth.*—These two lines are very similar to ll. 1169-70. The Lincoln MS. reads, " that hend knyght."

L. 1603. " Prevaly I ȝow highte," Lincoln MS.
L. 1604. " And coverde thame fra syghte," Lincoln MS.
L. 1611. *Bac.*—" Blake," Lincoln MS.
L. 1632. *For wele ne for wo.*—" Bestad, or wythe-holdyn yn wele or wo,"—*Prompt. Parv.* p. 33.
L. 1641. The Lincoln MS. reads,—

> So syr Degrevaunt faride,
> He mad thame in hert sterid.

L. 1645. *Syxty.*—" Fourty," Lincoln MS.
L. 1648. " Ne noghte wynne awaye," Lincoln MS.
L. 1654. " For the fyght that thay sees," Lincoln MS.
L. 1656. " And covers tham fulle clene," Lincoln MS.
L. 1658. The Lincoln MS. reads,—

> Of that chevalrouse case;
> He hase vencust his fase.

L. 1662. *Marchal.*—" Uschere," Lincoln MS.
L. 1672. Or dey in the playne?
L. 1675. *Eorlus castel.*—" Chambir," Lincoln MS.
L. 1702. *And ofte with mowthus thei mete.*—That is, they kiss each other.
L. 1714. *Eymere.*—The Lincoln MS. reads " Gaymere."
L. 1735. *What.*—The Lincoln MS. has " whatkyns," which is a better reading.
L. 1742. The Lincoln MS. reads,—

> Syr, we hafe no childe bot ane!
> For the lufe of sayne Jame
> Off hir haff mercy!

L. 1750. " That he went hym to playe," Lincoln MS.
L. 1753. The Lincoln MS. reads,—

> When he werid in Spayne,
> ȝe made his landis barrayne.

L. 1756. " His wylde and his tame," Lincoln MS.

L. 1779. " And talde hym alle hir atent," Lincoln MS.

L. 1794. Compare l. 1153.

L. 1807. *And.*—The Lincoln MS. has " he," which seems to be a better reading.

L. 1833. " Of Almayne the emperour," Lincoln MS.

L. 1838. " Mare thane thre hundreth pounde," Lincoln MS.

L. 1841. *The sale.*—The Lincoln MS. reads " in sale," which is doubtlessly correct. Compare Sir Perceval, 1586.

L. 1848. " And frely to folde," Lincoln MS.

L. 1850. *Wyne in condyt rane.*—A common incident in the old pageants. See Lydgate's Minor Poems, p. 14. The l. 1854 of course refers to the pageant.

L. 1866. " The lorde come with a knyghte," Lincoln MS.

L. 1868. " Abowte in that haulle," Lincoln MS.

L. 1872. " With wirchipe tuk alle," Lincoln MS.

L. 1891. *Sevene.*—" Ten," Lincoln MS.

L. 1897. " Sertanly he was slayne," Lincoln MS.

L. 1901. The Lincoln MS. concludes thus,—

> Jhesu Lorde in Trinité,
> Graunt us alle in hevene to be,
> Thy worthy face for to see,
>   And gyff us wele to spede ! Amen.
> *Amen. Explicit syr Degrevaunt.*

GLOSSARIAL NOTES.

⁎ It was my original intention to have furnished a Glossary to the Romances contained in the present volume, but it was found that so large a portion of the words were also to be met with in similar collections, and, for the most part, sufficiently well explained, that it scarcely appeared necessary to increase the size of the work, the proposed limits of which have already been exceeded, by any extensive compilation of the kind. The few notes which follow are selected from memoranda made with the above-mentioned object in view, and comprise *inter alia* explanations of some of the more difficult words, with remarks on others of very unusual occurrence.

SIR PERCEVAL.

L. 1. *Lef.*—Dear, beloved. The substantive *people* is here understood, a practice more common in Anglo-Norman than in English.

L. 4. *Felle.*—Fierce, strong. In line 6 it has another meaning, viz. hill, or moor. Brockett says, " Frequently used for any moor or open waste, though properly a high or alpine tract only."

L. 31. *Bothers.*—Of both, *gen. pl.*

L. 35. *Mobles.*—Moveables, goods. Fr. Meubles.

L. 159. *Siche.*—Such. This, and many other words of the same kind, now considered vulgarisms, are found in respectable use at an earlier period. There are many who would disdain to use the verb *to ax*, who are not aware it is pure Anglo-Saxon, *acsian*, or *axian*.

L. 179. *Raye.*—King. Fr. Ré.

L. 185. *Nayte.*—So I printed the word, on Sir F. Madden's authority, Gloss. to Syr Gawayne, in v. *Nayted*, where it is left without explanation; but we should rather read *vayte*, from Teut. Vaten, *comprehendere*, or Vatten, *tenere*, or Dut. Vatten, to take. So also in A.-S. Fatan wif, *ducere uxorem*, to marry. The phrase is the same, but perhaps *fatan* singly is not exactly explained by *ducere*.

L. 186. *Tryppe.*—A small flock. See Grose, in v. *Trip*.

L. 187. *Bayte.*—To avail; to be useful. Dut. Baten.

L. 207. *Marte.*—Wonders, marvels. A.-S. mærð.

L. 255. *Layte.*—To look for, to seek. Still used in Craven.

L. 294. *Smertly.*—Sharply, quickly. This, I believe, is classed among the American neonisms. See also l. 335.

L. 295. *Thyngez.*—This term is often applied to persons of both sexes. Cf. Sir Eglamour, 616.

L. 362. *Unroo.*—Vexation, trouble. *Roo* is not uncommon, but I have not observed another instance of the negative substantive.

L. 367. *Stode-mere.*—A mare in foal. A.-S. Stod-myre.

L. 393. *ʒole.*—Yule, or Christmas.

L. 411. *Fare.*—Fur? Roquefort has, "*Fare*, sorte de filet."

L. 424. *Kenylles.*—A misprint for *kevylles*, i. e. he passes the *wythe* through the mouth of the horse, not having a proper bit. The substantive *kevelles* occurs at l. 1426, "*kevelles* did thay caste," a phrase for stopping the horses. The word occurs in Prompt. Parv. p. 274.

L. 439. *Bett.*—Supplied with fuel.

L. 487. *Has.*—Haste.

L 583. *With thi that.*—On condition that.

L. 616. *Fadde.*—We have *fade* at ll. 1165, 1307, and in Syr Gawayne, p. 8, which seems to be the same word. Sir F. Madden conjectures *wan*, which suits only the context in the last instance.

L. 641. *Petir.*—A common oath in the old romances. See Weber's Glossary, in v. *Petur*.

L. 661. *How.*—Stop! See l. 1901.

L. 672. *Slongene.*—Flung.

L. 678. *Umbrere.*—The moveable part of a helmet.

GLOSSARIAL NOTES.

L. 717. *Bagged.*—Warner, as quoted by Nares, uses this term applied to Venus,—

"Well, Venus shortly *bagged*, and ere long was Cupid bred."

L. 754. *Fyre-irene.*—An iron used to strike a light with. "Fyyre yryne, to smyte wythe fyre, *fugillus, piricidium.*"—Prompt. Parv. p. 161.

L. 795. *Coste.*—Side.

L. 796. *Spalde.*—Shoulder.

L. 803. *Lete.*—Considered, supposed. A.-S. Lætan.

L. 825. *Forthe dayes.*—Close of the day. A.-S. Forð-dæges.

L. 848. *Ille farande.*—Bad-conditioned, ill-looking.

L. 891. *By-soughte.*—Sought after.

L. 911. *For-ferde.*—Very much afraid, terrified.

L. 923. *Theefe.*—A term of reproach, not necessarily a robber. See Sir Eglamour, 327.

L. 1022. *To-too.*—Exceedingly. See a paper of mine on this word in the Shakespeare Society's Papers, vol. i. p. 39.

L. 1052. *Took his knawlage.*—Knew him.

L. 1065. *Wansome.*—Inefficient. From A.-S. Wana.

L. 1136. *ʒemande.*—Ruling, keeping.

L. 1173. *Tide in townne who wille telle.*—Cf. Sir Tristrem, Fytte i. st. 1. l. 10.

L. 1202. *To-medis.*—In the midst. A.-S. To-middes.

L. 1375. *Roke.*—To roll.

L. 1440. *Fade.*—At variance? A.-N. Fadiu.

L. 1441. *Sister-sones.*—Nephews. See l. 1457.

L. 1481. *Wyde-whare.*—Far on every side. Cf. Eglamour, 445.

L. 1595. *Wynne thi schone.* A new-made knight was said *to win his spurs* when he first achieved some gallant action. See Ritson's Met. Rom. iii. 341, and Ipomydon, 978.

L. 1657. *Thofe he welde wede.*—Though he possessed accoutrements, *i. e.* was well armed.

L. 1704. *Laykes.*—Sports, games. This term is constantly applied by the romance writers to combats. War was called swerd-layke.

L. 1708. *Fyve stryde mett.*—This apparently means that the steed leapt over five usual paces.

L. 1709. *Forby.*—Past.

L. 1879. *For-waked.*—Tired for want of sleep.

L. 1929. *Forbere.*—Prevented from coming in.

L. 1996. *Toke.*—Gave, delivered up. *I-toke* would scarcely agree with the context.

L. 2077. *Now bese it, &c.*—Now the club may never be taken from the earth for any one; I reckon thy goings are all gone, by the good rood!

L. 2114. *Schott.*—Turned out. Exactly in the same sense as the announcement, "Rubbish may be *shot* here."

L. 2157. *Rafe.*—Præt. of *rive*.

SIR ISUMBRAS.

L. 6. *Arethede.*—Honour. Apparently connected with A.-S. Ar. See Degrevant, 8.

L. 18. *Se.*—So in the MS., but perhaps an error for *so*.

L. 26. *Thurte.*—Need. Præt. of *thare*, to need.

L. 83. *Vey.*—True. A.-N. Vé.

L. 159. *Wylle.*—Should we read *a wylle?*

L. 175. *To-whils.*—Whilst. See l. 590.

L. 222. *Toppe-castelles.*—Ledgings surrounding the mast head. In Eglamour, 1072, it is apparently applied to the upper turrets of a castle, or perhaps to the temporary wooden fortifications built at the tops of towers in preparing for a siege. According to Mr. Hunter, Hallamshire Glossary, p. 24, "any building which overtops those around it, will be called in derision a *cob-castle*."

L. 332. *Conntré.*—This would generally be read *countré*, but we have *cunntré* at l. 522.

L. 391. *Wille of wone.*—At a loss for a dwelling.

L. 453. *Growndyne.*—Bellowing.

L. 489. *For that.*—Because. A common idiom, which confirms Mr. Hunter's reading of a passage in Shakespeare in his New Illustrations, p. 290.

L. 508. *Lende.*—To land, to arrive. A.-S. Ge-landian.

L. 522. *A syde.*—One side.

L. 526. *Welle-streme.*—A well, a fountain.—Cf. Chaucer, ed. Urry, p. 415.

L. 599. *Thankes God of alle.*—That is, for all. A song with this burden is in Lydgate's Minor Poems, p. 225.

SIR EGLAMOUR.

L. 68. *On-henely.*—Ungently, uncourteously.

L. 300. *Schylle.*—Shrill. Not an error for *schrylle*, as conjectured in the Archæologia, xxi. 61.

L. 317. *Sowe.*—A blow. See Jamieson, Supp. in v. *Sough.* At l. 374, *sowe* means a rumbling noise.

L. 416. *Ley on.*—See Macbeth, v. 7.

L. 490. *Splatt.*—To cut up.

L. 612. *Roone.*—Vermilion. It occurs in Le Bone Florence of Rome, 1904, left unexplained by Ritson. Jamieson absurdly explains it, " the mountain-ash or roan tree."

L. 755. *Bayly.*—A district given in charge to a bailiff, or guard.

L. 995. *Toke a towre.*—Betook himself to a tower.

L. 1087. *By rome.*—About a room?

L. 1128. *Alle-be-dene.*—Perhaps we may read, " alle be-dene."

L. 1192. *Fane*—See Prompt. Parv. p. 148, note.

L. 1283. *On-sett stevyn.*—A time not previously appointed.

SIR DEGREVANT.

L. 86. *Her.*—To hear.

L. 239. *Launde.*—A lawn, a plain extended between woods.

L. 275. *No sege be ensoynd.*—No man be excused.

L. 291. *Jepun and jesseraund.* — The jepun was the pourpoint or doubtlet, not necessarily the coat-armour, as Sir F. Madden seems to say, notes to Syr Gawayne, p. 314. The jesseraunt, according to Mr. Planché, was a sort of jacket without sleeves, composed of small oblong plates of iron or steel, overlapping each other, and sometimes covered with velvet[1]; but the term was used in different senses. A chain of small gold or silver plates worn round the neck, and also a kind of cuirass, was so called. See Roquefort, in v. *Jaseran, Jaserans.* Compare l. 798.

L. 371. *Sted ferraunt.*—An African horse.

L. 424. *Wylde.*—Wild cattle.

L. 473. *Eyth.*—Easily.

L. 527. *Fausoned one florene.*—Fashioned into florence?

L. 626. *Overfret.*—Made into fret-work. A.-N. Freter.

L. 634. *Anamelede.* — Interwoven, mixed. See Strutt, ed. Planché, ii. 104.

L. 755. *Fay.*—Doomed to death, fated to die. A.-S. Fæge.

L. 757. *Astered.*—Moved with passion. A.-S. Astyrian.

L. 823. *Unwynly to wak.*—Unpleasantly to languish. A.-S. Wacan.

L. 824. *Wete.*—Left unexplained by Sir F. Madden, Gloss. to Syr Gawayne, in v. Mr. Robson has the word in his Romances, p. 4, explained *wet* in Glossary, which cannot be correct. Ray gives *weet* as a North-country word, meaning *nimble, swift;* so that perhaps we may explain it *expeditious.* Can it be connected with A.-N. Witart?

L. 832. *And honde I the hete.*—I promise you on my hand. See l. 1272.

L. 853. *Ensent.*—Advice, wish. A.-N. Esciant.

L. 907. *Watur-wal.*—A waterfall. Dut.

L. 930. *Reten.*—Garrison. A.-N.

L. 942. *Man.*—Should we read *woman?*

L. 1185. *Held.*—Hilled, covered.

THE END.